COMPLETE
BUSINESS
LAW
CASES
FOR
REVIEW

COMPLETE BUSINESS LAW CASES FOR REVIEW

COMPILED BY: MICHAEL A. KATZ

Delaware State University
Department of Accounting and Finance

Prentice Hall

Upper Saddle River, New Jersey 07458

Acquisitions editor: Linda Schreiber
Associate editor: Jennifer Surich
Production editor: Leah Crescenzo
Manufacturer: Victor Graphics, Inc.

ISBN 0-13-090631-X

10 9 8 7 6 5 4 3 2 1

Table of Contents

JANET RENO, ATTORNEY GENERAL, ET AL. v. CHARLIE CONDON, ATTORNEY GENERAL OF SOUTH CAROLINA, ET AL.

120 S. Ct. 666 (2000)

SUPREME COURT OF THE UNITED STATES

REHNQUIST, CHIEF JUSTICE

The DPPA regulates the disclosure and resale of personal information contained in the records of state DMVs. State DMVs require drivers and automobile owners to provide personal information, which may include a person's name, address, telephone number, vehicle description, Social Security number, medical information, and photograph, as a condition of obtaining a driver's license or registering an automobile. Congress found that many States, in turn, sell this personal information to individuals and businesses. These sales generate significant revenues for the States. [t]he Wisconsin Department of Transportation receives approximately $8 million each year from the sale of motor vehicle information.

The DPPA establishes a regulatory scheme that restricts the States' ability to disclose a driver's personal information without the driver's consent. The DPPA generally prohibits any state DMV, or officer, employee, or contractor thereof, from "knowingly disclosing or otherwise making available to any person or entity personal information about any individual obtained by the department in connection with a motor vehicle record. The DPPA defines "personal information" as any information "that identifies an individual, including an individual's photograph, social security number, driver identification number, name, address (but not the 5-digit zip code), telephone number, and medical or disability information," but not including "information on vehicular accidents, driving violations, and driver's status. A "motor vehicle record" is defined as "any record that pertains to a motor vehicle operator's permit, motor vehicle title, motor vehicle registration, or identification card issued by a department of motor vehicles.

The DPPA's ban on disclosure of personal information does not apply if drivers have consented to the release of their data. Under the amended DPPA, States may not imply consent from a driver's failure to take advantage of a state-afforded opportunity to block disclosure, but must rather obtain a driver's affirmative consent to disclose the driver's personal information for use in surveys, marketing, solicitations, and other restricted purposes.

South Carolina law conflicts with the DPPA's provisions. Under that law, the information contained in the State's DMV records is available to any person or entity that fills out a form listing the requester's name and address and stating that the information will not be used for telephone solicitation. South Carolina's DMV retains a copy of all requests for information from the State's motor vehicle records, and it is required to release copies of all requests relating to a person upon that person's written petition. State law authorizes the South Carolina DMV to charge a fee for releasing motor vehicle information, and it requires the DMV to allow drivers to prohibit the use of their motor vehicle information for certain commercial activities.

Following the DPPA's enactment, South Carolina and its Attorney General, respondent Condon, filed suit in the United States District Court for the District of South Carolina, alleging that the DPPA violates the Tenth and Eleventh Amendments to the United States Constitution. The District Court concluded that the Act is incompatible with the principles of federalism inherent in the Constitution's division of power between the States and the Federal Government. The court accordingly granted summary judgment for the State and permanently enjoined the Act's enforcement against the State and its officers. The Court of Appeals for the Fourth Circuit affirmed, concluding that the Act violates constitutional principles of federalism.

The United States asserts that the DPPA is a proper exercise of Congress' authority to regulate interstate commerce under the Commerce Clause, U.S. Const., Art. I, § 8, cl. 3. n2 The United States bases its Commerce Clause argument on the fact that the personal, identifying information that the DPPA regulates is a "thing in interstate commerce," and that the sale or release of that information in interstate commerce is therefore a proper subject of congressional regulation. We agree with the United States' contention. The motor vehicle information which the States have historically sold is used by insurers, manufacturers, direct marketers, and others engaged in interstate commerce to contact drivers with customized solicitations. The information is also used in the stream of interstate commerce by various public and private entities for matters related to interstate motoring. Because drivers' information is, in this context, an article of commerce, its sale or release into the interstate stream of business is sufficient to support congressional regulation.

But the fact that drivers' personal information is, in the context of this case, an article in interstate commerce does not conclusively resolve the constitutionality of the DPPA.

"While Congress has substantial powers to govern the Nation directly, including in areas of intimate concern to the States, the Constitution has never been understood to confer upon Congress the ability to the require the States to govern according to Congress' instructions.

The Federal Government may neither issue directives requiring the States to address particular problems, nor command the States' officers, or those of their political subdivisions, to administer or enforce a federal regulatory program.

South Carolina contends that the DPPA violates the Tenth Amendment because it "thrusts upon the States all of the day-to-day responsibility for administering its complex provisions," and thereby makes "state officials the unwilling implementors of federal policy. South Carolina emphasizes that the DPPA requires the State's employees to learn and apply the Act's substantive restrictions, which are summarized above, and notes that these activities will consume the employees' time and thus the State's resources.

"The NGA [National Governor's Association] nonetheless contends that § 310 has commandeered the state legislative and administrative process because many state legislatures had to amend a substantial number of statutes in order to issue bonds in registered form and because state officials had to devote substantial effort to determine how best to implement a registered bond system. Such 'commandeering' is, however, an inevitable consequence of regulating a state activity. Any federal regulation demands compliance. That a State wishing to engage in certain activity must take administrative and sometimes legislative action to comply with federal standards regulating that activity is a commonplace that presents no constitutional defect."

[t]he DPPA does not require the States in their sovereign capacity to regulate their own citizens. The DPPA regulates the States as the owners of databases. It does not require the South Carolina Legislature to enact any laws or regulations, and it does not require state officials to assist in the enforcement of federal statutes regulating private individuals. We accordingly conclude that the DPPA is consistent with the constitutional principles.

The judgment of the Court of Appeals is therefore Reversed.

DONALD E. NELSON v. ADAMS, USA, INC., ET AL.

120 S. Ct. 1579 (2000)

SUPREME COURT OF THE UNITED STATES

GINSBURG, JUSTICE delivered the opinion for a unanimous Court.

OCP and its successor corporation held two patents relating to the method of manufacturing a foamed padding used in athletic equipment. In 1994, OCP sued Adams for infringement. Adams maintained that the patents had been anticipated by prior art and were therefore invalid under 35 U.S.C. § 102(b). The District Court ruled in Adams' favor and dismissed the infringement complaint.

Adams then moved for attorney fees and costs. The District Court granted the motion on the ground that Nelson, who was at all relevant times president and sole shareholder of OCP, had deceitfully withheld the prior art from the United States Patent and Trademark Office. This behavior, the District Court concluded, constituted inequitable conduct chargeable to OCP. On January 20, 1998, the District Court awarded Adams costs and fees in the amount of $178,888.51 against OCP.

Adams feared, however, that it would be unable to collect the award. This was an altogether understandable concern; it stemmed from a letter OCP's counsel had sent Adams warning that OCP would be liquidated if exposed to a judgment for fees more than nominal in amount. Adams therefore moved to amend its pleading to add Nelson, personally, as a party from whom fees could be collected. In this postjudgment endeavor, Adams reasoned that Nelson was the flesh-and-blood party behind OCP, the person whose conduct in withholding prior art precipitated [***537] the fee award, and a person with funds sufficient to satisfy that award. The District Court granted the motion.

Adams' motion, however, sought more than permission to amend the pleading. It sought simultaneously an amended judgment, subjecting Nelson to liability as soon as he was made a party. In presenting the motion, Adams offered no reason why the judgment should be altered immediately. The motion did contend that an amendment to the judgment was "necessary to prevent manifest injustice," but it did not explain why Nelson, once joined as a party, should not be permitted to state his side of that argument. The District Court seems not to have paused over this question. The memorandum explaining the District Court's decision addressed only the propriety of adding Nelson as a party. It did not address the propriety of altering the judgment at the very same time.

The Court of Appeals for the Federal Circuit affirmed the amended judgment against Nelson. It was "uncommon," the appeals court acknowledged, to add a party after the entry of judgment. The court concluded, however, that Nelson had not been prejudiced by the postjudgment joinder. The Federal Circuit based that conclusion on Nelson's failure to show that "anything different or additional would have been done" to stave off the judgment had Nelson been a party, in his individual capacity, from the outset of the litigation. The panel, over a vigorous dissent, was apparently satisfied that adding Nelson as a party and simultaneously amending the judgment to obligate him individually met due process requirements.

Seeking review in this Court, Nelson did not dispute the portion of the District Court's order that granted Adams leave to amend its pleading to add Nelson as a party against whom costs and fees were sought. What he does challenge, and what is now before us, is the portion of the District Court's order that immediately adjudged Nelson personally liable the moment he was made a party.

The Federal Rules of Civil Procedure are designed to further the due process of law that the Constitution guarantees. Cf. Fed. Rule Civ. Proc. 1 (Rules "shall be construed and administered to secure the just, speedy, and inexpensive determination of every action."). Rule 15 sets out the requirements for amended and supplemental pleadings. On that score, the Court of Appeals observed that as long as no undue prejudice is shown, "due process requirements are met if the requirements of Rule 15 are met." But in the instant case, the requirements of Rule 15 were not met. [d]ue process does not countenance such swift passage from pleading to judgment in the pleader's favor.

The propriety of allowing a pleading alteration depends not only on the state of affairs prior to amendment but also on what happens afterwards. Accordingly, Rule 15 both conveys the circumstances under which leave to amend shall be granted and directs how the litigation will move forward following an amendment. When a court grants leave to amend to add an adverse party after the time for responding to the original pleading has lapsed, the party so added is given "10 days after service of the amended pleading" to plead in response. This opportunity to respond, fundamental to due process, is the echo of the opportunity to respond to original pleadings secured by Rule 12. Thus, Rule 15 assumes an amended pleading will be filed and anticipates service of that pleading on the adverse party.

Nelson was never served with an amended pleading. Indeed, no such pleading was ever actually composed and filed in court. Nor, after the amendment naming him as a party, was Nelson accorded 10 days to state his defenses against personal liability for costs and fees. Instead, judgment was entered against him the moment permission to amend the pleading was granted. Appeal after judgment, in the circumstances this case presents, did not provide an adequate opportunity to defend against the imposition of liability. Adams points to nothing in the record indicating that Nelson affirmatively relinquished his right to respond on the merits of the case belatedly stated against him in his individual capacity. Accordingly, the proceedings did not comply with Rule 15, and neither did they comport with due process. 'The fundamental requisite of due process of law is the opportunity to be heard.

It is true that Nelson knew as soon as Adams moved to amend the pleading and alter the judgment that he might ultimately be subjected to personal liability. One could ask, therefore, whether Nelson in fact had a fair chance, before alteration of the judgment, to respond and be heard. Rule 15 and the due process for which it provides, however, demand a more reliable and orderly course. First, as the Rule indicates, pleading in response to an amended complaint is a prerogative of parties, and Nelson was not a party prior to the District Court's ruling on Adams' motion to amend. Second, as Rule 15 further prescribes, the clock on an added party's time to respond does not start running until the new pleading naming that party is served, see ibid., just as the clock on an original party's time to respond does not start running until the original pleading is served. This is not to say that Rule 15 is itself a constitutional requirement. Beyond doubt, however, a prospective party cannot fairly be required to answer an amended pleading not yet permitted, framed, and served.

Even when an amendment relates back to the original date of pleading under Rule 15(c), as Adams contends its amendment does, the relation back cannot, consistently with due process, deny a party all opportunity to be heard in response to the amendment.

To summarize, Nelson was never afforded a proper opportunity to respond to the claim against him. Instead, he was adjudged liable the very first moment his personal liability was legally at issue. Procedure of this style has been questioned even in systems, real and imaginary, less concerned than ours with the right to due process.

A well-known work offers this example:
"'Herald, read the accusation!' said the King.
On this the White Rabbit blew three blasts on the trumpet, and then unrolled the parchment scroll, and read as follows:
'The Queen of Hearts, she made some tarts,
All on a summer day:
The Knave of Hearts, he stole those tarts,
And took them quite away!'
'Consider your verdict,' the King said to the jury.
'Not yet, not yet!' the Rabbit interrupted. 'There's a great deal to come before that!'" L. Carroll, Alice in Wonderland and Through the Looking Glass 108 (Messner, 1982) (emphasis in original).

Adams strongly urges, however, that Nelson waived his objections to the swift process of the District Court. Adams first maintains that Nelson waived arguments based on personal jurisdiction and the absence of service of process by failing to raise them promptly after being added as a party. Nelson's winning argument, however, is based neither on personal jurisdiction nor on service of process. It rests on his right to have time and opportunity to respond to the claim once Adams gained leave to sue Nelson in his individual capacity, and thereby to reach beyond OCP's corporate till into Nelson's personal pocket. Waiver of arguments based on personal jurisdiction and service of process is therefore beside the point.

In a similar vein, and this time coming closer to the dispositive issue, Adams submits that the Federal Circuit "did not address the 'due process' issues now sought to be presented, . . . because these issues were never raised by Petitioner" before that court. It is indeed the general rule that issues must be raised in lower courts in order to be preserved as potential grounds of decision in higher courts. But this principle does not demand the incantation of particular words; rather, it requires that the lower court be fairly put on notice as to the substance of the issue. And the general rule does not prevent us from declaring what due process requires in this case, for that matter was fairly before the Court of Appeals.

In response to questioning from the appellate bench, Nelson's counsel explained that the core of his client's argument was the fundamental unfairness of imposing judgment without going through the process of litigation our rules of civil procedure prescribe. Both the majority and the dissent in the Federal Circuit understood that an issue before them concerned the process due after Adams' postjudgment motion. Our resolution of the case as a matter of due process therefore rests on a ground considered and passed upon by the court below.

For the reasons stated, the judgment of the Court of Appeals is reversed, and the case is remanded for further proceedings consistent with this opinion.

It is so ordered.

SANTA FE INDEPENDENT SCHOOL DISTRICT v. JANE DOE,
INDIVIDUALLY AND AS NEXT FRIEND FOR HER MINOR CHILDREN, JANE
AND JOHN DOE, ET AL.

2000 U.S. LEXIS 4154; 68 U.S.L.W. 4525 (2000)

SUPREME COURT OF THE UNITED STATES

STEVENS, JUSTICE,

Prior to 1995, the Santa Fe High School student who occupied the school's elective office of student council chaplain delivered a prayer over the public address system before each varsity football game for the entire season. This practice, along with others, was challenged in District Court as a violation of the Establishment Clause of the First Amendment. While these proceedings were pending in the District Court, the school district adopted a different policy that permits, but does not require, prayer initiated and led by a student at all home games. The District Court entered an order modifying that policy to permit only nonsectarian, nonproselytizing prayer. The Court of Appeals held that, even as modified by the District Court, the football prayer policy was invalid.

The Santa Fe Independent School District (District) is a political subdivision of the State of Texas, responsible for the education of more than 4,000 students in a small community in the southern part of the State. The District includes the Santa Fe High School, two primary schools, an intermediate school and the junior high school. Respondents are two sets of current or former students and their respective mothers. One family is Mormon and the other is Catholic. The District Court permitted respondents (Does) to litigate anonymously to protect them from intimidation or harassment.

Respondents commenced this action in April 1995 and moved for a temporary restraining order to prevent the District from violating the Establishment Clause at the imminent graduation exercises. In their complaint the Does alleged that the District had engaged in several proselytizing practices, such as promoting attendance at a Baptist revival meeting, encouraging membership in religious clubs, chastising children who held minority religious beliefs, and distributing Gideon Bibles on school premises. They also alleged that the District allowed students to read Christian invocations and benedictions from the stage at graduation ceremonies and to deliver overtly Christian prayers over the public address system at home football games.

On May 10, 1995, the District Court entered an interim order addressing a number of different issues. With respect to the impending graduation, the order provided that "non-denominational prayer" consisting of "an invocation and/or benediction" could be presented by a senior student or students selected by members of the graduating class. The text of the prayer was to be determined by the students, without scrutiny or preapproval by school officials. References to particular religious figures "such as Mohammed, Jesus, Buddha, or the like" would be permitted "as long as the general thrust of the prayer is non-proselytizing.".

In response to that portion of the order, the District adopted a series of policies over several months dealing with prayer at school functions. The policies enacted in May and July for graduation ceremonies provided the format for the August and October policies for football games. The May policy provided:

"'The board has chosen to permit the graduating senior class, with the advice and counsel of the senior class principal or designee, to elect by secret ballot to choose whether an invocation and benediction shall be part of the graduation exercise. If so chosen the class shall elect by secret ballot, from a list of student volunteers, students to deliver nonsectarian, nonproselytizing invocations and benedictions for the purpose of solemnizing their graduation ceremonies.'"

The parties stipulated that after this policy was adopted, "the senior class held an election to determine whether to have an invocation and benediction at the commencement [and that the] class voted, by secret ballot, to include prayer at the high school graduation." In a second vote the class elected two seniors to deliver the invocation and benediction.

The student giving the invocation thanked the Lord for keeping the class safe through 12 years of school and for gracing their lives with two special people and closed: "Lord, we ask that You keep Your hand upon us during this ceremony and to help us keep You in our hearts through the rest of our lives. In God's name we pray. Amen.". The student benediction was similar in content and closed: "Lord, we ask for Your protection as we depart to our next destination and watch over us as we go our separate ways. Grant each of us a safe trip and keep us secure throughout the night. In Your name we pray. Amen."

In July, the District enacted another policy eliminating the requirement that invocations and benedictions be "nonsectarian and nonproselytising," but also providing that if the District were to be enjoined from enforcing that policy, the May policy would automatically become effective.

The August policy, which was titled "Prayer at Football Games," was similar to the July policy for graduations. It also authorized two student elections, the first to determine whether "invocations" should be delivered, and the second to select the spokesperson to deliver them. Like the July policy, it contained two parts, an initial statement that omitted any requirement that the content of the invocation be "nonsectarian and nonproselytising," and a fallback provision that automatically added that limitation if the preferred policy should be enjoined. On August 31, 1995, according to the parties' stipulation, "the district's high school students voted to determine whether a student would deliver prayer at varsity football games . . . . The students chose to allow a student to say a prayer at football games. A week later, in a separate election, they selected a student "to deliver the prayer at varsity football games."

The final policy (October policy) is essentially the same as the August policy, though it omits the word "prayer" from its title, and refers to "messages" and "statements" as well as "invocations." It is the validity of that policy that is before us.

We granted the District's petition for certiorari, limited to the following question: "Whether petitioner's policy permitting student-led, student-initiated prayer at football games violates the Establishment Clause."

The first Clause in the First Amendment to the Federal Constitution provides that "Congress shall make no law respecting an establishment of religion, or prohibiting the free exercise thereof." The Fourteenth Amendment imposes those substantive limitations on the legislative power of the States and their political subdivisions.

The principle that government may accommodate the free exercise of religion does not supersede the fundamental limitations imposed by the Establishment Clause. It is beyond dispute that, at a minimum, the Constitution guarantees that government may not coerce anyone to support or participate in religion or its exercise, or otherwise act in a way which 'establishes a [state] religion or religious faith, or tends to do so.

In this case the District first argues that this principle is inapplicable to its October policy because the messages are private student speech, not public speech. It reminds us that "there is a crucial difference between government speech endorsing religion, which the Establishment Clause forbids, and private speech endorsing religion, which the Free Speech and Free Exercise Clauses protect." We certainly agree with that distinction, but we are not persuaded that the pregame invocations should be regarded as "private speech."

These invocations are authorized by a government policy and take place on government property [*22] at government-sponsored school-related events. Of course, not every message delivered under such circumstances is the government's own. We have held, for example, that an individual's contribution to a government-created forum was not government speech.

Granting only one student access to the stage at a time does not, of course, necessarily preclude a finding that a school has created a limited public forum. Here, however, Santa Fe's student election system ensures that only those messages deemed "appropriate" under the District's policy may be delivered. That is, the majoritarian process implemented by the District guarantees, by definition, that minority candidates will never prevail and that their views will be effectively silenced.

[T]his student election does nothing to protect minority views but rather places the students who hold such views at the mercy of the majority. Because "fundamental rights may not be submitted to vote; they depend on the outcome of no elections,"

[W]hile Santa Fe's majoritarian election might ensure that most of the students are represented, it does nothing to protect the minority; indeed, it likely serves to intensify their offense.

Moreover, the District has failed to divorce itself from the religious content in the invocations. It has not succeeded in doing so, either by claiming that its policy is "'one of neutrality rather than endorsement'" or by characterizing the individual student as the "circuit-breaker" in the process. Contrary to the District's repeated assertions that it has adopted a "hands-off" approach to the pregame invocation, the realities of the situation plainly reveal that its policy involves both perceived and actual endorsement of religion.

The District has attempted to disentangle itself from the religious messages by developing the two-step student election process. The text of the October policy, however, exposes the extent of the school's entanglement. The elections take place at all only because the school "board has chosen to permit students to deliver a brief invocation and/or message." The elections thus "shall" be conducted "by the high school student council" and "upon advice and direction of the high school principal." The decision whether to deliver a message is first made by majority vote of the entire student body, followed by a choice of the speaker in a separate, similar majority election. Even though the particular words used by the speaker are not determined by those votes, the policy mandates that the "statement or invocation" be "consistent with the goals and purposes of this policy," which are "to solemnize the event, to promote good sportsmanship and student safety, and to establish the appropriate environment for the competition."

In addition to involving the school in the selection of the speaker, the policy, by its terms, invites and encourages religious messages. The policy itself states that the purpose of the message is "to solemnize the event." A religious message is the most obvious method of solemnizing an event. Moreover, the requirements that the message "promote good citizenship" and "establish the appropriate environment for competition" further narrow the types of message deemed appropriate, suggesting that a solemn, yet nonreligious, message, such as commentary on United States foreign policy, would be prohibited. Indeed, the only type of message that is expressly endorsed in the text is an "invocation" -- a term that primarily describes an appeal for divine assistance. In fact, as used in the past at Santa Fe High School, an "invocation" has always entailed a focused religious message. Thus, the expressed purposes of the policy encourage the selection of a religious message, and that is precisely how the students understand the policy. The results of the elections make it clear that the students understood that the central question before them was whether prayer should be a part of the pregame ceremony. We recognize the important role that public worship plays in many communities, as well as the sincere desire to include public prayer as a part of various occasions so as to mark those occasions' significance. But such religious activity in public schools, as elsewhere, must comport with the First Amendment.

The District next argues that its football does not coerce students to participate in religious observances. Its argument has two parts: first, that there is no impermissible government coercion because the pregame messages are the product of student choices; and second, that there is really no coercion at all because attendance at an extracurricular event, unlike a graduation ceremony, is voluntary.

The reasons just discussed explaining why the alleged "circuit-breaker" mechanism of the dual elections and student speaker do not turn public speech into private speech also demonstrate why these mechanisms do not insulate the school from the coercive element of the final message.

One of the purposes served by the Establishment Clause is to remove debate over this kind of issue from governmental supervision or control.. The two student elections authorized by the policy, coupled with the debates that presumably must precede each, impermissibly invade that private sphere. The election mechanism, when considered in light of the history in which the policy in question evolved, reflects a device the District put in place that determines whether religious messages will be delivered at home football games. The mechanism encourages divisiveness along religious lines in a public school setting, a result at odds with the Establishment Clause. Although it is true that the ultimate choice of student speaker is "attributable to the students," the District's decision to hold the constitutionally problematic election is clearly "a choice attributable to the State,"

The District further argues that attendance at the commencement ceremonies "differs dramatically" from attendance at high school football games, which it contends "are of no more than passing interest to many students" and are "decidedly extracurricular," thus dissipating any coercion. Attendance at a high school football game, unlike showing up for class, is certainly not required in order to receive a diploma. Moreover, we may assume that the District is correct in arguing that the informal pressure to attend an athletic event is not as strong as a senior's desire to attend her own graduation ceremony.

There are some students, however, such as cheerleaders, members of the band, and, of course, the team members themselves, for whom seasonal commitments mandate their attendance, sometimes for class credit. The District also minimizes the importance to many students of attending and participating in extracurricular activities as part of a complete educational experience. High school home football games are traditional gatherings of a school community; they bring together students and faculty as well as friends and family from years present and past to root for a common cause. Undoubtedly, the games are not important to some students, and they voluntarily choose not to attend. For many others, however, the choice between whether to attend these games or to risk facing a personally offensive religious ritual is in no practical sense an easy one. The Constitution, moreover, demands that the school may not force this difficult choice upon these students for "it is a tenet of the First Amendment that the State cannot require one of its citizens to forfeit his or her rights and benefits as the price of resisting conformance to state-sponsored religious practice."

The Religion Clauses of the First Amendment prevent the government from making any law respecting the establishment of religion or prohibiting the free exercise thereof. By no means do these commands impose a prohibition on all religious activity in our public schools. Indeed, the common purpose of the Religion Clauses "is to secure religious liberty." Thus, nothing in the Constitution as interpreted by this Court prohibits any public school student from voluntarily praying at any time before, during, or after the schoolday. But the religious liberty protected by the Constitution is abridged when the State affirmatively sponsors the particular religious practice of prayer.

To properly examine this policy on its face, we "must be deemed aware of the history and context of the community and forum," Our examination of those circumstances above leads to the conclusion that this policy does not provide the District with the constitutional safe harbor it sought. The policy is invalid on its face because it establishes an improper majoritarian election on religion, and unquestionably has the purpose and creates the perception of encouraging the delivery of prayer at a series of important school events.

The judgment of the Court of Appeals is, accordingly, affirmed.

DISSENT: CHIEF JUSTICE REHNQUIST, with whom JUSTICE SCALIA and JUSTICE THOMAS join, dissenting.

The Court distorts existing precedent to conclude that the school district's student-message program is invalid on its face under the Establishment Clause. But even more disturbing than its holding is the tone of the Court's opinion; it bristles with hostility to all things religious in public life. Neither the holding nor the tone of the opinion is faithful to the meaning of the Establishment Clause, when it is recalled that George Washington himself, at the request of the very Congress which passed the Bill of Rights, proclaimed a day of "public thanksgiving and prayer, to be observed by acknowledging with grateful hearts the many and signal favors of Almighty God." Presidential Proclamation, 1 Messages and Papers of the Presidents, 1789-1897, p. 64 (J. Richardson ed. 1897).

First, the Court misconstrues the nature of the "majoritarian election" permitted by the policy as being an election on "prayer" and "religion to the contrary, the election permitted by the policy is a two-fold process whereby students vote first on whether to have a student speaker before football games at all, and second, if the students vote to have such a speaker, on who that speaker will be. It is conceivable that the election could become one in which student candidates campaign on platforms that focus on whether or not they will pray if elected. It is also conceivable that the election could lead to a Christian prayer before 90 percent of the football games. If, upon implementation, the policy operated in this fashion, we would have a record before us to review whether the policy, as applied, violated the Establishment Clause or unduly suppressed minority viewpoints. But it is possible that the students might vote not to have a pregame speaker, in which case there would be no threat of a constitutional violation. It is also possible that the election would not focus on prayer, but on public speaking ability or social popularity. And if student campaigning did begin to focus on prayer, the

school might decide to implement reasonable campaign restrictions.

But the Court ignores these possibilities by holding that merely granting the student body the power to elect a speaker that may choose to pray, "regardless of the students' ultimate use of it, is not acceptable." The Court so holds despite that any speech that may occur as a result of the election process here would be private, not government, speech. The elected student, not the government, would choose what to say. Support for the Court's holding cannot be found in any of our cases. And it essentially invalidates all student elections. A newly elected student body president, or even a newly elected prom king or queen, could use opportunities for public speaking to say prayers. Under the Court's view, the mere grant of power to the students to vote for such offices, in light of the fear that those elected might publicly pray, violates the Establishment Clause.

Second, with respect to the policy's purpose, the Court holds that "the simple enactment of this policy, with the purpose and perception of school endorsement of student prayer, was a constitutional violation." But the policy itself has plausible secular purposes: "To solemnize the event, to promote good sportsmanship and student safety, and to establish the appropriate environment for the competition." Where a governmental body "expresses a plausible secular purpose" for an enactment, "courts should generally defer to that stated intent."

For example, the Court dismisses the secular purpose of solemnization by claiming that it "invites and encourages religious messages." The Court so concludes based on its rather strange view that a "religious message is the most obvious means of solemnizing an event." But it is easy to think of solemn messages that are not religious in nature, for example urging that a game be fought fairly. And sporting events often begin with a solemn rendition of our national anthem, with its concluding verse "And this be our motto: 'In God is our trust.'" Under the Court's logic, a public school that sponsors the singing of the national anthem before football games violates the Establishment Clause. Although the Court apparently believes that solemnizing football games is an illegitimate purpose, the voters in the school district seem to disagree. Nothing in the Establishment Clause prevents them from making this choice.

The Court also determines that the use of the term "invocation" in the policy is an express endorsement of that type of message over all others. See ante, at 14-15. A less cynical view of the policy's text is that it permits many types of messages, including invocations. That a policy tolerates religion does not mean that it improperly endorses it. Indeed, as the majority reluctantly admits, the Free Exercise Clause mandates such tolerance. See ante, at 21 ("Nothing in the Constitution as interpreted by this Court prohibits any public school student from voluntarily praying at any time before, during, or after the schoolday"); see also Lynch v. Donnelly, 465 U.S. 668, 673, 79 L. Ed. 2d 604, 104 S. Ct. 1355 (1984) ("Nor does the Constitution require complete separation of church and state; it affirmatively mandates accommodation, not merely tolerance, of all religions, and forbids hostility toward any").

The Court bases its conclusion that the true purpose of the policy is to endorse student prayer on its view of the school district's history of Establishment Clause violations and the context in which the policy was written, that is, as "the latest step in developing litigation brought as a challenge to institutional practices that unquestionably violated the Establishment Clause." The District Court ordered the school district to formulate a policy consistent with Fifth Circuit precedent, which permitted a school district to have a prayer-only policy. But the school district went further than required by the District Court order and eventually settled on a policy that gave the student speaker a choice to deliver either an invocation or a message. In so doing, the school district exhibited a willingness to comply with, and exceed, Establishment Clause restrictions. Thus, the policy cannot be viewed as having a sectarian purpose.

The "crucial difference between government speech endorsing religion, which the Establishment Clause forbids, and private speech endorsing religion, which the Free Speech and Free Exercise Clauses protect," applies with particular force to the question of endorsement.

Had the policy been put into practice, the students may have chosen a speaker according to wholly secular criteria -- like good public speaking skills or social popularity -- and the student speaker may have chosen, on her own accord, to deliver a religious message. Such an application of the policy would likely pass constitutional muster.

The policy at issue here may be applied in an unconstitutional manner, but it will be time enough to invalidate it if that is found to be the case. I would reverse the judgment of the Court of Appeals.

STEPHEN P. CROSBY, ET AL., v. NATIONAL FOREIGN TRADE COUNCIL

2000 U.S. LEXIS 4153; 68 U.S.L.W. 4545; (2000)

SUPREME COURT OF THE UNITED STATES

SOUTER, JUSTICE

In June 1996, Massachusetts adopted "An Act Regulating State Contracts with Companies Doing Business with or in Burma (Myanmar)." The statute generally bars state entities from buying goods or services from any person (defined to include a business organization) identified on a "restricted purchase list" of those doing business with Burma. Although the statute has no general provision for waiver or termination of its ban, it does exempt from boycott any entities present in Burma solely to report the news, or to provide international telecommunication goods or services, or medical supplies.

In September 1996, three months after Massachusetts law was enacted, Congress passed a statute imposing a set of mandatory and conditional sanctions on Burma. The federal act has five basic parts, three substantive and two procedural.

First, it imposes three sanctions directly on Burma. It bans all aid to the Burmese Government except for humanitarian assistance, counternarcotics efforts, and promotion of human rights and democracy. The statute instructs United States representatives to international financial institutions to vote against loans or other assistance to or for Burma, and it provides that no entry visa shall be issued to any Burmese government official unless required by treaty or to staff the Burmese mission to the United Nations,. These restrictions are to remain in effect "until such time as the President determines and certifies to Congress that Burma has made measurable and substantial progress in improving human rights practices and implementing democratic government.

Second, the federal Act authorizes the President to impose further sanctions subject to certain conditions. He may prohibit "United States persons" from "new investment" in Burma, and shall do so if he determines and certifies to Congress that the Burmese Government has physically harmed, rearrested, or exiled Daw Aung San Suu Kyi (the opposition leader selected to receive the Nobel Peace Prize), or has committed "large-scale repression of or violence against the Democratic opposition

Third, the statute directs the President to work to develop "a comprehensive, multilateral strategy to bring democracy to and improve human rights practices and the quality of life in Burma. He is instructed to cooperate with members of the Association of Southeast Asian Nations (ASEAN) and with other countries having major trade and investment interests in Burma to devise such an approach, and to pursue the additional objective of fostering dialogue between the ruling State Law and Order Restoration Council (SLORC) and democratic opposition groups.

As for the procedural provisions of the federal statute, the fourth section requires the President to report periodically to certain congressional committee chairmen on the progress toward democratization and better living conditions. And the fifth part of the federal Act authorizes the President "to waive, temporarily or permanently, any sanction [under the federal Act] . . . if he determines and certifies to Congress that the application of such sanction would be contrary to the national security interests of the United States."

On May 20, 1997, the President issued the Burma Executive Order. He certified that the Government of Burma had "committed large-scale repression of the democratic opposition in Burma" and found that the Burmese Government's actions and policies constituted "an unusual and extraordinary threat to the national security and foreign policy of the United States," a threat characterized as a national emergency. The President then prohibited new investment in Burma "by United States persons," any approval or facilitation by a United States person of such new investment by foreign persons, and any transaction meant to evade or avoid the ban.

Respondent National Foreign Trade Council (Council) is a nonprofit corporation representing companies engaged in foreign commerce; 34 of its members were on the Massachusetts restricted purchase list in 1998. Three withdrew from Burma after the passage of the state Act, and one member had its bid for a procurement contract increased by 10 percent under the provision of the state law allowing acceptance of a low bid from a listed bidder only if the next-to-lowest bid is more than 10 percent higher.

In April 1998, the Council filed suit in the United States District Court for the District of Massachusetts, seeking declaratory and injunctive relief against the petitioner state officials charged with administering and enforcing the state Act (whom we will refer to simply as the State). The Council argued that the state law unconstitutionally infringed on the federal foreign affairs power, violated the Foreign Commerce Clause, and was preempted by the federal Act. After detailed stipulations, briefing, and argument, the District Court permanently enjoined enforcement of the state Act, holding that it "unconstitutionally impinged on the federal government's exclusive authority to regulate foreign affairs."

The United States Court of Appeals for the First Circuit affirmed on three independent grounds. It found the state Act unconstitutionally interfered with the foreign affairs power of the National Government; violated the dormant Foreign Commerce Clause; and was preempted by the congressional Burma Act.

A fundamental principle of the Constitution is that Congress has the power to preempt state law. Even without an express provision for preemption, we have found that state law must yield to a congressional Act in at least two circumstances. When Congress intends federal law to "occupy the field," state law in that area is preempted. And even if Congress has not occupied the field, state law is naturally preempted to the extent of any conflict with a federal statute. We will find preemption where it is impossible for a private party to comply with both state and federal law. What is a sufficient obstacle is a matter of judgment, to be informed by examining the federal statute as a whole and identifying its purpose and intended effects:

We recognize, of course, that the categories of preemption are not "rigidly distinct." Because a variety of state laws and regulations may conflict with a federal statute, whether because a private party cannot comply with both sets of provisions or because the objectives of the federal statute are frustrated, "field pre-emption may be understood as a species of conflict pre-emption."

"For when the question is whether a Federal act overrides a state law, the entire scheme of the statute must of course be considered and that which needs must be implied is of no less force than that which is expressed. If the purpose of the act cannot otherwise be accomplished -- if its operation within its chosen field else must be frustrated and its provisions be refused their natural effect -- the state law must yield to the regulation of Congress within the sphere of its delegated power."

Applying this standard, we see the state Burma law as an obstacle to the accomplishment of Congress's full objectives under the federal Act. We find that the state law undermines the intended purpose and "natural effect" of at least three provisions of the federal Act, that is, its delegation of effective discretion to the President to control economic sanctions against Burma, its limitation of sanctions solely to United States persons and new investment, and its directive to the President to proceed diplomatically in developing a comprehensive, multilateral strategy towards Burma.

First, Congress clearly intended the federal act to provide the President with flexible and effective authority over economic sanctions against Burma. Although Congress immediately put in place a set of initial sanctions It invested the President with the further power to ban new investment by United States persons, dependent only on specific Presidential findings of repression in Burma. And, most significantly, Congress empowered the President "to waive, temporarily or permanently, any sanction [under the federal act] . . . if he determines and certifies to Congress that the application of such sanction would be contrary to the national security interests of the United States."

Within the sphere defined by Congress, then, the statute has placed the President in a position with as much discretion to exercise economic leverage against Burma, with an eye toward national security, as our law will admit. And it is just this plenitude of Executive authority that we think controls the issue of preemption here. The President has been given this authority not merely to make a political statement but to achieve a political result, and the fullness of his authority shows the importance in the congressional mind of reaching that result. It is simply implausible that Congress would have gone to such lengths to empower the President if it had been willing to compromise his effectiveness by deference to every provision of state statute or local ordinance that might, if enforced, blunt the consequences of discretionary Presidential action.

And that is just what the Massachusetts Burma law would do in imposing a different, state system of economic pressure against the Burmese political regime. As will be seen, the state statute penalizes some private action that the federal Act (as administered by the President) may allow, and pulls levers of influence that the federal Act does not reach. This unyielding application undermines the President's intended statutory authority by making it impossible for him to restrain fully the coercive power of the national economy when he may choose to take the discretionary action open to him, whether he believes that the national interest requires sanctions to be lifted, or believes that the promise of lifting sanctions would move the Burmese regime in the democratic direction. Quite simply, if the Massachusetts law is enforceable the President has less to offer and less economic and diplomatic leverage as a consequence.

Congress manifestly intended to limit economic pressure against the Burmese Government to a specific range. The federal Act confines its reach to United States persons imposes limited immediate sanctions, places only a conditional ban on a carefully defined area of "new investment," and pointedly exempts contracts to sell or purchase goods, services, or technology, These detailed provisions show that Congress's calibrated Burma policy is a deliberate effort "to steer a middle path,"

The State has set a different course, and its statute conflicts with federal law at a number of points by penalizing individuals and conduct that Congress has explicitly exempted or excluded from sanctions. While the state Act differs from the federal in relying entirely on indirect economic leverage through third parties with Burmese connections, it otherwise stands in clear contrast to the congressional scheme in the scope of subject matter addressed. It restricts all contracts between the State and companies doing business in Burma, except when purchasing medical supplies and other essentials (or when short of comparable bids). It is specific in targeting contracts to provide financial services, and general goods and services to the Government of Burma, and thus prohibits contracts between the State and United States persons for goods, services, or technology, even though those transactions are explicitly exempted from the ambit of new investment prohibition when the President exercises his discretionary authority to impose sanctions under the federal Act.

Finally, the state Act is at odds with the President's intended authority to speak for the United States among the world's nations in developing a "comprehensive, multilateral strategy to bring democracy to and improve human rights practices and the quality of life in Burma."

Again, the state Act undermines the President's capacity, in this instance for effective diplomacy. It is not merely that the differences between the state and federal Acts in scope and type of sanctions threaten to complicate discussions; they compromise the very capacity of the President to speak for the Nation with one voice in dealing with other governments.

Because the state Act's provisions conflict with Congress's specific delegation to the President of flexible discretion, with limitation of sanctions to a limited scope of actions and actors, and with direction to develop a comprehensive, multilateral strategy under he federal Act, it is preempted, and its application is unconstitutional, under the Supremacy Clause.

The judgment of the Court of Appeals for the First Circuit is affirmed

Kmart Corporation v. Christine Bassett

2000 Ala. LEXIS 151 (2000)

SUPREME COURT OF ALABAMA

SEE, Justice.

In January 1995, Christine Bassett, an 83-year-old woman who walked with the aid of a cane, went to a Kmart store in Montgomery. Bassett stepped on a rubber mat outside the store to open the automatic doors. The doors swung open, and she began walking into the store. When she was about one-third of the way onto the rubber safety mat inside the store, the doors began to close. Bassett alleges that one of the doors struck her left hip and caused her to fall. In the fall, Bassett suffered a broken hip. After the accident, the store manager examined the doors. They worked properly and did not need to be repaired.

In January 1996, Bassett sued Kmart, alleging negligent or wanton maintenance or repair. The jury returned a verdict in favor of Kmart. The trial court, however, granted Bassett a new trial because, before the jury entered its deliberations, one of the jurors had gone to the store and had inspected the automatic doors. After the retrial, the court submitted to the jury only Bassett's claims alleging negligent maintenance or negligent repair. The jury returned a verdict in favor of Bassett, awarding her $289,000 in damages. Kmart moved for a judgment as a matter of law or, alternatively, for a new trial or a remittitur. The motion was denied by operation of law.

"It is a well-established rule of law in this state that in order to prove a claim of negligence a plaintiff must establish that the defendant breached a duty owed by the defendant to the plaintiff and that the breach proximately caused injury or damage to the plaintiff." The duty owed by a premises owner to an invitee is also well established:

"The owner of premises owes a duty to business invitees to use reasonable care and diligence to keep the premises in a safe condition, or, if the premises are in a dangerous condition, to give sufficient warning so that, by the use of ordinary care, the danger can be avoided."

This duty does not, however, convert a premises owner into an insurer of its invitees' safety. Moreover, the mere fact that a business invitee is injured does not create a presumption of negligence on the part of the premises owner. Rather, a premises owner is liable in negligence only if it "fails to use reasonable care in maintaining its premises in a reasonably safe manner."

Thus, in order to defeat Kmart's motion for a judgment as a matter of law on her negligence claim, Bassett had to present substantial evidence indicating that Kmart had failed to use reasonable care to maintain its automatic doors in a reasonably safe condition, and that Kmart's failure proximately caused the doors to malfunction in such a way as to injure her. Bassett, however, did not produce any evidence at trial to indicate what caused the automatic doors to malfunction as she entered the store.

Kmart argues that Bassett failed to make out a prima facie case of negligence because, it argues, she failed to produce substantial evidence indicating that Kmart breached its duty of care to her. She argues that she produced substantial circumstantial evidence indicating that Kmart had negligently maintained the automatic doors. Specifically, she argues that she presented evidence indicating that the company that installed the doors sold maintenance contracts as part of its business; that Kmart had no maintenance contract for the doors; that Kmart had a policy of waiting until the doors needed repair or maintenance before calling someone to work on them; that the Kmart store manager.

However, Bassett's evidence is insufficient to prove a breach of duty, an element of her negligence cause of action. She did not produce substantial evidence indicating that Kmart failed to maintain the automatic doors in a reasonably safe condition or that the maintenance Kmart provided was unreasonable. Bassett impliedly argues that Kmart's failure to have a preventive-maintenance contract was a breach of duty. However, Bassett's own expert, Jack Cherry, the owner of the door company that had installed the automatic doors, testified that he did not try to sell such a contract to Kmart because he did not think Kmart needed one. Cherry also testified that if the doors had been inspected six months before the date of Bassett's fall, that would have been reasonable maintenance on

However, Cherry did not testify that a failure to inspect the doors for a period exceeding six months would have been unreasonable. Hence, Kmart's policy of not contracting with the door company for its preventive-maintenance program, but, instead, waiting until a door needed repair or maintenance and then calling for repairs, standing alone, is not substantial evidence of negligence.

Bassett also argues that she produced evidence that, under the doctrine of res ipsa loquitur, permitted the jury to infer that Kmart had negligently maintained the automatic doors. Specifically, she argues that evidence that the automatic doors closed while she was still standing on the inside mat is sufficient to allow the jury to infer that Kmart was negligent.

The res ipsa loquitur doctrine allows "an inference of negligence where there is no direct evidence of negligence." For the doctrine to apply, a plaintiff must show that:

"(1) the defendant ... had full management and control of the instrumentality which caused the injury; (2) the circumstances [are] such that according to common knowledge and the experience of mankind the accident could not have happened if those having control of the [instrumentality] had not been negligent; [and] (3) the plaintiff's injury ... resulted from the accident."

However, "if one can reasonably conclude that the accident could have happened without any negligence on the part of the defendant[], then the res ipsa loquitur presumption does not apply."

Thus, the issue is whether the malfunctioning of Kmart's automatic doors is something that "according to common knowledge and the experience of mankind ... could not have happened if those having control of [the doors] had not been negligent." A court may take judicial notice of certain facts that are within the common knowledge. Whether a fact is a matter of common knowledge is an issue to be determined by the court

Bassett argues that it is common knowledge and the experience of the community that the malfunctioning of an automatic door is "unusual

"'An inference cannot be derived from another inference.' An inference must be based on a known or proved fact." Even if the door's malfunction were proved by direct evidence (and, thus, was not an inference), a mere malfunction would be insufficient to invoke the doctrine of res ipsa loquitur under Alabama law, because "one can reasonably conclude that the accident could have happened without any negligence on the part of the defendant[]."

For example, the malfunction could have occurred because the doors were defective or because the company that serviced the doors had been negligent. Also, "mechanical devices, such as [the automatic doors] here involved, get out of working order, and sometimes become dangerous and cause injury without negligence on the part of anyone." Therefore, we do not consider it to be common knowledge that automatic doors cannot malfunction unless the premises owner is negligent in maintaining the doors.

The doctrine of res ipsa loquitur can still be applied if expert testimony is presented. Therefore, we must consider whether Bassett produced sufficient expert testimony indicating that Kmart's automatic doors could not have malfunctioned unless Kmart had failed to use reasonable care to keep its automatic doors in a safe condition.

Jack Cherry testified by deposition that, "without preventive maintenance, eventually the doors are going to malfunction or stop working properly." That is the extent of Cherry's testimony as to the circumstances in which automatic doors malfunction. That testimony is insufficient to show that automatic doors cannot malfunction unless the premises owner fails to use reasonable care to keep them in a safe condition. Therefore, Bassett did not satisfy the second requirement for applying the doctrine of res ipsa loquitur, because she did not show that "according to common knowledge and the experience of mankind [or according to expert testimony] the accident could not have happened" absent Kmart's failure to "use reasonable care in maintaining its premises in a reasonably safe manner."

Our conclusion that the doctrine of res ipsa loquitur does not apply in this case is in accord with the holdings of the Supreme Court of New Mexico and the Court of Appeals of Georgia in similar automatic-door cases.

We conclude that the doctrine of res ipsa loquitur does not apply to the facts of this case. Because Bassett did not produce substantial evidence indicating that Kmart breached its duty to her, the trial court erred in denying Kmart's motion for a judgment as a matter of law.

OPINION OF NOVEMBER 19, 1999, WITHDRAWN; OPINION SUBSTITUTED; APPLICATION OVERRULED; REVERSED AND REMANDED.

ALEXIS GEIER, ET AL. v. AMERICAN HONDA MOTOR COMPANY, INC., ET AL.

120 S. Ct. 1913 (2000)

SUPREME COURT OF THE UNITED STATES

BREYER, JUSTICE

This case focuses on the 1984 version of a Federal Motor Vehicle Safety Standard promulgated by the Department of Transportation under the authority of the National Traffic and Motor Vehicle Safety Act of 1966. The standard, FMVSS 208, required auto manufacturers to equip some but not all of their 1987 vehicles with passive restraints.

In 1992, petitioner Alexis Geier, driving a 1987 Honda Accord, collided with a tree and was seriously injured. The car was equipped with manual shoulder and lap belts which Geier had buckled up at the time. The car was not equipped with airbags or other passive restraint devices.

Geier and her parents, also petitioners, sued the car's manufacturer, American Honda Motor Company, Inc., and its affiliates (hereinafter American Honda), under District of Columbia tort law. They claimed, among other things, that American Honda had designed its car negligently and defectively because it lacked a driver's side airbag. The District Court dismissed the lawsuit. The court noted that FMVSS 208 gave car manufacturers a choice as to whether to install airbags. And the court concluded that petitioners' lawsuit, because it sought to establish a different safety standard -- i.e., an airbag requirement -- was expressly pre-empted by a provision of the Act which pre-empts "any safety standard" that is not identical to a federal safety standard applicable to the same aspect of performance.

The Court of Appeals agreed with the District Court's conclusion but on somewhat different reasoning. It had doubts, given the existence of the Act's "saving" clause, that petitioners' lawsuit involved the potential creation of the kind of "safety standard" to which the Safety Act's express pre-emption provision refers. But it declined to resolve that question because it found that petitioners' state-law tort claims posed an obstacle to the accomplishment of FMVSS 208's objectives. For that reason, it found that those claims conflicted with FMVSS 208, and that, under ordinary pre-emption principles, the Act consequently pre-empted the lawsuit. The Court of Appeals thus affirmed the District Court's dismissal.

We first ask whether the Safety Act's express pre-emption provision pre-empts this tort action. The provision reads as follows:

"Whenever a Federal motor vehicle safety standard established under this subchapter is in effect, no State or political subdivision of a State shall have any authority either to establish, or to continue in effect, with respect to any motor vehicle or item of motor vehicle equipment[,] any safety standard applicable to the same aspect of performance of such vehicle or item of equipment which is not identical to the Federal standard." 15 U.S.C. § 1392(d) (1988 ed.).

The saving clause assumes that there are some significant number of common-law liability cases to save. And a reading of the express pre-emption provision that excludes common-law tort actions gives actual meaning to the saving clause's literal language, while leaving adequate room for state tort law to operate -- for example, where federal law creates only a floor, i.e., a minimum safety standard. Without the saving clause, a broad reading of the express pre-emption provision arguably might pre-empt those actions, for, as we have just mentioned, it is possible to read the pre-emption provision, standing alone, as applying to standards imposed in common-law tort actions, as well as standards contained in state legislation or regulations. And if so, it would pre-empt all nonidentical state standards established in tort actions covering the same aspect of performance as an applicable federal standard, even if the federal standard merely established a minimum standard.

Nothing in the language of the saving clause suggests an intent to save state-law tort actions that conflict with federal regulations.

Neither do we believe that the pre-emption provision, the saving provision, or both together, create some kind of "special burden" beyond that inherent in ordinary pre-emption principles -- which "special burden" would specially disfavor pre-emption here The two provisions, read together, reflect a neutral policy, not a specially favorable or unfavorable policy, towards the application of ordinary conflict pre-emption principles. On the one hand, the pre-emption provision itself reflects a desire to subject the industry to a single, uniform set of federal safety standards. Its pre-emption of all state standards, even those that might stand in harmony with federal law, suggests an intent to avoid the conflict, uncertainty, cost, and occasional risk to safety itself that too many different safety-standard cooks might otherwise create

Why, in any event, would Congress not have wanted ordinary pre-emption principles to apply where an actual conflict with a federal objective is at stake? Some such principle is needed. In its absence, state law could impose legal duties that would conflict directly with federal regulatory. Insofar as petitioners' argument would permit common-law actions that "actually conflict" with federal regulations, it would take from those who would enforce a federal law the very ability to achieve the law's congressionally mandated objectives that the Constitution, through the operation of ordinary pre-emption principles, seeks to protect.

The dissent, as we have said, contends nonetheless that the express pre-emption and saving provisions here, taken together, create a "special burden," which a court must impose "on a party" who claims conflict pre-emption under those principles. But nothing in the Safety Act's language refers to any "special burden." Nor can one find the basis for a "special burden" in this Court's precedents.

A "special burden" would also promise practical difficulty by further complicating well-established pre-emption principles that already are difficult to apply.

Nothing in the statute suggests Congress wanted to complicate ordinary experience-proved principles of conflict pre-emption with an added, "special burden." Indeed, the dissent's willingness to impose a "special burden" here stems ultimately from its view that "frustration-of-purpose" conflict pre-emption is a freewheeling. In a word, ordinary pre-emption principles, grounded in longstanding precedent apply. We would not further complicate the law with complex new doctrine.

The basic question, then, is whether a common-law "no airbag" action like the one before us actually conflicts with FMVSS 208.

In petitioners' and the dissent's view, FMVSS 208 sets a minimum airbag standard. As far as FMVSS 208 is concerned, the more airbags, and the sooner, the better. But that was not the Secretary's view. DOT's comments, which accompanied the promulgation of FMVSS 208, make clear that the standard deliberately provided the manufacturer with a range of choices among different passive restraint devices. Those choices would bring about a mix of different devices introduced gradually over time; and FMVSS 208 would thereby lower costs, overcome technical safety problems, encourage technological development, and win widespread consumer acceptance -- all of which would promote FMVSS 208's safety objectives.

Regardless, the language of FMVSS 208 and the contemporaneous 1984 DOT explanation is clear enough -- even without giving DOT's own view special weight. FMVSS 208 sought a gradually developing mix of alternative passive restraint devices for safety-related reasons. The rule of state tort law for which petitioners

argue would stand as an "obstacle" to the accomplishment of that objective. And the statute foresees the application of ordinary principles of pre-emption in cases of actual conflict. Hence, the tort action is pre-empted.

The judgment of the Court of Appeals is affirmed.

DISSENT: JUSTICE STEVENS, with whom JUSTICE SOUTER, JUSTICE THOMAS, and JUSTICE GINSBURG join, dissenting.

Airbag technology has been available to automobile manufacturers for over 30 years. There is now general agreement on the proposition "that, to be safe, a car must have an airbag." Indeed, current federal law imposes that requirement on all automobile manufacturers.

The question presented is whether either the National Traffic and Motor Vehicle Safety Act of 1966 (Safety Act or Act), pre-empts common-law tort claims that an automobile manufactured in 1987 was negligently and defectively designed because it lacked "an effective and safe passive restraint system, including, but not limited to, airbags."

The 1984 standard provided for a phase-in of passive restraint requirements beginning with the 1987 model year. In that year, vehicle manufacturers were required to equip a minimum of 10% of their new passenger cars with such restraints. While the 1987 Honda Accord driven by Ms. Geier was not so equipped, it is undisputed that Honda complied with the 10% minimum by installing passive restraints in certain other 1987 models. This minimum passive restraint requirement increased to 25% of 1988 models and 40% of 1989 models; the standard also mandated that "after September 1, 1989, all new cars must have automatic occupant crash protection." In response to a 1991 amendment to the Safety Act, the Secretary amended the standard to require that, beginning in the 1998 model year, all new cars have an airbag at both the driver's and right front passenger's positions.

Although the standard did not require airbags in all cars, it is clear that the Secretary did intend to encourage wider use of airbags. One of her basic conclusions was that "automatic occupant protection systems that do not totally rely upon belts, such as airbags . . . , offer significant additional potential for preventing fatalities and injuries, at least in part because the American public is likely to find them less intrusive; their development and availability should be encouraged through appropriate incentives." The Secretary therefore included a phase-in period in order to encourage manufacturers to comply with the standard by installing airbags and other (perhaps more effective) nonbelt technologies that they might develop, rather than by installing less expensive automatic seatbelts

When a state statute, administrative rule, or common-law cause of action conflicts with a federal statute, it is axiomatic that the state law is without effect.

When a federal statute contains an express pre-emption provision, "the task of statutory construction must in the first instance focus on the plain wording of [that provision], which necessarily contains the best evidence of Congress' pre-emptive intent." The Safety Act contains both an express pre-emption provision, and a saving clause that expressly preserves common-law claims. The relevant part of the former provides:

"Whenever a Federal motor vehicle safety standard established under this subchapter is in effect, no State or political subdivision of a State shall have any authority either to establish, or to continue in effect, with respect to any motor vehicle or item of motor vehicle equipment[,] any safety standard applicable to the same aspect of performance of such vehicle or item of equipment which is not identical to the Federal standard."

The latter states:

"Compliance with any Federal motor vehicle safety standard issued under this subchapter does not exempt any person from any liability under common law."

Relying on § 1392(d) and legislative history discussing Congress' desire for uniform national safety standards, Honda argues that petitioners' common-law no-airbag claims are expressly pre-empted because success on those claims would necessarily establish a state "safety standard" not identical to Standard 208.

Even though the Safety Act does not expressly pre-empt common-law claims, Honda contends that Standard 208 -- of its own force -- implicitly pre-empts the claims in this case.

"We have recognized that a federal statute implicitly overrides state law either when the scope of a statute indicates that Congress intended federal law to occupy a field exclusively, or when state law is in actual conflict with federal law.

In addition, we have concluded that regulations "intended to pre-empt state law" that are promulgated by an agency acting non-arbitrarily and within its congressionally delegated authority may also have pre-emptive force. Honda relies on the last of the implied pre-emption principles arguing that the imposition of common-law liability for failure to install an airbag would frustrate the purposes and objectives of Standard 208.

Both the text of the statute and the text of the standard provide persuasive reasons for rejecting this argument. The saving clause of the Safety Act arguably denies the Secretary the authority to promulgate standards that would pre-empt common-law remedies. Moreover, the text of Standard 208 says nothing about pre-emption, and

I am not persuaded that Honda has overcome our traditional presumption that it lacks any implicit pre-emptive effect.

Honda argues, and the Court now agrees, that the risk of liability presented by common-law claims that vehicles without airbags are negligently and defectively designed would frustrate the policy decision that the Secretary made in promulgating Standard 208. This decision, in their view, was that safety -- including a desire to encourage "public acceptance of the airbag technology and experimentation with better passive restraint systems," would best be promoted through gradual implementation of a passive restraint requirement making airbags only one of a variety of systems that a manufacturer could install in order to comply, rather than through a requirement mandating the use of one particular system in every vehicle. In its brief supporting Honda, the United States agreed with this submission. It argued that if the manufacturers had known in 1984 that they might later be held liable for failure to install airbags, that risk "would likely have led them to install airbags in all cars," thereby frustrating the Secretary's safety goals and interfering with the methods designed to achieve them.

There are at least three flaws in this argument that provide sufficient grounds for rejecting it. First, the entire argument is based on an unrealistic factual predicate. Whatever the risk of liability on a no-airbag claim may have been prior to the promulgation of the 1984 version of Standard 208, that risk did not lead any manufacturer to install airbags in even a substantial portion of its cars.

Second, even if the manufacturers' assessment of their risk of liability ultimately proved to be wrong, the purposes of Standard 208 would not be frustrated. In light of the inevitable time interval between the eventual filing of a tort action alleging that the failure to install an airbag is a design defect and the possible resolution of such a claim against a manufacturer, as well as the additional interval between such a resolution (if any) and manufacturers' "compliance with the state law duty in question," by modifying their designs to avoid such liability in the future, it is obvious that the phase-in period would have ended long before its purposes could have been frustrated by the specter of tort liability.

Third, despite its acknowledgement that the saving clause "preserves those actions that seek to establish greater safety than the minimum safety achieved by a federal regulation intended to provide a floor," the Court completely ignores the important fact that by definition all of the standards established under the Safety Act -- like the British regulations that governed the number and capacity of lifeboats aboard the Titanic -- impose minimum, rather than fixed or maximum, requirements. The phase-in program authorized by Standard 208 thus set minimum percentage requirements for the installation of passive restraints, increasing in annual stages of 10, 25, 40, and 100%. Those requirements were not ceilings, and it is obvious that the Secretary favored a more rapid increase. The possibility that exposure to potential tort liability might accelerate the rate of increase would actually further the only goal explicitly mentioned in the standard itself: reducing the number of deaths and severity of injuries of vehicle occupants.

For these reasons, it is evident that Honda has not crossed the high threshold established by our decisions regarding pre-emption of state laws that allegedly frustrate federal purposes: it has not demonstrated that allowing a common-law no-airbag claim to go forward would impose an obligation on manufacturers that directly and irreconcilably contradicts any primary objective that the Secretary set forth with clarity in Standard 208.

Our presumption against pre-emption is rooted in the concept of federalism. It recognizes that when Congress legislates "in a field which the States have traditionally occupied . . . [,] we start with the assumption that the historic police powers of the States were not to be superseded by the Federal Act unless that was the clear and manifest purpose of Congress." The signal virtues of this presumption are its placement of the power of pre-emption squarely in the hands of Congress, which is far more suited than the Judiciary to strike the appropriate state/federal balance (particularly in areas of traditional state regulation), and its requirement that Congress speak clearly when exercising that power. [**83] In this way, the structural safeguards inherent in the normal operation of the legislative process operate to defend state interests from undue infringement.

Because neither the text of the statute nor the text of the regulation contains any indication of an intent to pre-empt petitioners' cause of action, and because I cannot agree with the Court's unprecedented use of inferences from regulatory history and commentary as a basis for implied pre-emption, I am convinced that Honda has not overcome the presumption against pre-emption in this case. I therefore respectfully dissent.

ILLINOIS v. WILLIAM AKA SAM WARDLOW

120 S. Ct. 673 (2000)

SUPREME COURT OF THE UNITED STATES

REHNQUIST, CHIEF JUSTICE

On September 9, 1995, Officers Nolan and Harvey were working as uniformed officers in the special operations section of the Chicago Police Department. The officers were driving the last car of a four car caravan converging on an area known for heavy narcotics trafficking in order to investigate drug transactions. The officers were traveling together because they expected to find a crowd of people in the area, including lookouts and customers.

As the caravan passed 4035 West Van Buren, Officer Nolan observed respondent Wardlow standing next to the building holding an opaque bag. Respondent looked in the direction of the officers and fled. Nolan and Harvey turned their car southbound, watched him as he ran through the gangway and an alley, and eventually cornered him on the street. Nolan then exited his car and stopped respondent. He immediately conducted a protective pat-down search for weapons because in his experience it was common for there to be weapons in the near vicinity of narcotics transactions. During the frisk, Officer Nolan squeezed the bag respondent was carrying and felt a heavy, hard object similar to the shape of a gun. The officer then opened the bag and discovered a .38-caliber handgun with five live rounds of ammunition. The officers arrested Wardlow.

The Illinois trial court denied respondent's motion to suppress, finding the gun was recovered during a lawful stop and frisk. Following a stipulated bench trial, Wardlow was convicted of unlawful use of a weapon by a felon. The Illinois Appellate Court reversed Wardlow's conviction, concluding that the gun should have been suppressed because Officer Nolan did not have reasonable suspicion sufficient to justify an investigative stop pursuant to Terry v. Ohio, 392 U.S. 1, 20 L. Ed. 2d 889, 88 S. Ct. 1868 (1968). 287 Ill. App. 3d 367, 678 N.E.2d 65, 222 Ill. Dec. 658 (1997).

The Illinois Supreme Court agreed. While rejecting the Appellate Court's conclusion that Wardlow was not in a high crime area, the Illinois Supreme Court determined that sudden flight in such an area does not create a reasonable suspicion justifying a Terry stop. The court then determined that flight may simply be an exercise of this right to "go on one's way," and, thus, could not constitute reasonable suspicion justifying a Terry stop.

The Illinois Supreme Court also rejected the argument that flight combined with the fact that it occurred in a high crime area supported a finding of reasonable suspicion because the "high crime area" factor was not sufficient standing alone to justify a Terry stop. Finding no independently suspicious circumstances to support an investigatory detention, the court held that the stop and subsequent arrest violated the Fourth Amendment.

This case, involving a brief encounter between a citizen and a police officer on a public street, is governed by the analysis we first applied in Terry. In Terry, we held that an officer may, consistent with the Fourth Amendment, conduct a brief, investigatory stop when the officer has a reasonable, articulable suspicion that criminal activity is afoot. While "reasonable suspicion" is a less demanding standard than probable cause and requires a showing considerably less than preponderance of the evidence, the Fourth Amendment requires at least a minimal level of objective justification for making the stop. The officer must be able to articulate more than an "inchoate and unparticularized suspicion or 'hunch'" of criminal activity.

We granted certiorari solely on the question of whether the initial stop was supported by reasonable suspicion. Therefore, we express no opinion as to the lawfulness of the frisk independently of the stop.

Nolan and Harvey were among eight officers in a four car caravan that was converging on an area known for heavy narcotics trafficking, and the officers anticipated encountering a large number of people in the area, including drug customers and individuals serving as lookouts. It was in this context that Officer Nolan decided to investigate Wardlow after observing him flee. An individual's presence in an area of expected criminal activity, standing alone, is not enough to support a reasonable, particularized suspicion that the person is committing a crime. But officers are not required to ignore the relevant characteristics of a location in determining whether the circumstances are sufficiently suspicious to warrant further investigation. Accordingly, we have previously noted the fact that the stop occurred in a "high crime area" among the relevant contextual considerations in a Terry analysis.

In this case, moreover, it was not merely respondent's presence in an area of heavy narcotics trafficking that aroused the officers' suspicion but his unprovoked flight upon noticing the police. Our cases have also recognized that nervous, evasive behavior is a pertinent factor in determining reasonable suspicion.. Headlong flight -- wherever it occurs -- is the consummate act of evasion: it is not necessarily indicative of wrongdoing, but it is certainly suggestive of such. [t]he determination of reasonable suspicion must be based on commonsense judgments and inferences about human behavior. We conclude Officer Nolan was justified in suspecting that Wardlow was involved in criminal activity, and, therefore, in investigating further.

Respondent and amici also argue that there are innocent reasons for flight from police and that, therefore, flight is not necessarily indicative of ongoing criminal activity. This fact is undoubtedly true, but does not establish a violation of the Fourth Amendment. Even in Terry, the conduct justifying the stop was ambiguous and susceptible of an innocent explanation. The officer observed two individuals pacing back and forth in front of a store, peering into the window and periodically conferring. . All of this conduct was by itself lawful, but it also suggested that the individuals were casing the store for a planned robbery. Terry recognized that the officers could detain the individuals to resolve the ambiguity.

In allowing such detentions, Terry accepts the risk that officers may stop innocent people. Indeed, the Fourth Amendment accepts that risk in connection with more drastic police action; persons arrested and detained on probable cause to believe they have committed a crime may turn out to be innocent. The Terry stop is a far more minimal intrusion, simply allowing the officer to briefly investigate further. If the officer does not learn facts rising to the level of probable cause, the individual must be allowed to go on his way. But in this case the officers found respondent in possession of a handgun, and arrested him for violation of an Illinois firearms statute. No question of the propriety of the arrest itself is before us.

The judgment of the Supreme Court of Illinois is reversed, and the cause is remanded for further proceedings not inconsistent with this opinion.

It is so ordered. [***578]

DISSENT: JUSTICE STEVENS, with whom JUSTICE SOUTER, JUSTICE GINSBURG, and JUSTICE BREYER join, concurring in part and dissenting in part.

The State of Illinois asks this Court to announce a "bright-line rule" authorizing the temporary detention of anyone who flees at the mere sight of a police officer..

Respondent counters by asking us to adopt the opposite per se rule -- that the fact that a person flees upon seeing the police can never, by itself, be sufficient to justify a temporary investigative stop of the kind authorized by Terry v. Ohio, 392 U.S. 1, 20 L. Ed. 2d 889, 88 S. Ct. 1868 (1968).

The Court today wisely endorses neither per se rule. Instead, it rejects the proposition that "flight is . . . necessarily indicative of ongoing criminal activity," ante, at 5, adhering to the view that "the concept of reasonable suspicion . . . is not readily, or even usefully, reduced [**14] to a neat set of legal rules," but must be determined by looking to "the totality of the circumstances -- the whole picture." Abiding by this framework, the Court concludes that "Officer Nolan was justified in suspecting that Wardlow was involved in criminal activity."

Although I agree with the Court's rejection of the per se rules proffered by the parties, unlike the Court, I am persuaded that in this case the brief testimony of the officer who seized respondent does not justify the conclusion that he had reasonable suspicion to make the stop.

The question in this case concerns "the degree of suspicion that attaches to" a person's flight -- or, more precisely, what "commonsense conclusions" can be drawn respecting the motives behind that flight. A pedestrian may break into a run for a variety of reasons -- to catch up with a friend a block or two away, to seek shelter from an impending storm, to arrive at a bus stop before the bus leaves, to get home in time for dinner, to resume jogging after a pause for rest, to avoid contact with a bore or a bully, or simply to answer the call of nature -- any of which might coincide with the arrival of an officer in the vicinity. A pedestrian might also run because he or she has just sighted one or more police officers. In the latter instance, the State properly points out "that the fleeing person may be, inter alia, (1) an escapee from jail; (2) wanted on a warrant, (3) in possession of contraband, (i.e. drugs, weapons, stolen goods, etc.); or (4) someone who has just committed another type of crime." In short, there are unquestionably circumstances in which a person's flight is suspicious, and undeniably instances in which a person runs for entirely innocent reasons.

Given the diversity and frequency of possible motivations for flight, it would be profoundly unwise to endorse either per se rule. The inference we can reasonably draw about the motivation for a person's flight, rather, will depend on a number of different circumstances. Factors such as the time of day, the number of people in the area, the character of the neighborhood, whether the officer was in uniform, the way the runner was dressed, the direction and speed of the flight, and whether the person's behavior was otherwise unusual might be relevant in specific cases.

This number of variables is surely sufficient to preclude either a bright-line rule that always justifies, or that never justifies, an investigative stop based on the sole fact that flight began after a police officer appeared nearby.

"It is a matter of common knowledge that men who are entirely innocent do sometimes fly from the scene of a crime through fear of being apprehended as the guilty parties, or from an unwillingness to appear as witnesses. Nor is it true as an accepted axiom of criminal law that 'the wicked flee when no man pursueth, but the righteous are as bold as a lion.' Innocent men sometimes hesitate to confront a jury -- not necessarily because they fear that the jury will not protect them, but because they do not wish their names to appear in connection with criminal acts, are humiliated at being obliged to incur the popular odium of an arrest and trial, or because they do not wish to be put to the annoyance or expense of defending themselves." In addition to these concerns, a reasonable person may conclude that an officer's sudden appearance indicates nearby criminal activity. And where there is criminal activity there is also a substantial element of danger -- either from the criminal or from a confrontation between the criminal and the police. These considerations can lead to an innocent and understandable desire to quit the vicinity with all speed.

Among some citizens, particularly minorities and those residing in high crime areas, there is also the possibility that the fleeing person is entirely innocent, but, with or without justification, believes that contact with the police can itself be dangerous, apart from any criminal activity associated with the officer's sudden presence. For such a person, unprovoked flight is neither "aberrant" nor "abnormal." Moreover, these concerns and fears are known to the police officers themselves, and are validated by law enforcement investigations into their own practices. Accordingly, the evidence supporting the reasonableness of these beliefs is too pervasive to be dismissed as random or rare, and too persuasive to be disparaged as inconclusive or insufficient. In any event, just as we do not require "scientific certainty" for our commonsense conclusion that unprovoked flight can sometimes indicate suspicious motives, neither do we require scientific certainty to conclude that unprovoked flight can occur for other, innocent reasons

II

Guided by that totality-of-the-circumstances test, the Court concludes that Officer Nolan had reasonable suspicion to stop respondent. Ante, at 5. In this respect, my view differs from the Court's. The entire justification for the stop is articulated in the brief testimony of Officer Nolan. Some facts are perfectly clear; others are not. This factual insufficiency leads me to conclude that the Court's judgment is mistaken.

Respondent Wardlow was arrested a few minutes after noon on September 9, 1995. Nolan was part of an eight-officer, four-car caravan patrol team. The officers were headed for "one of the areas in the 11th District [of Chicago] that's high [in] narcotics traffic. The reason why four cars were in the caravan was that "normally in these different areas there's an enormous amount of people, sometimes lookouts, customers." Officer Nolan testified that he was in uniform on that day, but he did not recall whether he was driving a marked or an unmarked car

Officer Nolan and his partner were in the last of the four patrol cars that "were all caravaning eastbound down Van Buren." Id. at 8. Nolan first observed respondent "in front of 4035 West Van Buren." Id. at 7. Wardlow "looked in our direction and began fleeing." Id. at 9. Nolan then "began driving southbound down the street observing [respondent] running through the gangway and the alley southbound," and observed that Wardlow was carrying a white, opaque bag under his arm. Id. at 6, 9. After the car turned south and intercepted respondent as he "ran right towards us," Officer Nolan stopped him and conducted a "protective search," which revealed that the bag under respondent's arm contained a loaded handgun. Id. at 9-11.

This terse testimony is most noticeable for what it fails to reveal. Though asked whether he was in a marked or unmarked car, Officer Nolan could not recall the answer. He was not asked whether any of the other three cars in the caravan were marked, or whether any of the other seven officers were in uniform. Though he explained that the size of the caravan was because "normally in these different areas there's an enormous amount of people, sometimes lookouts, customers," Officer Nolan did not testify as to whether anyone besides Wardlow was nearby 4035 West Van Buren. Nor is it clear that that address was the intended destination of the caravan. As the Appellate Court of Illinois interpreted the record, "it appears that the officers were simply driving by, on their way to some unidentified location, when they noticed defendant standing at Officer Nolan's testimony also does not reveal how fast the officers were driving. It does not indicate whether he saw respondent notice the other patrol cars. And it does not say whether the caravan, or any part of it, had already passed Wardlow by before he began to run.

No other factors sufficiently support a finding of reasonable suspicion. Though respondent was carrying a white, opaque bag under his arm, there is nothing at all suspicious about that. Certainly the time of day -- shortly after noon -- does not support Illinois' argument. Nor were the officers "responding to any call or report of suspicious activity in the area." Officer Nolan did testify that he expected to find "an enormous amount of people," including drug customers or lookouts, and the Court points out that "it was in this context that Officer

Nolan decided to investigate Wardlow after observing him flee." Ante, at 4. This observation, in my view, lends insufficient weight to the reasonable suspicion analysis; indeed, in light of the absence of testimony that anyone else was nearby when respondent began to run, this observation points in the opposite direction.

The State, along with the majority of the Court, relies as well on the assumption that this flight occurred in a high crime area. Even if that assumption is accurate, it is insufficient because even in a high crime neighborhood unprovoked flight does not invariably lead to reasonable suspicion. On the contrary, because many factors providing innocent motivations for unprovoked flight are concentrated in high crime areas, the character of the neighborhood arguably makes an inference of guilt less appropriate, rather than more so. Like unprovoked flight itself, presence in a high crime neighborhood is a fact too generic and susceptible to innocent explanation to satisfy the reasonable suspicion inquiry.

It is the State's burden to articulate facts sufficient to support reasonable suspicion. In my judgment, Illinois has failed to discharge that burden. I am not persuaded that the mere fact that someone standing on a sidewalk looked in the direction of a passing car before starting to run is sufficient to justify a forcible stop and frisk.

I therefore respectfully dissent from the Court's judgment to reverse the court below.

CHAPTER 8
TO ACCOMPANY
ETHICS AND SOCIAL RESPONSIBILITY
OF BUSINESS 160

MARC KASKY v. NIKE, INC., ET AL.,

79 Cal. App. 4th 165 (2000)

COURT OF APPEAL OF CALIFORNIA, FIRST APPELLATE DISTRICT,
DIVISION ONE

SWAGER JUDGE

Nike, Inc., a marketer of athletic shoes and sports apparel, has grown into a large multinational enterprise through a marketing strategy centering on a favorable brand image, which is associated with a distinctive logo and the advertising slogan, "Just do it." To maintain this image, the company invests heavily in advertising and brand promotion, spending no less than $978,251,000 for the year ending May 31, 1997. Reviewing the company's successful marketing strategy, the 1997 annual report asserts, "We are a company . . . that is based on a brand, one with a genuine and distinct personality, and tangible, emotional connections to consumers the world over.

Like other major marketers of athletic shoes and sports apparel, Nike contracts for the manufacture of its products in countries with low labor costs. In Nike's case, the actual production facilities are owned by South Korean and Taiwanese companies that manufacture the products under contract with Nike. The bulk of Nike products are manufactured in China, Thailand, and Indonesia, though some components or products involving more complex technology are manufactured in South Korea or Taiwan. In 1995, a Korean company opened up a major new facility in Vietnam, giving that country also a significant share of Nike's production. The record indicates that between 300,000 and 500,000 workers are employed in Asian factories producing Nike products. The complaint alleges that the vast majority of these workers are women under the age of 24.

The company has sought to foster the appearance and reality of good working conditions in the Asian factories producing its products. All contractors are required to sign a Memorandum of Understanding that, in general, commits them to comply with local laws regarding minimum wage, overtime, child labor, holidays and vacations, insurance benefits, working conditions, and other similar matters and to maintain records documenting their compliance. To assure compliance, the company conducts spot audits of labor and environmental conditions by accounting firms. Early in 1997, Nike retained a consulting firm, co-

chaired by Andrew Young, the former ambassador to the United Nations, to carry out an independent evaluation of the labor practices in Nike factories. After visits to 12 factories, Young issued a report that commented favorably on working conditions in the factories and found no evidence of widespread abuse or mistreatment of workers.

Nevertheless, Nike was beset in 1996 and 1997 with a series of reports on working conditions in its factories that contrasted sharply with the favorable view in the Young report. An accounting firm's spot audit of the large Vietnamese factory, which was leaked to the press by a disgruntled employee, reported widespread violations of local regulations and atmospheric pollution causing respiratory problems in 77 percent of the workers. An investigator for Vietnam Labor Watch found evidence of widespread abuses and a pervasive "sense of desperation" from 35 interviews with Vietnamese workers. An Australian organization published a highly critical case study on Nike's Indonesian factories. And the Hong Kong Christian Industrial Committee released an extensively documented study of several Chinese factories, including three used by Nike, which reported 11- to 12-hour work days, compulsory overtime, violation of minimum wage laws, exposure to dangerous levels of dust and toxic fumes, and employment of workers under the age of 16.

Nike countered with a public relations campaign that defended the benefits of its Asian factories to host countries and sought to portray the company as being in the vanguard of responsible corporations seeking to maintain adequate labor standards in overseas facilities. Press releases responded to sweatshop allegations, addressed women's issues, stressed the company's code of conduct, and broadly denied exploitation of underage workers. A more lengthy press release, entitled "Nike Production Primer" answered a series of allegations with detailed information and footnoted sources. Another release drew attention to the favorable Young report and invited readers to consult it on-line. A letter to the presidents and athletic directors of those colleges sponsoring Nike products defended the company's labor practices. And company officials sought to rebut specific charges in letters to the editor and to nonprofit organizations.

The complaint alleges that, in the course of this public relations campaign, Nike made a series of six misrepresentations regarding its labor practices: (1) "that workers who make NIKE products are . . . not subjected to corporal punishment and/or sexual abuse;" (2) "that NIKE products are made in accordance with applicable governmental laws and regulations governing wages and hours;" (3) "that NIKE products are made in accordance with applicable laws and regulations governing health and safety conditions;" (4) "that NIKE pays average line-workers double-the-minimum wage in Southeast Asia;" (5) "that workers who produce NIKE products receive free meals and health care;" and (6) "that NIKE guarantees a 'living wage' for all workers who make NIKE products." In addition, the complaint alleges that NIKE made the false claim that the Young report proves that it "is doing a good job and 'operating morally.' "

The first and second causes of action, based on negligent misrepresentation and intentional or reckless misrepresentation, alleged that Nike engaged in an unlawful business practice in violation of Business and Professions Code section 17200 by making the above misrepresentations "In order to maintain and/or increase its sales and profits . . . through its advertising, promotional campaigns, public statements and marketing . . . ." The third cause of action alleged unfair business practices within the meaning of section 17200, and the fourth cause of action alleged false advertising in violation of Business and Professions Code section 17500. The prayer sought an injunction ordering Nike "to disgorge all monies" that it acquired by the alleged unlawful and unfair practices, "to undertake a Court-approved public information campaign" to remedy the misinformation disseminated by its false advertising and unlawful and unfair practices, and to cease "misrepresenting the working conditions under which NIKE products are made . . . ."

A line of decisions has sanctioned restraints on commercial speech that is false, deceptive or misleading. [a]dvertising that is false, deceptive, or misleading of course is subject to restraint. Since the advertiser knows his product and has a commercial interest in its dissemination, we have little worry that regulation to assure truthfulness will discourage protected speech. The public and private benefits from commercial speech derive from confidence in its accuracy and reliability. Thus, the leeway for untruthful or misleading expression that has been allowed in other contexts has little force in the commercial arena."

Nike exemplifies the perceived evils or benefits of labor practices associated with the processes of economic globalization. Though participants in purely private labor disputes are entitled to certain First Amendment protections, Nike's strong corporate image and widespread consumer market places its labor practices in the context of a broader debate about the social implications of employing low-cost foreign labor for manufacturing functions once performed by domestic workers. We take judicial notice that this debate has given rise to urgent calls for action ranging from international labor standards to consumer boycotts. Information about the labor practices at Nike's overseas plants thus constitutes data relevant to a controversy of great public interest in our times.

Freedom of " 'expression on public issues "has always rested on the highest rung of the hierarchy of First Amendment values." "[t]he general proposition that freedom of expression upon public questions is secured by the First Amendment has long been settled by our decisions. The constitutional safeguard . . . 'was fashioned to assure unfettered interchange of ideas for the bringing about of political and social changes desired by the people.'

It follows that "under the free speech guaranty the validity and truth of declarations in political disputes over issues of public interest must be resolved by the public and not by a judge "In the context of . . . public debate on a matter of public interest, the truth of the statement is irrelevant." In the famous words of Judge Learned Hand, the First Amendment "presupposes that right conclusions are more likely to be gathered out of a multitude of tongues, than through any kind of authoritative selection. To many this is, and always will be, folly; but we have staked upon it our all."

The press releases and letters at issue here cross the boundary between political and private decisionmaking. The citizen may want to translate personal discontent over Nike's labor practices into political action or may merely wish to refrain from purchasing its products manufactured by undesired labor practices, just as he or she may wish to buy products with a union identification. In either case, "the First Amendment protects the public's interest in receiving information

Finally, we note that "commercial motivation does not transform noncommercial speech into commercial speech . . The present case is not one in which commercial speech is linked to noncommercial speech again one in which commercial and noncommercial speech are " 'inextricably intertwined.'" Rather, the record discloses noncommercial speech, addressed to a topic of public interest and responding to public criticism of Nike's labor practices. The fact that Nike has an economic motivation in defending its corporate image from such criticism does not alter the significance of the speech to the "listeners" --the consumers or other members of the public concerned with labor practices attending the process of economic globalization.

The judgment is affirmed.

CHAPTER 9
TO ACCOMPANY
UNIT III. CONTRACTS AND ELECTRONIC
COMMERCE
NATURE OF TRADITIONAL AND INTERNET
CONTRACTS 179

SHARON FLOSS, V. RYAN'S FAMILY STEAK
HOUSES, INC., ET AL., v. RYAN'S FAMILY STEAK HOUSES, INC.,

211 F.3d 306 (2000)

UNITED STATES COURT OF APPEALS FOR THE SIXTH CIRCUIT

GWIN, DISTRICT JUDGE.

With these appeals, consolidated for purposes of decision, the Court reviews whether employees effectively waived their rights to bring actions in federal court under the Americans with Disabilities Act, 42 U.S.C. § 12101, et seq. ("ADA"), and the Fair Labor Standards Act, 29 U.S.C. § 201, et seq. ("FLSA"). At the district court, the plaintiffs attempted to sue their former employer, Ryan's Family Steak Houses, Inc. ("Ryan's"). However, when applying for employment at Ryan's, both plaintiffs had signed a form indicating they would arbitrate all employment-related disputes. In both cases, Ryan's filed a motion to compel arbitration.

Finding no valid arbitration agreement, the United States District Court for the Eastern District of Tennessee refused to require Plaintiff-Appellee Kyle Daniels to arbitrate his claim under the ADA. In contrast, the United States District Court for the Eastern District of Kentucky found that Plaintiff-Appellant Sharon Floss was required to arbitrate her dispute and could thus not pursue her claim under the FLSA in federal court.

Ryan's now appeals the district court's refusal to require Daniels to arbitrate his ADA claim. Similarly, Floss appeals the district court's order requiring her to submit her FLSA claim to arbitration.

In support of its argument that the plaintiffs agreed to waive their right to bring an action in federal court and instead agreed to arbitrate all employment disputes, Ryan's relies upon a document identified as the "Job Applicant Agreement to Arbitration of Employment-Related Disputes." Ryan's includes this purported agreement in its employment application packet. Only those applicants who sign the agreement are considered for employment at Ryan's. Both Daniels and Floss acknowledge signing the agreement.

A notice on the inside cover of the packet informs applicants that they must agree to the terms and conditions outlined in the agreement in order to be considered for employment with Ryan's.

The employee's agreement to arbitrate is not with Ryan's. Instead, the agreement runs between the employee and a third-party arbitration services provider, Employment Dispute Services, Inc. ("EDSI"). In the agreement, EDSI agrees to provide an arbitration forum in exchange for the employee's agreement to submit any dispute with his potential employer to arbitration with EDSI. Although Ryan's is not explicitly identified as a party to the agreement, the agreement says the employee's potential employer is a third-party beneficiary of the employee's agreement to waive a judicial forum and arbitrate all employment-related disputes.

The agreement gives EDSI complete discretion over arbitration rules and procedures. The agreement says that all arbitration proceedings will be conducted under "EDSI Rules and Procedures." The agreement then gives EDSI the unlimited right to modify the rules without the employee's consent.

In July 1994, Kyle Daniels applied for employment with Ryan's and received this agreement as part of the employment application packet. n2 Similarly, Ryan's gave Sharon Floss the agreement when she applied for employment in December 1997. Both Daniels and Floss signed the agreement and began their employment at Ryan's shortly thereafter.

The agreement received by Daniels designated Employment Dispute Resolution, Inc. ("EDR") as the arbitration services provider. EDR is now apparently referred to as Employment Dispute Services, Inc. ("EDSI").

Daniels ceased working at Ryan's on August 13, 1997. On that date, Daniels claims he attempted to resume his employment with Ryan's after taking a medical leave to treat his viral hepatitis. However, Daniels says Ryan's terminated him upon his return to the restaurant.

Floss ceased working at Ryan's on January 23, 1998. Floss left her position with Ryan's after a confrontation with two management employees. According to Floss, these management employees intimidated and harassed her after learning that she had complained to the United States Department of Labor regarding Ryan's pay practices.

On February 17, 1998, Floss sued Ryan's in the United States District Court for the Eastern District of Kentucky for violation of the Fair Labor Standards Act. n3 Floss claimed that Ryan's (1) did not pay employees legally-required minimum and overtime wages, (2) failed to pay employees for certain hours worked, and (3) retaliated against her because she complained of these practices to the United States Department of Labor. Floss sued in both her individual capacity and on behalf of similarly situated Ryan's employees.

Floss also asserted state-law claims for false imprisonment and intentional infliction of emotional distress, naming as codefendants the two management employees involved in the alleged confrontation.

On May 19, 1998, Daniels filed his action against Ryan's in the United States District Court for the Eastern District of Tennessee. In this action, Daniels asserted a claim under the ADA, alleging that Ryan's terminated him on account of his handicapped status despite his ability to perform the essential functions of his job with or without reasonable accommodation.

Daniels also asserted a claim under a state disability discrimination statute.

In both actions, Ryan's filed motions to compel arbitration. In ruling on these motions, the respective district courts reached different conclusions as to whether the agreements were enforceable.

In Daniels's action, the district court ruled that the agreement was not enforceable. The court reasoned that EDSI did not provide Daniels with any consideration for his promise to arbitrate his dispute with Ryan's. Though EDSI promised to provide an arbitration forum, the court found that only Ryan's and EDSI, rather than Daniels, actually benefited from that promise. The court also found that the arbitration document did not bind EDSI. Specifically, the court noted that the agreement gave EDSI an unlimited right to unilaterally modify or amend the rules and procedures of the arbitration proceeding without providing notice to Daniels. Finally, the court noted that even if enforceable the agreement was not sufficiently clear so as to represent a knowing and intelligent waiver of Daniels's right to pursue his disability discrimination claim in federal court.

However, the district court in Floss's case enforced the agreement The court rejected Floss's argument that claims under the FLSA could not be made subject to mandatory arbitration.

The district court enforced the agreement under the Federal Arbitration Act ("FAA"). The FAA authorizes federal district courts to stay a proceeding if any matter raised therein is subject to an arbitration agreement and to issue an order compelling arbitration if a party has filed suit in contravention of an arbitration agreement.

Both Ryan's and Floss now appeal the rulings adverse to them.

The Federal Arbitration Act declares that arbitration agreements "shall be valid, irrevocable, and enforceable, save upon grounds that exist at law or in equity for the revocation of any contract." However, "the FAA was not enacted to force parties to arbitrate in the absence of an agreement. Indeed, "the sine qua non of the FAA's applicability to a particular dispute is an agreement to arbitrate the dispute in a contract which evidences a transaction in interstate commerce."

Floss and Daniels say the arbitration agreements they signed as part of their employment applications with Ryan's are unenforceable. In deciding whether the agreements are enforceable, we examine applicable state-law contract principles.

Consideration is an essential element of every contract. In other words, a promise is legally enforceable only if the promisor receives in exchange for that promise some act or forbearance, or the promise thereof. Consideration consists when the promisee does something that he is under no legal obligation to do or refrains from doing [that] which he has a legal right to do. 'It is invariably held that the promise of one party is a valid consideration for the promise of the other party.

A promise constitutes consideration for another promise only when it creates a binding obligation. Thus, absent a mutuality of obligation, a contract based on reciprocal promises lacks consideration.. Put more succinctly, such a contract "must be binding on both or else it is binding on neither.

Promises may fail to create legally binding obligations for a variety of reasons. Most notably, a promise may in effect promise nothing at all. Such an illusory promise arises when a promisor retains the right to decide whether or not to perform the promised act

In the purported agreement at issue in this case, EDSI offered its promise to provide an arbitral forum as consideration for Floss and Daniels's promise to submit any dispute they may have with their employer to arbitration with EDSI. In ruling in favor of Daniels, the district court found that EDSI's promise did not create a binding obligation. We agree.

EDSI's promise to provide an arbitral forum is fatally indefinite. Though obligated to provide some type of arbitral forum, EDSI has unfettered discretion in choosing the nature of that forum. Specifically, EDSI has reserved the right to alter the applicable rules and procedures without any obligation to notify, much less receive consent from, Floss and Daniels. EDSI's right to choose the nature of its performance renders its promise illusory. As Professor Williston has explained:

Where a promisor retains an unlimited right to decide later the nature or extent of his performance, the promise is too indefinite for legal enforcement. The unlimited choice in effect destroys the promise and makes it merely illusory.

EDSI's illusory promise does not create a binding obligation. The purported arbitration agreement therefore lacks a mutuality of obligation. Without a mutuality of obligation, the agreement lacks consideration and, accordingly, does not constitute an enforceable arbitration agreement. n8

Ryan's has pursued an acceptable objective in an unacceptable manner. An employer may enter an agreement with employees requiring the arbitration of all employment disputes, including those involving federal statutory claims. Yet an employer cannot seek to do so in such a way that leaves employees with no consideration for their promise to submit their disputes to arbitration. Here, we find that Floss and Daniels did not receive any consideration for their promise to arbitrate their disputes. We thus refuse to enforce their promise in favor of Ryan's.

The judgment of the United States District Court for the Eastern District of Tennessee is AFFIRMED, and the judgment of the United States District Court for the Eastern District of Kentucky is REVERSED.

CHAPTER 10
TO ACCOMPANY
AGREEMENT 194

SCOTT D. MCCOMAS, DAVID A. NAULT AND JAMMERS WEST, INC, AND MIXED NUTS, INC V.
CHRISTOPHER C. BOCCI,

166 Ore. App. 150; 996 P.2d 506 (2000)

COURT OF APPEALS OF OREGON

BREWER, JUDGE

Plaintiffs appeal from summary judgment for defendant on their legal malpractice and breach of contract claims, as well as from the denial of their cross-motion for summary judgment on the malpractice claim.

Plaintiffs are a corporation, its president, and its secretary. This case arises out of plaintiffs' attempt to obtain a Retail Malt Beverage (RMB) license from the Oregon Liquor Control Commission (OLCC) for a tavern they had contracted to purchase in Independence, Oregon. The purchase of the business, which was to be known as "Jammers West," and the accompanying 25-year lease of the premises both were contingent on issuance of the RMB license. In March 1994, after conducting an investigation, OLCC regulatory staff recommended that the license be denied. Plaintiffs hired defendant in late March or early April 1994 to represent them in connection with their continuing efforts to obtain the license. Plaintiffs requested a hearing on the proposed denial. The hearing, at which defendant represented plaintiffs, was held in June 1994.

According to the affidavit of the corporation's president Scott McComas, submitted in opposition to a motion for summary judgment, defendant made the following contractual guarantee after the OLCC hearing:

"On or about June 23, 1994, plaintiff David Nault and I had lunch with [defendant] following an OLCC hearing in the Jammers West licensing matter.

"The primary topic discussed at this lunch was how to proceed in the event that the OLCC denied an RMB license for Jammers West.

"[Defendant] repeatedly assured [plaintiffs] that if the OLCC denied a license to Jammers West, we would prevail at the Oregon Court of Appeals. [He] stated that he was completely confident that we would prevail in that forum. He stated further that if we received an adverse OLCC determination, we would 'kick ass' at the Court of Appeals."

Defendant contends that he "never guaranteed plaintiffs a result at the Court of Appeals * * * [,] that he did not believe an appeal from the OLCC's adverse Final Order would be successful[,] and that he communicated his belief to the plaintiffs."

In October 1994, the hearings examiner recommended that a license be issued with restrictions. In March 1995, after considering exceptions to the hearings examiner's recommendation, OLCC denied the license on two grounds: (1) The establishment was located in a "problem" area, and (2) McComas had "a record of using alcoholic beverages to excess," Plaintiffs moved for reconsideration, which OLCC denied. Although defendant proceeded with the plan to seek review of the final OLCC order, the petition for judicial review that he filed was untimely. As a consequence, we dismissed the appeal. Thus, OLCC's order stood un challenged and plaintiffs were unable to obtain an RMB license and complete the purchase of Jammers West.

Plaintiffs then filed this action against defendant. They alleged that defendant's failure to file a timely petition for judicial review constituted professional negligence. Furthermore, plaintiffs asserted that defendant's omission constituted a breach of the alleged contractual guarantee to obtain a reversal of OLCC's decision in this court. Defendant moved for summary judgment, contending, among other arguments, that plaintiffs were not damaged by his failure to file in time, because plaintiffs would not have succeeded in obtaining reversal of the adverse OLCC decision. Plaintiffs filed a cross-motion for summary judgment on the issue of liability with respect to the malpractice claim.

The trial court granted defendant's motion for summary judgment and denied plaintiffs' cross-motion for summary judgment, concluding that:

"[With respect to the professional negligence claim,] if the plaintiffs would not have prevailed at the Court of Appeals, it could also be fairly said that the plaintiffs would not have been damaged and therefore it makes no difference whether the defendant missed the filing deadline.

"In my opinion the result must be the same vis-a-vis the contract claim as it is the malpractice claim. The plaintiffs say the damages arose due to the failure of the defendant to perfect the appeal. Because the appeal, in my opinion, would not have been successful, the failure to perfect [the appeal] caused the plaintiffs no damages."

With respect to the malpractice claim, our review of the record discloses that OLCC's findings of fact were supported by substantial evidence and its conclusions were supported by substantial reason. Plaintiffs do not suggest that the order was vulnerable for any other reason. Therefore, plaintiffs would not have prevailed on the merits of their petition for review of the final OLCC order, even if the petition for judicial review had been timely filed. For that reason, we agree with the trial court that plaintiffs were not damaged in the ways they alleged in their malpractice claim by defendant's failure to timely file a petition for review. However, our analysis of plaintiffs' contract claim takes a different path.

In their third assignment of error, plaintiffs argue that the trial court erred in granting summary judgment to defendant on their breach of contract claim. Plaintiffs argue that defendant's guarantee arose in the context of the parties' existing contract of representation and is, therefore, enforceable. Plaintiffs also challenge the trial court's conclusion that their entitlement to damages for breach of contract depends on whether they would have prevailed on the merits following appellate review of the OLCC order. Plaintiffs assert that, unlike the rule governing professional negligence claims, the measure of damages for breach of a contract to produce a particular result does not require a plaintiff to prove the "case within a case." Defendant denies making a guarantee and contends, among other arguments, that plaintiffs' evidence opposing summary judgment was insufficient to create a genuine issue of material fact with respect to the existence of an enforceable contractual guarantee.

According to plaintiffs' pleadings and evidentiary submissions, defendant undertook his representation of them in a contract made between the parties in late March or early April 1994. Defendant's alleged guarantee occurred, plaintiffs assert, on or about June 23, 1994--following OLCC's hearing, but before OLCC made its decision to deny the license. Plaintiffs contend that the guarantee was made in the context of a discussion about "how to proceed in the event that OLCC denied an RMB license for Jammers West." In their brief to the trial court, plaintiffs themselves characterized the guarantee, as one made "in the course of [the] representation."

If, as plaintiffs argue, a promise of appellate success was made in the context of defendant's pre-existing contractual undertaking, it is unenforceable. A promise made after the creation of a contract and arising in the course of its performance is gratuitous and establishes no duty unless it is supported by new consideration. Plaintiffs have not alleged or proven that they treated defendant's statement as a contractual offer by accepting it or that they furnished any consideration for the alleged promise. Therefore, the statements, if made, merely constituted defendant's prediction or opinion, unfettered by contractual constraints.

Nor have plaintiffs pleaded or proven an enforceable modification of the existing contract for legal services, which requires the same elements.

As pleaded, it could reasonably be inferred that the alleged undertaking was an integral part of the defendant's offer of services and, therefore, furnished consideration for the plaintiff's acceptance. Here, on the summary judgment record, the timing of the alleged promise does not permit such an inference. It is undisputed that defendant's alleged statement was made months after the parties' existing contractual arrangement was established and there is no evidence that it was supported by consideration. Therefore, defendant's statement, if made, constituted a gratuitous prediction that defendant had no contractual duty to produce. The trial court did not err in granting summary judgment in favor of defendant and in denying plaintiffs' cross-motion for summary judgment.

Affirmed.

CHAPTER 11
TO ACCOMPANY
CONSIDERATION 211

GARY KREMEN, ET AL., V. STEPHEN MICHAEL COHEN, ET AL.

2000 U.S. Dist. LEXIS 8476 (2000)

UNITED STATES DISTRICT COURT FOR THE NORTHERN DISTRICT OF CALIFORNIA

WARE, JUDGE

Plaintiff Gary Kremen registered the domain name sex.com with NSI on May 9, 1994. Plaintiff identified Online Classified, Inc. ("Online Classified") as the registering organization. Plaintiff never constructed a Web site or otherwise commercially exploited the domain name. In a letter dated October 15, 1995, Sharon Dimmick, purportedly on behalf of Online Classified informed Defendant Stephen Cohen that Online Classified had "decided to abandon the domain name sex.com" and requested that Mr. Cohen "notify the internet registration on our behalf, to delete [their] domain name sex.com." It further stated that "we have no objection to your use of the domain name sex.com and this letter shall serve as our authorization to the internet registration to transfer sex.com to your corporation." The letter was on Online Classified letterhead and was signed by Ms. Dimmick, who represented herself as the President of the company. Shortly thereafter, Mr. Cohen registered sex.com in the name of a company he operated.

Plaintiff contends that the October 15, 1995 letter is a forgery by Mr. Cohen. On October 16, 1998, Plaintiff filed suit against numerous defendants, including NSI for its deletion of the domain name. Plaintiff alleges the following causes of action against NSI: (1) breach of contract, (2)...NSI now moves for summary judgment as to all claims against it.

A. Breach of Contract

A party must prove the following to establish a claim for breach of contract: the existence and terms of the contract, plaintiff's performance, defendant's breach, and damages. Student Loan Marketing Ass'n v. Hanes, 181 F.R.D. 629, 633 (S.D. Cal. 1998). The essential elements required to demonstrate the existence of a contract are: "(1) parties capable of contracting, (2) their consent, (3) a lawful object, and (4) a sufficient cause or consideration." "Consideration is a benefit conferred or agreed to be conferred upon the promisor or prejudice suffered or agreed to be suffered 'as an inducement' to the promisor." Conservatorship of O'Connor, 48 Cal. App. 4th 1076 (1996).

Plaintiff contends NSI breached the contract governing Kremen's registration of the domain name. Plaintiff registered the domain name on May 4, 1994. In 1994, the registration process involved completing a short administrative template which was then submitted to NSI via e-mail. Graves Decl. P 20. At that time, NSI received no registration fee or other form of payment from registrants in exchange for the service. Thus, the registration form is not supported by consideration because there was no benefit conferred or agreed to be conferred upon NSI. Accordingly, Plaintiff's motion for summary judgment as to the breach of contract claim is granted because Plaintiff has failed to demonstrate an essential element of the claim- the existence of a contract.

Based upon the foregoing, the Court grants Defendant NSI's motion for summary judgment.

CHAPTER 12
TO ACCOMPANY
CAPACITY AND LEGALITY 225

CHARLES O. GRIGSON, v. CREATIVE ARTISTS AGENCY,

210 F.3d 524 (2000)

UNITED STATES COURT OF APPEALS FOR THE FIFTH CIRCUIT

BARKSDALE, Circuit Judge:

"Return of the Texas Chain Saw Massacre" (the movie) was filmed in 1993-94; then "obscure actors" Matthew McConaughey and Renee Zellweger acted in it. The movie was produced by Ultra Muchos, Inc., and River City Films, Inc. The trustee for the movie's owners is Charles Grigson.

In October 1995, Ultra Muchos and River City entered into a distribution agreement with Columbia TriStar Home Video, Inc. It was given exclusive distribution rights and complete discretion on how to exercise them; the producers were to receive a percentage of the movie's gross revenue. And, by separate, earlier agreement, the owners were to receive a portion of the producers' percentage.

In the period post-acting in the movie and prior to the fall of 1996, McConaughey signed an agency contract with Creative Artists Agency, L.L.C. The movie's distribution was delayed by TriStar to take advantage of Zellweger and McConaughey's success in subsequent movies. Subsequently, however, TriStar gave the movie only a limited distribution.

In district court in mid-1997, Grigson, as trustee, sued Ultra Muchos, River City, and TriStar for breach of the distribution agreement. But, Grigson quickly and voluntarily had the action dismissed that fall, when TriStar sought to enforce the distribution agreement's arbitration clause, which contains a forum selection provision (Los Angeles County, California).

In late 1997, a few months after the voluntary dismissal of the first action, Grigson, now joined by Ultra Muchos and River City, filed this action in state court against McConaughey and Creative Artists (Defendants) for, inter alia, tortious interference with the distribution agreement, claiming that such interference occurred between McConaughey's signing with Creative Artists and the movie's limited distribution. In this regard, Defendants allegedly pressured TriStar to limit the release because they viewed it as an improper exploitation of McConaughey's success post-acting in the movie.

This is an issue of first impression for our circuit. Other circuits have, in a few instances, allowed a non-signatory to a contract with an arbitration clause to compel arbitration under an equitable estoppel theory,

including when the action is intertwined with, and dependent upon, that contract.

Existing case law demonstrates that equitable estoppel allows a nonsignatory to compel arbitration in two different circumstances. First, equitable estoppel applies when the signatory to a written agreement containing an arbitration clause must rely on the terms of the written agreement in asserting its claims against the nonsignatory. When each of a signatory's claims against a nonsignatory makes reference to or presumes the existence of the written agreement, the signatory's claims arise out of and relate directly to the written agreement, and arbitration is appropriate. Second, application of equitable estoppel is warranted when the signatory to the contract containing an arbitration clause raises allegations of substantially interdependent and concerted misconduct by both the nonsignatory and one or more of the signatories to the contract. Otherwise the arbitration proceedings between the two signatories would be rendered meaningless and the federal policy in favor of arbitration effectively thwarted.

We agree with the intertwined-claims test formulated by the Eleventh Circuit. Each case, of course, turns on its facts. Such equitable estoppel is much more readily applicable when the case presents both independent bases advanced by the Eleventh Circuit for applying the intertwined-claims doctrine. That is the situation here. The linchpin for equitable estoppel is equity -- fairness. For the case at hand, to not apply this intertwined-claims basis to compel arbitration would fly in the face of fairness.

Moreover, it would be especially inequitable where, as here, a signatory non-defendant is charged with interdependent and concerted misconduct with a non-signatory defendant. In such instances, that signatory, in essence, becomes a party, with resulting loss, inter alia, of time and money because of its required participation in the proceeding. Concomitantly, detrimental reliance by that signatory cannot be denied: it and the signatory-plaintiff had agreed to arbitration in lieu of litigation (generally far more costly in terms of time and expense); but, the plaintiff is seeking to avoid that agreement by bringing the action against a non-signatory charged with acting in concert with that non-defendant signatory. Of course, detrimental reliance is one of the elements for the usual application of equitable estoppel.

Accordingly, whether to utilize equitable estoppel in this fashion is within the district court's discretion; we review to determine only whether it has been abused. To constitute an abuse of discretion, the district court's decision must be either premised on an application of the law that is erroneous, or on an assessment of the evidence that is clearly erroneously.

Creative Artists is also charged with such interference with McConaughey's actor's contract for the movie (another exhibit to the complaint); he is charged with breach of that contract. Among other things, he was required by that actor's contract to allow use of "his name and photographs ... for commercial and advertising purposes".

The complaint uses that specific requirement in the actor's contract in describing how, for the theatrical release (as defined in the distribution agreement) mandated by the distribution agreement, TriStar had planned to distribute Chainsaw movie posters prominently featuring the likeness and name of McConaughey and, in fact, had printed posters reflecting this plan. Creative Artists, acting for McConaughey, contacted Columbia Tristar and successfully pressured it to retreat from its plan for the posters on the grounds that McConaughey's fame should not be exploited in such a manner in connection with the Chainsaw movie.

This is but part of the charged interference. In addition, the complaint alleges that the theatrical release was delayed initially to take advantage of Zellweger's post-movie success in another movie, also released by TriStar; that the plan changed to take advantage of both actors' success; that Creative Artists, on behalf of McConaughey, "pressured" TriStar to not make a major release of the movie and, instead, to make only a limited one, to Appellants' great financial detriment; and that, because of Defendants' actions, "TriStar failed to exercise its good faith judgment in promoting, exploiting, and distributing" the movie.

As is obvious from the foregoing, and as the district court concluded, these allegations and claims are intertwined with, and dependent upon, the distribution agreement. In addition to Appellants relying on the terms of the agreement in asserting their claims, TriStar and Defendants are charged with interdependent and concerted misconduct.

The distribution agreement, in describing the movie, lists Zellweger and two others as "starring" in it; McConaughey is not so listed. All rights to the movie are given to TriStar; and, subject to it making a required minimum expenditure in connection with the theatrical release, TriStar has "absolute discretion concerning the exploitation of the [movie] in any and all media".

In that provision, which obviously lies at the heart of this action, Appellants agreed that the good faith judgment of [TriStar] regarding any matter affecting the exploitation of the [movie] shall be binding and conclusive upon [Appellants] ([TriStar] shall make the determination, within its sole discretion, whether or not to release the [movie] in a given media and/or in a given territory). (Emphasis added.) "Territory" includes, with some exceptions, "the entire universe", while "media" includes, but is not limited to, movie theaters.

And, as noted, the distribution agreement's arbitration clause pertains, inter alia, to the "interpretation of [the distribution] agreement, ... the performance by the Parties of their respective obligations thereunder, and ... all other causes of action (whether sounding in contract or in tort) arising out of or relating to this Agreement". (Emphasis added.)

In short, the scope of the distribution, the "discretion", both "absolute" and "sole", vested in TriStar, and its "good faith judgment" are at the center of this dispute. Among other things, TriStar is charged with, as a result of the claimed interference ("pressure"), not using its "good faith judgment". Although not sued (an obvious attempt to make an end-run around the arbitration clause, as discussed infra), TriStar nevertheless will be involved extensively -- and, no doubt, quite expensively -- in this dispute, including whether it performed properly under the distribution agreement.

In any event, comparison of the two actions demonstrates, quite vividly, why the district court, which presided over both actions, did not abuse its discretion in compelling arbitration in the second, by applying the equitable estoppel doctrine crafted for such situations. The claims are intertwined with, and dependent upon, the distribution agreement, including, but not limited to, Defendants (non-signatories) and TriStar (non-defendant signatory) being charged with interdependent and concerted misconduct. Indeed, this action is the quintessential situation for when the doctrine should be applied.

For the foregoing reasons, the judgment is AFFIRMED.

ROBERT D. GREENE v. SAFEWAY STORES, INC.

210 F.3d 1237 (2000)

UNITED STATES COURT OF APPEALS FOR THE TENTH CIRCUIT

ALARCON, Circuit Judge.

Safeway Stores, Inc. ("Safeway"), appeals from the July 1997 judgment entered following a jury's verdict in favor of Robert Greene ("Greene"), a former Safeway employee. The jury found that Safeway engaged in willful discrimination in violation of the Age Discrimination in Employment Act, 29 U.S.C. § 621 et seq. ("ADEA"), and awarded Greene $6.7 million in damages.

The first trial in this matter commenced on February 13, 1995. The district court granted Safeway's motion for judgment as a matter of law at the close of Greene's case-in-chief. On October 15, 1996, a panel of this court reversed and remanded the case for a new trial. This court held that the evidence presented was legally sufficient to support an inference of age discrimination. The retrial of the action began on June 2, 1997. The district court denied Safeway's motions for judgment as a matter of law at the close of Greene's case-in-chief, at the close of all evidence, and after the jury found in favor of Greene.

Safeway appeals the denial of its motions for judgment as a matter of law. Because the evidence presented at the second trial was not substantially different from that presented at the first trial, we affirm. Safeway also appeals from the judgment awarding Greene $4.4 million for unrealized stock option appreciation. We conclude that the unrealized appreciation was compensable under the ADEA.

In his cross-appeal, Greene appeals from the district court's decision that the $4.4 million in unrealized stock option appreciation was not subject to doubling under the ADEA's provision for liquidated damages. We reject this contention and hold that the unrealized stock option appreciation was not an amount owing at the time of trial. We also uphold the district court's decision to deny prejudgment interest because an award of liquidated damages precludes an award of prejudgment interest.

Greene was born November 7, 1940. He went to work for Safeway as a courtesy clerk in 1957. In 1961, he became a produce manager at a Safeway store in Denver, Colorado. He became a store manager in 1966. Ten years later, he became a retail operations manager in Little Rock, Arkansas. Two years later, he returned to Denver as a retail operations manager. Five years later, Greene became a marketing operations manager in Houston. In 1986, Greene was appointed to the post of manager of Safeway's Denver Division.

On June 10, 1993, Greene was summoned to a meeting with Safeway's president, Steven Burd, and Safeway's executive vice president, Kenneth Oder. Burd fired Greene at that meeting. Greene was then 52. A document introduced at trial entitled "Senior Executive Supplemental Benefit Plan" showed that Greene's interest in Safeway's supplemental executive pension plan would have vested a little over two years later, when he turned 55. Greene testified at the Greene II trial that Burd said that he was "assembling his new team and unfortunately, he didn't have a place for me on his team." Burd testified that he told Greene at the meeting that "he didn't fit in with the new management style." Greene testified that Burd told him at the meeting that Safeway would "give [him] the chance to resign if [he thought] that would be better."

The specific reasons Burd gave for firing Greene were that Greene was a poor merchandiser, that sales had flattened or declined at established stores in the Denver Division, that Greene was pessimistic about competition with another supermarket chain in Denver, and that Greene was intimidating to the employees he supervised. Burd, Oder, and Bob Kinnie, who had been Greene's direct supervisor, each testified at trial that he had not mentioned these concerns to Greene prior to his termination on June 10, 1993. Also in evidence at trial were three internal memoranda that praised Greene's work and the performance of the Denver Division. The memoranda were dated November 5, 1992, February 8, 1993, and April 6, 1993.

John King, a marketing operations manager from Safeway's Seattle Division, replaced Greene as Denver Division Manager. King was 57 at the time. Denita Renfrew, a Denver Division employee, testified that King "seemed shocked" by his appointment to the position of Denver Division Manager. Renfrew testified that King said "he was very happy living in Seattle," that "he said he wanted to retire in Seattle," and that he indicated that he expected to be with the Denver Division for "a short period." King has remained with the Denver Division throughout the pendency of this litigation.

Greene elicited testimony and introduced documents showing that eight other executives left Safeway in the months leading up to and following Greene's termination. All eight men were in their fifties or sixties. Younger people succeeded all eight men.

Greene originally filed this action on March 24, 1994. The case proceeded to trial for the first time on February 13, 1995. At the close of Greene's case-in-chief, Safeway moved for judgment as a matter of law on Greene's ADEA claim. The district court granted Safeway's motion. This court reversed and remanded for a new trial. This appeal arises out of the judgment entered following the second trial in this matter.

The jury awarded Greene a total of $6.7 million, which encompassed three categories of damages: (1) $600,000 for loss of salary, bonuses, and health insurance benefits; (2) $1.7 million for loss of retirement plan benefits; and (3) $4.4 million for unrealized stock option appreciation. On Greene's motion to alter or amend the judgment, the district court awarded an additional $810,786 under the ADEA's provision for liquidated damages. This amount was equal to the amount the jury awarded Greene for salary, bonuses, and employee and retirement benefits that Greene would have received before the June 1997 trial but for his termination. The district court declined, however, to double the $4.4 million awarded for unrealized stock option appreciation.

At the time of his termination, Greene had 250,000 fully vested Safeway stock options. The exercise price was $1 per share. He also had roughly 250,000 more options that had not yet vested. The subscription agreement required Greene to exercise his vested options within ninety-five days of his October 15, 1993, separation from Safeway. Had he not exercised the vested options within ninety-five days, they would have expired. He exercised all of his vested options on December 21, 1993. He acquired Safeway stock with a market value in excess of $3,000,000. His gain on the transaction, on paper, was roughly $2,160,000. He immediately incurred a tax liability of roughly $850,000.

Greene testified that, had he not been terminated, he would have refrained from exercising his stock options until shortly after November 7, 1995, the date he planned to retire upon reaching the age of 55. Greene testified that he sold all the shares he acquired within a few months of exercising his options because he needed cash to pay the Internal Revenue Service and because he was without income to cover his daily living expenses.

Leslie Patten, an accountant who was Greene's expert witness on damages, testified that, had Greene exercised his vested options on January 31, 1996, instead of December 21, 1993, he would have reaped the benefit of increases in the market price of Safeway stock for an incremental gain in excess of $3,000,000. Patten also testified that, had Greene retired from Safeway in November 1995 as he planned, the options that had not yet vested at the time of Greene's termination would have vested and could have been exercised to purchase additional Safeway stock for a gain of more than $1,000,000.

The ADEA includes a broad remedial provision:

In any action brought to enforce this chapter the court shall have jurisdiction to grant such legal or equitable relief as may be appropriate to effectuate the purposes of this chapter, including without limitation judgments compelling employment, reinstatement or promotion, or enforcing the liability for amounts deemed to be unpaid minimum wages or unpaid overtime compensation under this section.

Deterrence and providing compensation for injuries caused by illegal discrimination are goals of the ADEA. The purpose of the . . . remedies under the ADEA is to make a plaintiff whole--to put the plaintiff, as nearly as possible, into the position he or she would have been in absent the discriminatory conduct.

An "Employment Agreement" dated February 15, 1988, provides that Safeway (1) agreed to employ Greene at his specified base rate of pay of $105,000 and (2) "further agreed to provide certain investment opportunities to Employee pursuant to a Subscription Agreement and the Stock Option Agreement referred to therein." Greene's stock options were a component of his compensation package. When Safeway terminated Greene's employment, it forced him to exercise his stock options sooner than he had planned to do so. The difference in the value of the options at the time Greene was forced to exercise them, and their value when he otherwise would have exercised them, is contingent compensation Greene would have received but for his termination. Failure to compensate Greene for his unrealized stock option appreciation would be a failure to "return[] him as nearly as possible to the economic situation he would have enjoyed but for the defendant's illegal conduct." Safeway cites no case holding that stock options cannot be a basis for ADEA damages or that the appreciated value of the options is not the correct measure of damages.

Finally, Safeway contends that the jury's award was too speculative. "In reviewing a jury's award of damages, this court should sustain the award unless it is clearly erroneous or there is no evidence to support the award." The jury's award of $4.4 million in stock option damages is close in amount to the tabulations presented by Greene's expert witness on damages, Leslie Patten. Patten's testimony supports the award. The judgment of the district court is AFFIRMED.

CHAPTER 14
TO ACCOMPANY
WRITING AND CONTRACT FORM 261

ARNOLD R. RISSMAN, V. OWEN RANDALL
RISSMAN AND ROBERT DUNN GLICKY

213 F.3d 381 (2000)

UNITED STATES COURT OF APPEALS FOR THE SEVENTH CIRCUIT

EASTERBROOK, CIRCUIT JUDGE

Gerald Rissman formed Tiger Electronics to make toys and games. In 1979 Gerald gave his sons Arnold, Randall, and Samuel large blocks of stock in the firm: Gerald kept 400 shares and gave Randall 400, Arnold 100, and Samuel 100. In 1986 both Gerald and Samuel withdrew from the venture. Tiger bought Gerald's stock, and Arnold bought Samuel's, leaving Randall with 2/3 of the shares and Arnold with the rest. Randall managed the business while Arnold served as a salesman. Arnold did not elect himself to the board of directors, though Tiger employed cumulative voting, which would have enabled him to do so. When the brothers had a falling out, Arnold sold his shares to Randall for $17 million. Thirteen months later, Tiger sold its assets (including its name and trademarks) for $335 million to Hasbro, another toy maker, and was renamed Lion Holdings. Arnold contends in this suit under the federal securities laws (with state-law claims under the supplemental jurisdiction) that he would not have sold for as little as $17 million, and perhaps would not have sold at all, had Randall not deceived him into thinking that Randall would never take Tiger public or sell it to a third party. Arnold says that these statements convinced him that his stock would remain illiquid and not pay dividends, so he sold for whatever Randall was willing to pay. Arnold now wants the extra $95 million he would have received had he retained his stock until the sale to Hasbro. Because the district judge granted summary judgment to the defendants, we must assume that Randall told Arnold that he was determined to keep Tiger a family firm. Likewise we must assume that Randall secretly planned to sell after acquiring Arnold's shares. But we need not assume that Arnold relied on Randall's statements (equivalently, that the statements were material to and caused Arnold's decision), and without reliance Arnold has no claim. Arnold asked Randall to put in writing, as part of the agreement, a representation that Randall would never sell Tiger. Randall refused to make such a representation. Instead he warranted (accurately) that he was not aware of any offers to purchase Tiger and was not engaged in negotiations for its sale. The parties also agreed that if Tiger were sold before Arnold had received all installments of the purchase price, then payment of

the principal and interest would be accelerated. Having sought broader assurances, and having been refused, Arnold could not persuade a reasonable trier of fact that he relied on Randall's oral statements. Having signed an agreement providing for acceleration as a consequence of sale, Arnold is in no position to contend that he relied on the impossibility of sale.

Indeed, Arnold represented as part of the transaction that he had not relied on any prior oral statement:

The parties further declare that they have not relied upon any representation of any party hereby released [Randall] or of their attorneys [Glick], agents, or other representatives concerning the nature or extent of their respective injuries or damages.

That is pretty clear, but to foreclose quibbling Arnold made these warranties to Randall:

(a) no promise or inducement for this Agreement has been made to him except as set forth herein; (b) this Agreement is executed by [Arnold] freely and voluntarily, and without reliance upon any statement or representation by Purchaser, the Company, any of the Affiliates or O.R. Rissman or any of their attorneys or agents except as set forth herein; (c) he has read and fully understands this Agreement and the meaning of its provisions; (d) he is legally competent to enter into this Agreement and to accept full responsibility therefor; and (e) he has been advised to consult with counsel before entering into this Agreement and has had the opportunity to do so.

Arnold does not contend that any representation in the stock purchase agreement is untrue or misleading; his entire case rests on Randall's oral statements. Yet Arnold assured Randall that he had not relied on these statements. Securities law does not permit a party to a stock transaction to disavow such representations--to say, in effect, "I lied when I told you I wasn't relying on your prior statements" and then to seek damages for their contents. Stock transactions would be impossibly uncertain if federal law precluded parties from agreeing to rely on the written word alone. Without such a principle, sellers would have no protection against plausible liars and gullible jurors.

Two courts of appeals have held that non-reliance clauses in written stock-purchase agreements preclude any possibility of damages under the federal securities laws for prior oral statements. [A] written anti-reliance clause precludes any claim of deceit by prior representations. The principle is functionally the same as a doctrine long accepted in this circuit: that a person who has received written disclosure of the truth may not claim to rely on contrary oral falsehoods. A non-reliance clause is not identical to a truthful disclosure, but it has a similar function: it ensures that both the transaction and any subsequent litigation proceed on the basis of the parties' writings, which are less subject to the vagaries of memory and the risks of fabrication.

Memory plays tricks. Acting in the best of faith, people may "remember" things that never occurred but now serve their interests. Or they may remember events with a change of emphasis or nuance that makes a substantial difference to meaning. Express or implied qualifications may be lost in the folds of time. A statement such as "I won't sell at current prices" may be recalled years later as "I won't sell." Prudent people protect themselves against the limitations of memory (and the temptation to shade the truth) by limiting their dealings to those memorialized in writing, and promoting the primacy of the written word is a principal function of the federal securities laws.

Negotiation could have avoided this litigation. Instead of taking the maximum Randall was willing to pay unconditionally, Arnold could have sought a lower guaranteed payment (say, $10 million) plus a kicker if Tiger were sold or taken public. Because random events (or Randall's efforts) would dominate Tiger's prosperity over the long run, the kicker would fall with time. Perhaps Arnold could have asked for 25% of any proceeds on a sale within a year, diminishing 1% every other month after that (so that Randall would keep all proceeds of a sale more than 62 months after the transaction with Arnold). Many variations on this formula were possible; all would have put Randall to the test, for if he really planned not to sell, the approach would have been attractive to him because it reduced his total payment. Likewise it would have been attractive to Arnold if he believed that Randall wanted to sell as soon as he could receive more than 2/3 of the gains. Yet Arnold never proposed a payment formula that would share the risk (and rewards) between the brothers, and the one he proposes after the fact in this litigation--$17 million with certainty and a perpetual right to 1/3 of any later premium--is just about the only formula that could not conceivably have been the outcome of bargaining.

Arnold calls the no-reliance clauses "boilerplate," and they were; transactions lawyers have language of this sort stored up for reuse. But the fact that language has been used before does not make it less binding when used again. Phrases become boilerplate when many parties find that the language serves their ends. That's a reason to enforce the promises, not to disregard them. People negotiate about the presence of boilerplate clauses.

Contractual language serves its functions only if enforced consistently. This is one of the advantages of boilerplate, which usually has a record of predictable interpretation and application. If as Arnold says the extent of his reliance is a jury question even after he warranted his non-reliance, then the clause has been nullified, and people in Arnold's position will be worse off tomorrow for reasons we have explained.

The agreement between Randall and Arnold contains a global settlement and release. Our conclusion that the agreement is valid means that the agreement extinguishes all of Arnold's claims, under both state and federal law. Affirmed.

FIRST VIRGINIA BANKS, INCORPORATED V. BP EXPLORATION & OIL,
INCORPORATED ET AL

206 F.3d 404 (2000)

UNITED STATES COURT OF APPEALS FOR THE FOURTH CIRCUIT

LUTTIG, Circuit Judge:

From 1977 to 1986, BP operated a gasoline station on a parcel of land owned by Eakin in Falls Church, Virginia. In 1986, BP ceased its operations at that site, and removed from the site the underground tanks in which it had stored gasoline. In July 1988, Eakin discovered that the former BP site contained petroleum contamination.

[First Virginia Banks, Incorporated] FVBI owns an undeveloped parcel of residentially-zoned land located across the street from the former BP site, which it has divided into fourteen contiguous lots. FVBI also owns two parcels of commercially-zoned land adjacent to the former BP cite. In the fall of 1988, Eakin alerted FVBI to the contamination on the former BP site and, in January 1989, FVBI obtained test results confirming that the contamination had reached the groundwater beneath its own commercial and residential parcels.

Pursuant to an agreement with Eakin, BP took measures to mitigate the damage to the site of its former gas station. Despite these measures, Eakin filed suit against BP, alleging that the contamination left behind by BP damaged the property and that the delay involved in decontaminating the property resulted in lost rent revenues for Eakin. This lawsuit ended in a confidential settlement agreement, unsealed after the present suit between BP and FVBI commenced, in which BP agreed, inter alia, to "remediate as required by the State Water Control Board."

On March 5, 1998, FVBI filed suit against BP, alleging trespass and negligence claims against BP resulting from the migration of petroleum hydrocarbons from the former BP site into the groundwater beneath FVBI's property. FVBI also brought a breach of contract claim against BP, asserting that it was a third-party beneficiary to the settlement agreement between BP and Eakin. The district court granted summary judgment to BP with respect to the negligence and trespass claims, and entered a final judgment in BP's favor on the contract claim after a bench trial. FVBI appeals the disposition below of its trespass and contract claims.

FVBI asserts that it was a third-party beneficiary to the settlement agreement between BP and Eakin, and that BP failed to fulfill its duties to FVBI under that contract. The district court ruled that, because BP and Eakin did not express a clear intent to benefit FVBI directly when they entered into the settlement agreement, FVBI was not a third-party beneficiary to that compact under Virginia law. On appeal, FVBI argues that the district court impermissibly prohibited it from introducing certain evidence in support of its third-party beneficiary theory. Alternatively, FVBI contends that, even on the evidence it was permitted to introduce, the district court's conclusion that BP and Eakin did not intend their agreement to benefit FVBI directly was clearly erroneous. We reject both claims.

As to the question whether the district court's determination on the record before it was clearly erroneous, FVBI asserts that the evidence it was permitted to introduce established that the provision of the agreement requiring BP to "remediate as required by the State Water Control Board," was intended to benefit FVBI, given that the Board required remedial measures that would limit the impact of the petroleum contamination on FVBI's property. However, under Virginia law, a party incidentally benefitted by an agreement does not attain third-party beneficiary status; rather a party claiming that status must show that the parties to the underlying agreement "clearly and definitely intended to bestow a direct benefit" upon it. In concluding that the settlement agreement in the present case does not evince such an intent on the part of BP and Eakin, the district court observed that: (1) the agreement does not expressly mention FVBI, (2) the agreement was kept confidential until after the present suit commenced, suggesting the lack of a specific intent to benefit third parties directly, and (3) the testimony of Charles Schneider, Eakin's lawyer at the time of the settlement agreement, stating his view that the agreement would have the effect of limiting the damage to FVBI's property, not only failed to establish that the parties intended the agreement to directly (as opposed to incidentally) benefit FVBI, but also was lacking in credibility and appeared "defensive." Given these considerations, and having reviewed the record on appeal, we cannot conclude that the district court's factual determination that BP and Eakin did not intend their settlement agreement to benefit FVBI directly was clearly erroneous.

For the reasons stated herein, we affirm the judgment of the district court.

CITY OF MIDLAND, ET AL V. MILTON O'BRYANT, ET AL

18 S.W.3d 209 (2000)

SUPREME COURT OF TEXAS

OWEN, JUSTICE

The five plaintiffs in this case, were certified law enforcement and police officers for the City of Midland. O'Bryant brought two prior lawsuits against the City that are pertinent to this case. In the first, O'Bryant sued in federal court alleging violations of the Americans with Disabilities Act (ADA). O'Bryant voluntarily dismissed that suit. About a year later, the City notified O'Bryant and seven other police officers (who included the plaintiffs) that their duties were slated to be reclassified as civilian positions within three months. Each officer was given the option of: (1) staying in his present position with reclassification as a civilian; (2) applying for a transfer to another position within the police department and continuing in the status of police officer; or (3) applying for a transfer to a civilian position in other City departments. If an officer chose a civilian position, then the pay and benefits would be less. The City also required its police officers to demonstrate greater physical abilities than it had in the past.

After these and other changes within the police department were announced but before they took effect, O'Bryant filed a second suit, and Hendon, Cross, Ortiz, and Rasco later joined as plaintiffs. That suit was filed in state court seeking to enjoin the City's alleged violations of the ADA and the Texas Commission on Human Rights Act. The plaintiffs voluntarily dismissed that action.

The City proceeded to reclassify many positions that police officers had held, and each of the plaintiffs was affected. Two of the plaintiffs, O'Bryant and Cross, were working in the telephone response unit and were reclassified as civilians. Cross suffered from a degenerative arthritic condition, and O'Bryant had previously injured his back and was under physician's orders to limit physical activity. Two other plaintiffs, Rasco and Ortiz, were transferred to evening shifts as patrol officers when their respective positions in the evidence room and in the telephone response unit were reclassified as civilian positions. Rasco suffered from heart and lung disease, and Ortiz has an artificial leg prostheses. Both men requested transfer to another position with police officer status, and patrol duty was the second choice of assignment for both. Plaintiff

Hendon, who had no disability, was transferred to an evening patrol after his position in crime analysis became a civilian one. A few months after these reclassifications took effect, the plaintiffs brought this suit against the City and later added as defendants Chief of Police Richard L. Czech, and another police officer, J.W. Marugg, in their official and individual capacities.

The plaintiffs alleged that the reclassifications were in retaliation for filing the two prior suits. Rasco and Ortiz asserted that because of their disabilities, their personal safety was endangered when they were transferred to evening patrol shifts instead of less hazardous and less strenuous airport duty. O'Bryant similarly claimed that he was placed in jeopardy by his new assignment as an unarmed, non-commissioned civilian officer who was at times the only person on duty at the police station. The plaintiffs also alleged that the City's new, more stringent physical requirements for police officers were unnecessary and discriminated against the plaintiffs who had disabilities. A number of other acts of discrimination and retaliation were alleged by all five plaintiffs. Their theories of recovery included violations of the Texas Labor Code, intentional infliction of emotional distress, breach of an alleged duty of good faith and fair dealing, tortious interference with contract, and violations of the due course of law and free speech provisions of the Texas Constitution. The plaintiffs also sought an injunction restoring them to their original positions with the status and benefits of police officers.

The defendants' responses to the factual allegations are detailed by the court of appeals. Briefly summarized, they were that the City faced budgetary constraints and that there were limited human and monetary resources to meet an increased need for law enforcement services. Chief of Police Czech stated in an affidavit that in light of these circumstances, he filled positions formerly held by police officers with civilians. There was also evidence that the City revised the job requirements for police officers in response to the enactment of the Americans With Disabilities Act.

The City contends that no cause of action exists in Texas for breach of a duty of good faith and fair dealing in the context of an employer/employee relationship. This Court has never decided the question. Courts in other jurisdictions that have considered the issue have reached varying conclusions.

In decisions that have considered employment at-will, the holdings seem to fall within one or more of several broad categories: 1) an employee cannot be terminated if to do so would violate public policy; 2) there is an implied covenant of good faith and fair dealing not to impair a right to receive a benefit an employee has already earned; 3) there is a general implied covenant of good faith and fair dealing; 4) there is an implied covenant of good faith and fair dealing, but any damages are limited to a contract measure, not a bad faith, tort measure; or 5) there is no implied covenant of good faith and fair dealing. A few courts also suggest that the terms of an employee handbook can create a similar obligation that limits the at-will nature of the employment.

In the relatively few cases in which the employment agreement at issue was not at-will, the decisions seem to fall into the following categories: 1) there is only a cause of action for breach of an express covenant; 2) there is an implied covenant of good faith and fair dealing not to nullify the benefits of the contract; 3) there is no covenant of good faith and fair dealing in a "just cause" contract because the factfinder will decide what is or is not just cause; or 4) there is a covenant of good faith and fair dealing in a "just cause" contract or a contract for a definite term.

This Court has held that not every contractual relationship creates a duty of good faith and fair dealing. We have "specifically rejected the implication of a general duty of good faith and fair dealing in all contracts."

As the plaintiffs recognize, this Court has imposed an actionable duty of good faith and fair dealing only when there is a special relationship, such as that between an insured and his or her insurance carrier. We have held that a special relationship exists in the insurance context because of "the parties' unequal bargaining power and the nature of insurance contracts which would allow unscrupulous insurers to take advantage of their insureds' misfortunes in bargaining for settlement or resolution of claims

But the elements which make the relationship between an insurer and an insured a special one are absent in the relationship between an employer and its employees. First, in Texas, the employment relationship is generally at-will unless the parties enter into an express agreement that provides otherwise. Second, insurance contracts are typically much more restrictive than employment agreements. If an insured suffers a loss, he cannot simply contract with another insurance company to cover that loss. By contrast, an employee who has been demoted, transferred, or discharged may seek alternative employment.

Moreover, this Court has thus far recognized only one limited common-law exception to the at-will employment doctrine. We held that an employer may not discharge an employee for the sole reason that the employee refused to perform an illegal act that carried criminal penalties. We have not, however, recognized other common-law exceptions to the employment at-will doctrine. We declined to recognize a common-law whistleblower cause of action. We did so primarily on the basis that the Legislature has been active in crafting whistleblower statutes that often vary from one another in material respects. The adoption of a general common-law whistleblower cause of action would have undercut the many distinctions drawn by the Legislature among the various statutory whistleblower causes of action.

Similarly, we decline to impose a duty of good faith and fair dealing on employers in light of the variety of statutes that the Legislature has already enacted to regulate employment relationships. Recognizing a new common-law cause of action based on the duty plaintiffs advocate would tend to subvert those statutory schemes by allowing employees to make an end-run around the procedural requirements and specific remedies the existing statutes establish.

In holding that there is no duty of good faith and fair dealing in the employment context, we perceive no distinction between government and private employers, inasmuch as both types of employers are subject to applicable laws, regulations, and contractual agreements. Nor do we see any meaningful basis to distinguish between employment at-will and employment governed by an express agreement. A court-created duty of good faith and fair dealing would completely alter the nature of the at-will employment relationship, which generally can be terminated by either party for any reason or no reason at all, and we accordingly decline to change the at-will nature of employment in Texas. If, as plaintiffs argue, they could only be terminated or transferred for reasons of "merit," that fact militates against imposing a common-law duty of good faith and fair dealing because such a contractual limitation would afford more rights to the plaintiffs than at-will employees possess. Moreover, such a duty would be unnecessary when there are express contractual limits on an employer's right to terminate.

Accordingly, we hold that the City of Midland was entitled to summary judgment on the plaintiffs' claims that the defendants breached a duty of good faith and fair dealing.

For the reasons considered above, we affirm the judgment of the court of appeals in part, reverse that judgment in part, and remand O'Bryant's claim for reinstatement to the trial court for further proceedings consistent with this opinion.

A & M RECORDS, INC. ET AL V. NAPSTER, INC.

2000 U.S. Dist. LEXIS 6243 (2000)

UNITED STATES DISTRICT COURT FOR THE NORTHERN DISTRICT OF CALIFORNIA

PATEL, CHIEF JUDGE

On December 6, 1999, plaintiff record companies filed suit alleging contributory and vicarious federal copyright infringement and related state law violations by defendant Napster, Inc. ("Napster"). Now before this court is defendant's motion for summary adjudication of the applicability of a safe harbor provision of the Digital Millennium Copyright Act ("DMCA").

Napster--a small internet start-up based in San Mateo, California--makes its proprietary MusicShare software freely available for Internet users to download. Users who obtain Napster's software can then share MP3 music files with others logged-on to the Napster system. MP3 files, which reproduce nearly CD-quality sound in a compressed format, are available on a variety of websites either for a fee or free-of-charge. Napster allows users to exchange MP3 files stored on their own computer hard-drives directly, without payment, and boasts that it "takes the frustration out of locating servers with MP3 files."

Although the parties dispute the precise nature of the service Napster provides, they agree that using Napster typically involves the following basic steps: After downloading MusicShare software from the Napster website, a user can access the Napster system from her computer. The MusicShare software interacts with Napster's server-side software when the user logs on, automatically connecting her to one of some 150 servers that Napster operates. The MusicShare software reads a list of names of MP3 files that the user has elected to make available. This list is then added to a directory and index, on the Napster server, of MP3 files that users who are logged-on wish to share. If the user wants to locate a song, she enters its name or the name of the recording artist on the search page of the MusicShare program and clicks the "Find It" button. The Napster software then searches the current directory and generates a list of files responsive to the search request. To download a desired file, the user highlights it on the list and clicks the "Get Selected Songs" button. The user may also view a list of files that exist on another user's hard drive and select a file from that list. When the requesting user clicks on the name of a file, the Napster server communicates with the requesting user's and host user's MusicShare browser software to facilitate a connection between the two users and initiate the downloading of the file without any further action on either user's part.

According to Napster, when the requesting user clicks on the name of the desired MP3 file, the Napster server routes this request to the host user's browser. The host user's browser responds that it either can or cannot supply the file. If the host user can supply the file, the Napster server communicates the host's address and routing information to the requesting user's browser, allowing the requesting user to make a connection with the host and receive the desired MP3 file. The parties disagree about whether this process involves a hypertext link that the Napster server-side software provides. However, plaintiffs admit that the Napster server gets the necessary IP address information from the host user, enabling the requesting user to connect to the host. The MP3 file is actually transmitted over the Internet, see, but the steps necessary to make that connection could not take place without the Napster server.

The Napster system has other functions besides allowing users to search for, request, and download MP3 files. For example, a requesting user can play a downloaded song using the MusicShare software. Napster also hosts a chat room.

Napster has developed a policy that makes compliance with all copyright laws one of the "terms of use" of its service and warns users that:

> Napster will terminate the accounts of users who are repeat infringers of the copyrights, or other intellectual property rights, of others. In addition, Napster reserves the right to terminate the account of a user upon any single infringement of the rights of others in conjunction with use of the Napster service.

However, the parties disagree over when this policy was instituted and how effectively it bars infringers from using the Napster service. Napster claims that it had a copyright compliance policy as early as October 1999, but admits that it did not document or notify users of the existence of this policy until February 7, 2000.

Napster claims that its business activities fall within the safe harbor provided by subsection 512(a). This subsection limits liability "for infringement of copyright by reason of the [service] provider's transmitting, routing, or providing connections for, material through a system or network controlled or operated by or for the service provider, or by reason of the intermediate and transient storage of that material in the course of such transmitting, routing, or providing connections," if five conditions are satisfied:

(1) the transmission of the material was initiated by or at the direction of a person other than the service provider;

(2) the transmission, routing, provision of connections, or storage is carried out through an automatic technical process without selection of the material by the service provider;

(3) the service provider does not select the recipients of the material except as an automatic response to the request of another person;

(4) no copy of the material made by the service provider in the course of such intermediate or transient storage is maintained on the system or network in a manner ordinarily accessible to anyone other than the anticipated recipients, and no such copy is maintained on the system or network in a manner ordinarily accessible to such anticipated recipients for a longer period than is reasonably necessary for the transmission, routing, or provision of connections; and

(5) the material is transmitted through the system or network without modification of its content.

Citing the "definitions" subsection of the statute, Napster argues that it is a "service provider" for the purposes of the 512(a) safe harbor. Finally, the Napster system does not modify the content of the transferred files. Defendant contends that, because it meets the definition of "service provider," it need only satisfy the five remaining requirements of the safe harbor to prevail in its motion for summary adjudication.

Subparagraph 512(k)(1)(A provides:

As used in subsection (a), the term "service provider" means as entity offering the transmission, routing, or providing of connections for digital online communications, between or among points specified by a user, of material of the user's choosing, without modification to the content of the material sent or received.

Subparagraph 512(k)(1)(B) states:

As used in this section, other than subsection (a), the term "service provider" means a provider of online services or network access, or the operator of facilities therefor, and includes an entity described in subparagraph (A).

It is not entirely clear to the court that Napster qualifies under the narrower subparagraph 512(k)(1)(A). However, plaintiffs appear to concede that Napster is a "service provider" within the meaning of subparagraph

512(k)(1)(A), arguing instead that Napster does not satisfy the additional limitations that the prefatory language of subsection 512(a) imposes. The court assumes, but does not hold, that Napster is a "service provider" under subparagraph 512(k)(1)(A).

Defendant then seeks to show compliance with these requirements by arguing: (1) a Napster user, and never Napster itself; initiates the transmission of MP3 files; (2) the transmission occurs through an automatic, technical process without any editorial input from Napster; (3) Napster does not choose the recipients of the MP3 files; (4) Napster does not make a copy of the material during transmission; and (5) the content of the material is not modified during transmission. Napster maintains that the 512(a) safe harbor thus protects its core function-- "transmitting, routing and providing connections for sharing of the files its users choose."

Plaintiffs disagree. They first argue that subsection 512(n) requires the court to analyze each of Napster's functions independently and that not all of these functions fall under the 512(a) safe harbor. In their view, Napster provides information location tools--such as a search engine, directory, index, and links--that are covered by the more stringent eligibility requirements of subsection 512(d), rather than subsection 512(a).

Plaintiffs also contend that Napster does not perform the function which the 512(a) safe harbor protects because the infringing material is not transmitted or routed through the Napster system, as required by subsection 512(a). They correctly note that the definition of "service provider" under subparagraph 512(k)(1)(A) is not identical to the prefatory language of subsection 512(a). The latter imposes the additional requirement that transmitting, routing, or providing connections must occur "through the system or network." Plaintiffs argue in the alternative that, if users' computers are part of the Napster system, copies of MP3 files are stored on the system longer than reasonably necessary for transmission, and thus subparagraph 512(a)(4) is not satisfied.

Finally, plaintiffs note that, under the general eligibility requirements established in subsection 512(i), a service provider must have adopted, reasonably implemented, and informed its users of a policy for terminating repeat infringers. Plaintiffs contend that Napster only adopted its copyright compliance policy after the onset of this litigation and even now does not discipline infringers in any meaningful way. Therefore, in plaintiffs' view, Napster fails to satisfy the DMCA's threshold eligibility requirements or show that the 512(a) safe harbor covers any of its functions.

Plaintiffs' principal argument against application of the 512(a) safe harbor is that Napster does not perform the passive conduit function eligible for protection under this subsection. The language of subsection 512(a) makes the safe harbor applicable, as a threshold matter, to service providers "transmitting, routing or providing connections for, material through a system or network controlled or operated by or for the service provider. . . ." 17 U.S.C. § 512(a) (emphasis added). According to plaintiffs, the use of the word "conduit" in the legislative history explains the meaning of "through a system."

Napster has expressly denied that the transmission of MP3 files ever passes through its servers. Indeed, Kessler declared that "files reside on the computers of Napster users, and are transmitted directly between those computers." MP3 files are transmitted "from the Host user's hard drive and Napster browser, through the Internet to the recipient's Napster browser and hard drive." The internet cannot be considered "a system or network controlled or operated by or for the service provider," however. 17 U.S.C. § 512(a). To get around this problem, Napster avers (and plaintiffs seem willing to concede) that "Napster's servers and Napster's MusicShare browsers on its users' computers are all part of Napster's overall system." Defendant narrowly defines its system to include the browsers on users' computers. In contrast, plaintiffs argue that either (1) the system does not include the browsers, or (2) it includes not only the browsers, but also the users' computers themselves.

Napster contends that providing connections between users' addresses "constitutes the value of the system to the users and the public." Def. Br. at 15. This connection cannot be established without the provision of the host's address to the Napster browser software installed on the requesting user's computer. See Kessler Dec. P 10-13. The central Napster server delivers the host's address. See id. While plaintiffs contend that the infringing material is not transmitted through the Napster system, they provide no evidence to rebut the assertion that Napster supplies the requesting user's computer with information necessary to facilitate a connection with the host.

Nevertheless, the court finds that Napster does not provide connections "through" its system. Although the Napster server conveys address information to establish a connection between the requesting and host users, the connection itself occurs through the Internet. The legislative history of section 512 demonstrates that Congress intended the 512(a) safe harbor to apply only to activities "in which a service provider plays the role of a 'conduit' for the communications of others." Drawing inferences in the light most favorable to the non-moving party, this court cannot say that Napster serves as a conduit for the connection itself, as opposed to the address information that makes the connection possible. Napster enables or facilitates the initiation of connections, but these connections do not pass through the system within the meaning of subsection 512(a).

Because Napster does not transmit, route, or provide connections through its system, it has failed to demonstrate that it qualifies for the 512(a) safe harbor,

The court thus declines to grant summary adjudication in its favor.

Even if the court had determined that Napster meets the criteria outlined in subsection 512(a), subsection 512(i) imposes additional requirements on eligibility for any DMCA safe harbor. This provision states:

The limitations established by this section shall apply to a service provider only if the service provider--

(A) has adopted and reasonably implemented, and informs subscribers and account holders of the service provider's system or network of, a policy that provides for the termination in appropriate circumstances of subscribers and account holders of the service provider's system or network who are repeat infringers; and

(B) accommodates and does not interfere with standard technical measures.

Plaintiffs challenge Napster's compliance with these threshold eligibility requirements on two grounds. First, they point to evidence from Kessler's deposition that Napster did not adopt a written policy of which its users had notice until on or around February 7, 2000--two months after the filing of this lawsuit. Kessler testified that, although Napster had a copyright compliance policy as early as October 1999, he is not aware that this policy was reflected in any document or communicated to any user. Congress did not intend to require a service provider to "investigate possible infringements, monitor its service or make difficult judgments as to whether conduct is or is not infringing," but the notice requirement is designed to insure that flagrant or repeat infringers "know that there is a realistic threat of losing [their] access."

Napster attempts to refute plaintiffs' argument by noting that subsection 512(i) does not specify when the copyright compliance policy must be in place. Although this characterization of subsection 512(i) is facially accurate, it defies the logic of making formal notification to users or subscribers a prerequisite to exemption from monetary liability. The fact that Napster developed and notified its users of a formal policy after the onset of this action should not moot plaintiffs' claim to monetary relief for past harms. Without further documentation, defendant's argument that it has satisfied subsection 512(i) is merely conclusory and does not support summary adjudication in its favor.

Summary adjudication is also inappropriate because Napster has not shown that it reasonably implemented a policy for terminating repeat infringers. If Napster is formally notified of infringing activity, it blocks the infringer's password so she cannot log on to the Napster service using that password. Napster does not block the IP addresses of infringing users, however, and the parties dispute whether it would, be feasible or effective to do so.

Plaintiffs aver that Napster willfully turns a blind eye to the identity of its users -- that is, their real names and physical addresses -- because their anonymity allows Napster to disclaim responsibility for copyright infringement. Hence, plaintiffs contend, "infringers may readily reapply to the Napster system to recommence their infringing downloading and uploading of MP3 music files."

Hence, plaintiffs raise genuine issues of material fact about whether Napster has reasonably implemented a policy of terminating repeat infringers. They have produced evidence that Napster's copyright compliance policy is neither timely nor reasonable within the meaning of subparagraph 512(i)(A).

This court has determined above that Napster does not meet the requirements of subsection 512(a) because it does not transmit, route, or provide connections for allegedly infringing material through its system. The court also finds summary adjudication inappropriate due to the existence of genuine issues of material fact about Napster's compliance with subparagraph 512(i)(A), which a service provider must satisfy to enjoy the protection of any section 512 safe harbor. Defendant's motion for summary adjudication is DENIED.

UNIVERSAL CITY STUDIOS, INC, ET AL V. SHAWN C. REIMERDES, ET AL

82 F. Supp. 2d 211 (2000)

UNITED STATES DISTRICT COURT FOR THE SOUTHERN DISTRICT OF
NEW YORK

KAPLAN, DISTRICT JUDGE.

This case is another step in the evolution of the law of copyright occasioned by advances in technology. Plaintiff motion picture studios brought this action to enjoin defendants from providing a computer program on their Internet Web sites that permits users to decrypt and copy plaintiffs' copyrighted motion pictures from digital versatile disks ("DVDs"). They rely on the recently enacted Digital Millennium Copyright Act ("DMCA").

On January 20, 2000, the Court granted plaintiffs' motion for a preliminary injunction and indicated that this opinion would follow.

Plaintiffs in this case are eight major motion picture studios which are engaged in the business of producing, manufacturing and/or distributing copyrighted and copyrightable material, including motion pictures. Motion pictures usually are first released for theatrical distribution and later to consumers in "home video" formats such as videotape, laserdisc and, most recently, DVD.

DVDs are five-inch wide discs that, in this application, hold full-length motion pictures. They are the latest technology for private home viewing of recorded motion pictures. This technology drastically improves the clarity and overall quality of a motion picture shown on a television or computer screen.

DVDs contain motion pictures in digital form, which presents an enhanced risk of unauthorized reproduction and distribution because digital copies made from DVDs do not degrade from generation to generation. Concerned about this risk, motion picture companies, including plaintiffs, insisted upon the development of an access control and copy prevention system to inhibit the unauthorized reproduction and distribution of motion pictures before they released films in the DVD format. The means now in use, Content Scramble System or CSS, is an encryption-based security and authentication system that requires the use of appropriately configured hardware such as a DVD player or a computer DVD drive to decrypt, unscramble and play back, but not copy, motion pictures on DVDs. CSS has been licensed to hundreds of DVD player manufacturers and DVD content distributors in the United States and around the world.

CSS has facilitated enormous growth in the use of DVDs for the distribution of copyrighted movies to consumers. DVD movies first were introduced in the United States in 1996. Over 4,000 motion pictures now have been released in that format in the United States, and movies are being issued on DVDs at the rate of over 40 new titles per month in addition to re-releases of classic films. More than 5 million DVD players have been sold, and DVD disc sales now exceed one million units per week.

In October 1999, an individual or group, believed to be in Europe, managed to "hack" CSS and began offering, via the Internet, a software utility called DeCSS that enables users to break the CSS copy protection system and hence to make and distribute digital copies of DVD movies.

The Motion Picture Association of America ("MPAA") almost immediately acted under the provisions of the DMCA by demanding that Internet service providers remove DeCSS from their servers and, where the identities of the individuals responsible were known, that those individuals stop posting DeCSS. These efforts succeeded in removing a considerable share of the known postings of DeCSS.

On December 29, 1999, the licensor of CSS, DVD CCA, commenced a state court action in California for the misappropriation of its trade secrets as embodied in the DeCSS software. On the same day, the state court judge without explanation denied the plaintiff's motion for a temporary restraining order. Members of the hacker community then stepped up efforts to distribute DeCSS to the widest possible audience in an apparent attempt to preclude effective judicial relief. One individual even announced a contest with prizes (copies of DVDs) for the greatest number of copies of DeCSS distributed, for the most elegant distribution method, and for the "lowest tech" method.

Defendants each are associated with Web sites that were distributing DeCSS at the time plaintiffs moved for injunctive relief.

Plaintiffs' sole claim is for violation of the anti-circumvention provisions of the DMCA. They contend that plaintiffs' posting of DeCSS violates Section 1201(a)(2) of the statute, which prohibits unauthorized offering of products that circumvent technological measures that effectively control access to copyrighted works.

Section 1201(a)(2) of the Copyright Act, part of the DMCA, provides that:

"No person shall . . . offer to the public, provide or otherwise traffic in any technology . . . that--

"(A) is primarily designed or produced for the purpose of circumventing a technological measure that effectively controls access to a work protected under [the Copyright Act];

"(B) has only limited commercially significant purpose or use other than to circumvent a technological measure that effectively controls access to a work protected under [the Copyright Act]; or

"(C) is marketed by that person or another acting in concert with that person with that person's knowledge for use in circumventing a technological measure that effectively controls access to a work protected under [the Copyright Act]."

"Circumvent a technological measure" is defined to mean descrambling a scrambled work, decrypting an encrypted work, or "otherwise to avoid, bypass, remove, deactivate, or impair a technological measure, without the authority of the copyright owner." The statute explains further that "a technological measure 'effectively controls access to a work' if the measure, in the ordinary course of its operation, requires the application of information or a process or a treatment, with the authority of the copyright owner, to gain access to a work.

Here, it is perfectly clear that CSS is a technological measure that effectively controls access to plaintiffs' copyrighted movies because it requires the application of information or a process, with the authority of the copyright owner, to gain access to those works. Indeed, defendants conceded in their memorandum that one cannot in the ordinary course gain access to the copyrighted works on plaintiffs' DVDs without a "player key" issued by the DVD CCA that permits unscrambling the contents of the disks. It is undisputed also that DeCSS defeats CSS and decrypts copyrighted works without the authority of the copyright owners. As there is no evidence of any commercially significant purpose of DeCSS other than circumvention of CSS, defendants' actions likely violated Section 1201(a)(2)(B). Moreover, although defendants contended at oral argument that DeCSS was not designed primarily to circumvent CSS, that argument is exceptionally unpersuasive.

Copyright protection exists to "encourage individual effort by personal gain" and thereby "advance public welfare" through the "promotion of the Progress of Science and useful Arts." The DMCA plainly was designed with these goals in mind. It is a tool to protect copyright in the digital age. It responds to the risks of technological circumvention of access controlling mechanisms designed to protect copyrighted works distributed in digital form. It is designed to further precisely the goals articulated above, goals of unquestionably high social value.

For the foregoing reasons, the Court granted plaintiffs' motion for a preliminary injunction and entered such an order on January 20, 2000. The foregoing, together with those made on the record on that date, constitute the Court's findings of fact and conclusions of law.

INTERNATIONAL PAPER COMPANY v. SCHWABEDISSEN
MASCHINEN & ANLAGEN GMBH

206 F.3d 411 (2000)

UNITED STATES COURT OF APPEALS FOR THE FOURTH CIRCUIT

MOTZ, CIRCUIT JUDGE

A buyer became dissatisfied with an industrial saw and brought suit against the manufacturer of the saw on the basis of a contract between the distributor and the manufacturer. The question presented to us is whether an arbitration clause in the distributor-manufacturer contract requires the buyer, a nonsignatory to that contract, to arbitrate its claims against the manufacturer. The district court held that it did. Concluding that the buyer cannot sue to enforce the guarantees and warranties of the distributor-manufacturer contract without complying with its arbitration provision.

Westinghouse Electric Corporation (a predecessor-in-interest of the International Paper Company) sought to purchase an industrial saw manufactured by Schwabedissen Maschinen & Anlagen GMBH, a German corporation. On April 1, 1991, Westinghouse sent to Wood Systems Incorporated, a United States distributor of Schwabedissen saws, a non-binding letter of intent to purchase a new Schwabedissen double trim saw. Westinghouse personnel then visited Schwabedissen's facility in Germany to observe its production process. Upon their return, in a purchase order from Westinghouse to Wood dated May 17, 1991, Westinghouse agreed to buy and Wood agreed to sell the Schwabedissen saw, in accordance with a performance guarantee and certain specifications.

On June 6, 1991, Schwabedissen sent Wood an "Order Confirmation/Contract" for the saw Westinghouse sought to purchase, which included extensive specifications. Schwabedissen contends, and the district court found, that this contract also included the terms of two additional documents--the "General Conditions for the Supply and Erection of Plant and Machinery for Import and Export No. 188A, prepared under the auspices of the United Nations Economic Commission for Europe" (the "General Conditions"), and the "Annex attached to the General Conditions for the Supply and Erection of Plant and Machinery for Import and Export by the German Mechanical Engineering Industry" (the "Annex"). The "General Conditions" contain an

arbitration clause providing that "any dispute arising out of the Contract shall be finally settled, in accordance with the Rules of Conciliation and Arbitration of the International Chamber of Commerce, by one or more arbitrators designated by those Rules," and establish the governing law as that of the country of the contractor. The "Annex" permits the contractor to bring an action before a court rather than an arbitrator "unless and until the dispute has been referred to arbitration by one of the parties."

On June 12, 1991, Wood sent a purchase order for the saw to Schwabedissen, together with the specifications from Westinghouse's purchase order. In response, Schwabedissen arranged for delivery of the saw, which was installed at Westinghouse's plant in late December 1991. According to Westinghouse, the saw "completely failed to properly operate once installed or at anytime thereafter." No written contract ever existed between Westinghouse and Schwabedissen, but Westinghouse maintains that when difficulty arose as to the saw's operation, Schwabedissen orally agreed to repair the saw, but failed to do so.

On July 9, 1993, after Wood declared bankruptcy, Westinghouse filed a complaint against Schwabedissen in South Carolina state court, alleging breach of contract, rejection, and breach of warranties based on the May 17, 1991, purchase order between Westinghouse and Wood. Westinghouse alleged that Wood acted as an agent for Schwabedissen and therefore Schwabedissen was liable under that purchase order. Schwabedissen removed the case to federal court.

On September 21, 1994, Westinghouse filed an amended complaint, in which it added allegations based on the Wood-Schwabedissen contract and asserted that it was a third-party beneficiary of that contract. Schwabedissen then moved to stay the federal court proceedings pending arbitration, relying on the arbitration clause contained in its contract with Wood.

At argument on the motion to stay, Westinghouse maintained that as a third-party beneficiary of the Wood-Schwabedissen contract, it could compel arbitration in any disputes with a party to the contract, but that a party could not compel a third-party beneficiary to arbitrate. Responding to the district court's skepticism about this contention, Westinghouse withdrew its third-party beneficiary claim. The district court then continued the hearing to allow the parties to brief the issues without that claim.

When the district court again heard argument, Westinghouse contended that it had no knowledge of, and so could not be bound by, the "General Conditions" (containing the arbitration clause) assertedly made part of the Wood-Schwabedissen contract. The district court rejected this argument, reasoning that because Westinghouse sought "to take advantage of certain commitments that were made by Schwabedissen to" Wood in the Wood-Schwabedissen contract, it was bound by all commitments in that contract, including the arbitration provision.

Westinghouse then argued that, notwithstanding an affidavit of a Schwabedissen employee that the Wood-Schwabedissen contract included the "General Conditions," nothing in the June 6 contract nor June 12 purchase order indicated that Wood had in fact accepted the "General Conditions" as part of its contract with Schwabedissen. The district court again continued the hearing on the motion to stay to allow further discovery. At the subsequent hearing, Schwabedissen produced an agreement between itself and Wood dated February 24, 1993, indicating that the "General Conditions" were part of the June 6 Wood-Schwabedissen contract. Westinghouse offered no contrary evidence. The district court found that the "General Conditions" were part of the Wood-Schwabedissen contract and that Westinghouse was subject to the arbitration provision; therefore, the court granted Schwabedissen's motion to stay proceedings pending arbitration. The district court also substituted the International Paper Company, which had purchased certain Westinghouse assets, for Westinghouse in the litigation.

International Paper filed a request for arbitration before the International Court of Arbitration in Geneva. At the conclusion of the arbitral proceedings, the arbitrators ruled in Schwabedissen's favor. The arbitrators concluded that International Paper had asserted no basis for recovery against Schwabedissen because no contract existed between Schwabedissen and Westinghouse (International Paper's predecessor-in-interest), Wood was not an agent for Schwabedissen, and Westinghouse was not a third-party beneficiary of the Wood-Schwabedissen contract. The arbitrators also assessed costs against International Paper.

When International Paper refused to comply with the arbitration award, Schwabedissen sought its enforcement in the district court. International Paper moved for leave to file a second amended complaint, seeking to allege a breach of both an implied warranty of workmanlike service and an oral contract to repair. The district court

granted Schwabedissen's motion to enforce the arbitral award and denied International Paper's motion for leave to amend. International Paper now appeals.

International Paper claims that the district court erred in finding that the Schwabedissen-Wood contract contains an arbitration clause. It further contends that even if the contract contains such a clause, it was not bound to adhere to it.

Initially, International Paper contends that the Wood-Schwabedissen contract contains no arbitration clause. International Paper argues that the June 12 purchase order Wood sent to Schwabedissen was "the actual contract" between Wood and Schwabedissen, and that the parties never incorporated the "General Conditions," which contain the arbitration clause, into that contract. Schwabedissen submitted an affidavit from one of its employees stating that the Wood-Schwabedissen contract included the "General Conditions." In addition, Schwabedissen offered a separate agreement signed by Schwabedissen and Wood, dated February 24, 1993, that referenced the contract for the saw sold to Westinghouse and stated that the "General Conditions" were attached to that contract. Although International Paper failed to contradict this evidence in any way, it nonetheless claims that the district court erred in finding that "the only reasonable inference that [it could] get from [the evidence] was that the arbitration agreement was a part of the Wood-Schwabedissen contract."

We review factual findings that form the basis of a decision as to whether the parties have agreed to submit a dispute to arbitration for clear error. We find no error in the district court's factual finding that the Wood-Schwabedissen contract included the "General Conditions" containing the arbitration clause. Indeed, International Paper offered nothing to counter Schwabedissen's evidence in support of this finding.

International Paper's principal contention is that even if the Wood-Schwabedissen contract contains an arbitration clause, that clause cannot be enforced against International Paper, a non-signatory to the Wood-Schwabedissen contract. Generally, "arbitration is a matter of contract and a party cannot be required to submit to arbitration any dispute which he has not agreed so to submit." While a contract cannot bind parties to arbitrate disputes they have not agreed to arbitrate, "it does not follow . . . that under the [Federal Arbitration] Act an obligation to arbitrate attaches only to one who has personally signed the written arbitration provision." Rather, a party can agree to submit to arbitration by means other than personally signing a contract containing an arbitration clause.

Well-established common law principles dictate that in an appropriate case a nonsignatory can enforce, or be bound by, an arbitration provision within a contract executed by other parties.

We believe that the doctrine of equitable estoppel applies here. Equitable estoppel precludes a party from asserting rights "he otherwise would have had against another" when his own conduct renders assertion of those rights contrary to equity. In the arbitration context, the doctrine recognizes that a party may be estopped from asserting that the lack of his signature on a written contract precludes enforcement of the contract's arbitration clause when he has consistently maintained that other provisions of the same contract should be enforced to benefit him. "To allow [a plaintiff] to claim the benefit of the contract and simultaneously avoid its burdens would both disregard equity and contravene the purposes underlying enactment of the Arbitration Act."

A nonsignatory is estopped from refusing to comply with an arbitration clause "when it receives a 'direct benefit' from a contract containing an arbitration clause."

Some courts have, at a nonsignatory's instance, required a signatory of an arbitration agreement to arbitrate with the nonsignatory because of "the close relationship between the entities involved, as well as the relationship of the alleged wrongs to the nonsignatory's obligations and duties in the contract . . . and [the fact that] the claims were 'intimately founded in and intertwined with the underlying contract obligations.'" The Second Circuit has held, however, that a "close relationship" and "intimate[ ]" factual connection provide no independent basis to require a nonsignatory of an arbitration agreement to arbitrate with a signatory, and therefore that a nonsignatory cannot be bound without receiving a "direct benefit" from or pursuing a "claim . . .

integrally related to the contract containing the arbitration clause.

Applying these principles here we can only conclude that International Paper is estopped from refusing to arbitrate its dispute with Schwabedissen. The Wood-Schwabedissen contract provides part of the factual foundation for every claim asserted by International Paper against Schwabedissen. In its amended complaint, International Paper alleges that Schwabedissen failed to honor the warranties in the Wood-Schwabedissen contract, and it seeks damages, revocation, and rejection "in accordance with" that contract. International Paper's entire case hinges on its asserted rights under the Wood-Schwabedissen contract; it cannot seek to enforce those contractual rights and avoid the contract's requirement that "any dispute arising out of" the contract be arbitrated. The district court did not err in so holding.

For the same reason, we reject International Paper's claim that the Convention on the Recognition and Enforcement of Foreign Arbitral Awards precludes enforcement of the arbitral award because it requires United States courts to enforce international arbitration agreements only against parties to "an agreement in writing." As we have previously recognized, the estoppel doctrine also applies to non-signatories to arbitration agreements governed by the Convention.

For all of these reasons, the judgment of the district court is AFFIRMED.

BEST BUY CO., INC V. FEDDERS NORTH AMERICA, INC.,

202 F.3d 1004 (2000)

UNITED STATES COURT OF APPEALS FOR THE EIGHTH CIRCUIT

LAY, CIRCUIT JUDGE

Best Buy, a Minnesota corporation, is a retail operation that sells a variety of household goods, including window unit air conditioners. Fedders is a wholly-owned subsidiary of Fedders Corporation, a Delaware corporation. Fedders manufactures window unit air conditioners. In the fall of 1993, the parties entered into a written contract where Fedders would sell Best Buy window units and the latter would then resell them during the following summer. This agreement, known as the 1994 Program, provided for product costs, payment terms, and freight charges. Most importantly for purposes of this appeal, the contract also included an "Inventory Assistance" provision (IAP) which provided:

Inventory Assistance-Fedders is offering Best Buy an Inventory Assistance program for 1994.

Any of the five "core" models that Best Buy has in inventory on June 30th can be returned for full credit. The units must be in factory sealed cartons.

This provision was inserted into the 1994 Program largely at the insistence of Best Buy, which had previously refused to do business with Fedders because of Fedders' failure to provide an acceptable return policy, and was sought as assurance that it would not end up with a huge inventory at the end of the season.

The 1994 season came and went without incident, and the parties entered into subsequent one-year programs for the 1995 and 1996 seasons. The language in the IAP remained the same with the exception that the covered "core" models changed from year to year.

Pursuant to the 1996 Program, Fedders sold Best Buy $3,988,863 in core model units. However, the summer of 1996 was unusually cool, and Best Buy's sell-through rate was not as good as in previous years. As a result, Best Buy attempted to invoke the IAP for the first time in 1996. Best Buy representatives contacted Fedders in mid-July of 1996 and requested Fedders take back the unsold core models and refund Best Buy the purchase price. Fedders refused. A meeting was held on July 23, 1996 to discuss the returns. During this meeting, Fedders' representatives stated that they would not accept the unsold units because, under the IAP, any such request needed to have been made by June 30, 1996, and the models shipped by July 10, 1996, in order to receive a full refund. Fedders claimed that these return deadlines were agreed upon orally as part of the IAP during its presentation of the 1994 Program and asserted that because the terms of the IAP remained unchanged throughout the parties' three-year relationship, the deadlines remained unchanged. Two Best Buy representatives present at the July 23 meeting testified to the effect that, up until that time, they were unaware of any return deadlines under the IAP.

Best Buy commenced this action in Minnesota state court on January 14, 1997. On February 12, 1997, Fedders removed the action to federal district court alleging diversity jurisdiction.

The district court issued its Order for Judgment on November 25, 1998. Rejecting Fedders' contention that the return deadlines were part of the IAP, the court held that Fedders breached the contract by refusing to accept the core models.

On cross-appeal Fedders challenges the district court's finding that the return deadlines were not "expressly incorporated" into the 1996 Program's IAP and its holding that Fedders breached by refusing to accept the units. In particular, Fedders faults the lower court for failing to give proper consideration to all its parol evidence, especially the testimony of Thomas Purcell, Senior Vice President of Sales and Marketing at Fedders (Purcell). Purcell was one of two Fedders employees who attended the 1993 meeting where the return deadlines were allegedly articulated. Purcell testified that he told Best Buy about the return deadlines during that meeting and that, to ensure understanding, he carefully explained the reasoning behind the deadlines. The district court rejected his testimony, along with the rest of the parol evidence offered, stating that it undermined rather than supported Fedders' position. The court found that Purcell's testimony "stood alone" for the argument that the return deadlines were included in the IAP and the testimony contrasted the written agreement.

The "uncorroborated" nature of Purcell's testimony is a question of fact which this court reviews for clear error. The district court received parol evidence in this case in an attempt to "resolve the ambiguity presented by the inventory assistance program in light of the parties' positions," and "explain the 'Inventory Assistance' portion of the agreement, especially as it relates to the

June 30th date." Under Minnesota Statute § 336.2-202, parties are barred from bringing evidence of any prior agreement or a contemporaneous oral agreement which contradicts the terms of a final, written contract. However, explanatory or supplemental evidence of the course of dealing or course of performance by the parties is admissible, as is evidence of consistent additional terms unless the writing is intended by the parties to be a complete and exclusive statement of the terms of the agreement.

Neither Best Buy nor Fedders challenge the admission of the parol evidence. Rather, the foundation of Fedders' cross-appeal is the court's allegedly insufficient consideration of the parol evidence. Fedders claims the district court was clearly erroneous in its finding that Purcell's testimony "stood alone," because the court failed to consider other evidence that supported the testimony.

Fedders lists six pieces of evidence in support of Purcell's testimony. They are: (1) Purcell's memo to Fedders' president, prepared shortly after the 1993 meeting, stating that Best Buy's representative "was pleased with the core model return on June 30th provision"; (2) Purcell's testimony that he told management after the 1993 meeting that he had explained the return deadlines to Best Buy, evidenced by Fedders' deal sheet for the 1994 Program which contains a handwritten note stating "June return on core models is in place"; (3) testimony of Thomas Kroll, corporate controller for Fedders Corp., stating that a group of Fedders' managers had discussed the fact that the 1994 Program contained a June 30 notification date and a July 10 return date; (4) testimony of George Stadler (Stadler), another attendee of the 1993 meeting and Fedders employee, that he believed Best Buy was required to notify Fedders by June 30 and return the product "sometime in July"; (5) Fedders' inventory tracking system and Inventory Weekly Report, which was only used with the Best Buy account because of the IAP; and (6) testimony of Purcell and Stadler describing communications between Best Buy and Fedders representatives in May and June of 1996 regarding Best Buy's plans for its remaining inventory.

After reviewing the district court's opinion, we find that the court was not clearly erroneous in its factual findings. In the bench trial below, the district court judge was the trier of fact. It is evident that the court weighed the extrinsic evidence and found it insufficient to support Purcell's testimony. As we see nothing in the record that suggests this finding to be clearly erroneous, we are bound to affirm it.

A district court's interpretation of state law is subject to de novo review. As we noted in the preceding subsection, we are bound by the district court's findings of fact regarding Purcell's testimony. Thus, the question becomes whether, upon independent review, there exists sufficient evidence of breach to support the lower court's decision.

Best Buy also presented evidence in the form of an October 25, 1994, memo directed to Purcell from Fedders' upper management asking that Best Buy's written program include the language: "any of the (X) core models that X has in inventory on June 30, can be returned for full credit no later than July 10, 1995. These units must be in factory sealed cartons." Purcell testified that this language was never inserted into either the 1995 or 1996 programs. Finally, Stadler, the individual at Fedders with perhaps the most contact with Best Buy during the relevant seasons, testified that he was never told by anyone at Fedders to revise the language of the 1996 Program. He also stated that he was never told prior to July of 1996 that he should tell Best Buy that product should be returned by a specified date. All this evidence is strong support for the conclusion that the return deadlines were not a part of the 1996 Program; thus, Fedders breached the agreement.

After detailed consideration of Fedders' counter-evidence, we find it insufficient to upset the district court's holding on this issue. Although Stadler's testimony is somewhat useful in determining whether program terms carried over from year to year, there is countervailing evidence that each new program stood independent of its predecessor. Furthermore, even if Stadler's testimony is accepted on this point, Fedders still must establish that Best Buy was aware of the return deadlines in 1993, and this it has failed to do. Thus, we affirm the lower court's holding that because the return deadlines were not part of the 1996 Program, Fedders breached the contract in refusing to accept Best Buy's tender of the core models.

We read the district court's opinion as declining to make a holding on the foreseeability of the sought-after damages. Thus, we have no basis to review the court on this issue. The actual calculation of damages is a question for the district court, and we leave that task for remand

For the foregoing reasons, we AFFIRM the district court on the issue of breach and we REVERSE on the issue of Best Buy's entitlement to buyer's remedies and REMAND for a damages calculation in accordance with this judgment.

STREEKS, INC. V. DIAMOND HILL FARMS, INC., ET AL

SUPREME COURT OF NEBRASKA

258 Neb. 581; 605 N.W.2d 110 (2000)

HENDRY, CHIEF JUDGE

Darrel Streeks, doing business as Streeks, Inc., brought an action against John D. Nielsen for fraudulent concealment based on Nielsen's failure to disclose certain information about potato seed. A jury rendered a verdict in favor of Streeks, Inc., in the amount of $25,000. Nielsen filed a notice of appeal and a petition to bypass. Streeks, Inc., cross-appealed.

Streeks, Inc. (Streeks), is a family corporation composed of Darrel Streeks and his wife, LeAnn Streeks. Nielsen, doing business as Diamond Hill Farms, Inc., is in the business of raising seed potatoes for his own use and for sale to other farmers. For a number of years, Streeks has been engaged in growing certified seed potatoes. Potato growing in Nebraska is a specialized area of farming, with only 16 certified potato growers in the state.

Since 1994, Streeks has grown certified seed potatoes for Frenchman Valley Produce, which is owned and operated by Timothy May, Streeks' brother-in-law. May grows commercial potatoes and had agreements with Streeks in 1994 through 1996 to supply seed for this purpose. Pursuant to their agreement, during each of the 3 years, May would purchase potato seed and sell it to Streeks. Streeks would then raise the seedling potatoes at his expense and sell them back to May at a specified price. May then used the seedling potatoes to grow a commercial potato crop. This arrangement guaranteed May the required seedlings at a certain price.

May's operation requires a supply of seedling potatoes of a certain quality. The quality of certified potatoes is determined by classifying them into "generations." The generation of potato seed is determined by the standards set forth by the Potato Certification Association of Nebraska. One of the factors that determines a potato's generational level is the percentages of certain diseases it contains. Generation I potatoes have the lowest percentage of allowable diseases, and Generation V potatoes have the highest. Seed is evaluated by the "Florida winter test," which tests the seed for viruses. Seed can be reclassified at a lower generational level if the Florida tests detect a virus content that is above the acceptable level for that generation. Seed at one generational level produces a potato classified at the next lower generational level. May produced Generation III or IV potatoes, which required Generation II or III potato seed.

In early December 1995, Streeks contacted May and asked May to locate a supplier of Generation II seed for Streeks' use in raising the 1996 crop of Generation III seedlings for May. May located the supplier because May is a larger grower who could obtain a better price on the seed. May learned that Nielsen had some Generation II seed available for sale and contacted Nielsen about purchasing a supply. Before signing a written contract for the purchase of the seed, May informed Nielsen that Streeks would be raising the seedlings. Nielsen was aware that this was a three-party transaction in which May purchased the seed from Nielsen for Streeks' use in raising Generation III seedlings for May.

In January 1996, May entered into a contract with Nielsen for the purchase of Generation II certified seed. The contract contained a limitation-of-damages provision and an exclusion of warranties, including any warranties that the seed was free of latent potato diseases. After entering into the contract with Nielsen, May and Nielsen had no further contact with one another regarding the seed. May told Streeks that Nielsen would be supplying the seed that Streeks would raise for May. All further communication regarding the seed was between Streeks and Nielsen.

In early February 1996, Nielsen learned that the results of the Florida tests, dated January 31, 1996, showed the seed had been downgraded from Generation II to the lowest generational level, Generation V, because it contained 3.2 percent leaf roll virus. The allowable percentage of leaf roll virus for Generation II seed is two-tenths of a percent. Nielsen did not inform May or Streeks that the seed had been downgraded.

In March 1996, May and Streeks reduced to writing their agreement regarding the seed May had purchased from Nielsen in January. Streeks purchased the Generation II seed from May for $25,300 and agreed to plant the seed to raise Generation III seedlings for May. May agreed to purchase the seedlings Streeks raised for $6.50 per hundredweight.

Nielsen was aware that Streeks was going to pick up the seed. Streeks and Nielsen spoke on the telephone on several occasions prior to Streeks' picking up the seed.

Streeks and Nielsen discussed the fact that the seed was supposed to be classified as Generation II and would be used to raise certified seedlings for May. Streeks claimed that during these conversations, Nielsen never told him the seed had been downgraded to Generation V and never mentioned any problem with leaf roll. Nielsen claimed he told Streeks that the seed was "loused up with leaf roll" when he spoke with Streeks on the telephone in mid-April 1996. It is undisputed in the record that Nielsen never told Streeks that the seed had been downgraded to Generation V. Only Nielsen knew that the seed had been downgraded.

On May 2, 1996, Streeks picked up the seed from Nielsen's storage Quonset and began planting later that same day, believing the seed to be classified as Generation II. After Streeks had planted the seed in early May, Nielsen informed Streeks that the seed was carrying leaf roll virus. According to Streeks, this was the first indication that the seed was not classified as Generation II. Both parties acknowledged that Streeks reacted with shock and surprise when Nielsen revealed this information.

Because the seed was classified as Generation V, instead of Generation II, Streeks could not meet the requirement under his contract with May to supply Generation III seedlings. Nielsen never requested payment from May for the seed.

Streeks was unable to sell much of his crop as seedlings because it was too early in the year to sell that type of seedling potatoes. Furthermore, a nationwide surplus of potatoes made it difficult to sell the crop as commercial potatoes. Streeks did sell some of the potatoes, but at much lower prices than originally provided for under the contract with May.

On April 8, 1997, Streeks filed an action in Banner County District Court against Nielsen based on negligence, fraudulent misrepresentation, and fraudulent concealment. The negligence and fraudulent misrepresentation claims were disposed of prior to trial. Streeks claimed approximately $152,322 in damages as the result of not being able to sell the seedlings to May at the specified price under their contract. Streeks claimed that Nielsen fraudulently concealed the fact that the seed Streeks received had been downgraded from Generation II to Generation V.

The fraudulent concealment claim was tried to a jury on January 26 through 30, 1998. At trial, Nielsen admitted that reclassification of seed is a material fact important to the grower of certified seedlings and that it is an accepted practice in the industry to disclose any reclassification. Nielsen admitted that there is an obligation to disclose a reclassification and that it would never be appropriate to fail to disclose such a fact.

The jury found in favor of Streeks in the amount of $25,000. Streeks filed a motion for new trial or for judgment notwithstanding the verdict on the issue of damages only, claiming that the verdict was too small and was not supported by the evidence. The motion was denied. Nielsen thereafter appealed, and Streeks cross-appealed.

Nielsen claims his motion for directed verdict should have been granted because he had no duty to disclose to Streeks that the seed had been downgraded. He claims there was no contractual, fiduciary, or other special relationship between the parties that would create a duty to disclose. However, Streeks claims that Nielsen did have a duty to disclose because of the three-party transaction involving May, Nielsen, and Streeks. Thus, the issue presented is whether Nielsen owed Streeks a duty to disclose and the parameters of such a duty.

[T]o prove fraudulent concealment, a plaintiff must show that (1) the defendant had a duty to disclose a material fact; (2) the defendant, with knowledge of the material fact, concealed the fact; (3) the material fact was not within the plaintiff's reasonably diligent attention, observation, and judgment; (4) the defendant concealed the fact with the intention that the plaintiff act in response to the concealment or suppression; (5) the plaintiff, reasonably relying on the fact or facts as the plaintiff believed them to be as the result of the concealment, acted or withheld action; and (6) the plaintiff was damaged by the plaintiff's action or inaction in response to the concealment.

Under the Restatement, supra, § 551, a duty to disclose may arise among parties to a business transaction. The term "business transaction" is not defined in § 551. Generally, a transaction consists of "'an act or agreement, or several acts or agreements having some connection with each other, in which more than one person is concerned, and by which the legal relations of such persons between themselves are altered. It is a broader term than "contract."'"

In the present case, Streeks, May, and Nielsen were parties to a business transaction involving potato seed. May and Streeks agreed that May would procure the seed for Streeks' use in growing seedlings for May. May's contract with Nielsen for the purchase of the seed would not have occurred had there been no agreement with Streeks to raise the seedlings. When May first contacted Nielsen, he informed Nielsen that Streeks would be raising the seedlings. Thereafter, Streeks and Nielsen communicated directly with one another regarding the seed. Although there was not a contract between Streeks and Nielsen; Streeks, May, and Nielsen were all parties to this specialized business transaction involving potato seed.

Existence of a contract between the plaintiff and the defendant is not necessary for a duty of disclosure to arise.

We have permitted an action for fraudulent concealment in a situation regarding a business transaction where there was no contract between the plaintiff and the defendant

Nielsen and Streeks were parties to the transaction involving the potato seed. Nielsen knew that it was basic to the transaction that the seed be classified as Generation II. Nielsen spoke to Streeks on several occasions after Nielsen knew that the seed had been downgraded, but before the seed was picked up. Nielsen did not disclose the fact that the seed had been downgraded to Generation V. Streeks planted the seed, mistakenly believing it was classified as Generation II. Streeks would not have picked up the seed and planted it had he known the seed was not classified as Generation II. Nielsen admitted that it is standard practice in the industry to disclose any reclassification of seed and that it would never be appropriate to fail to disclose such information. The transaction involving Streeks, May, and Nielsen; the customs of the potato trade; and the objective circumstances of the case make it reasonable for Streeks to expect Nielsen to disclose to him the fact that the seed had been downgraded. The trial court correctly denied Nielsen's motion for directed verdict because under the Restatement, supra, § 551(2)(e), Nielsen owed Streeks a duty to disclose the reclassification.

Nielsen claims the trial court erred by failing to give Nielsen's proposed instruction on the measure of damages using the "benefit of the bargain" rule. To establish reversible error from a court's failure to give a requested instruction, an appellant has the burden of showing that (1) the tendered instruction is a correct statement of the law, (2) the tendered instruction is warranted by the evidence, and (3) the appellant was prejudiced by the court's failure to give the tendered instruction. Nielsen's proposed instruction stated the measure of damages as the difference between the value of the seed Streeks expected to receive and the value of the seed actually received at the time of delivery.

The benefit of the bargain rule is an appropriate measure of damages when the fraud induces a party to enter a contract for sale of property.

However, in the present case, we are not presented with a situation in which Streeks was fraudulently induced to enter into a contract with Nielsen. Because this action is not based on a fraudulently induced contract, the benefit of the bargain rule is not the appropriate measure of damages.

Nielsen has failed to show that his proposed benefit of the bargain instruction is a correct statement of the law warranted by the evidence in this case. Thus, failure to give this proposed instruction is not reversible error.

The instruction given by the court was an appropriate measure of damages under the circumstances of this case. "In an action for fraud a party may recover such damages as will compensate him for the loss or injury actually caused by the fraud and place the defrauded

party in the same position as he would have been in had the fraud not occurred." Because of Nielsen's nondisclosure, Streeks could not perform the contract with May and was damaged as a result.

The May-Nielsen contract included exclusion of warranty provisions and limited damages to the price of the seed. Nielsen claims that Streeks should have no better rights against him than May would have had under the contract. However, Nielsen overlooks the fact that had May sued Nielsen, the May-Nielsen contract would not have prohibited May from bringing a separate claim for fraudulent concealment.

We have held that a purchaser is not limited to the contract when bringing claims against a seller, but may also bring claims for fraudulent concealment, fraudulent misrepresentation, and negligence.

Additionally, the disclaimer in the May-Nielsen contract provided that there were "no warranties which extend beyond the description on the face hereof." However, the face of the contract stated, and Nielsen expressly warranted, that the seed was classified as Generation II. Thus, had May sued Nielsen, the disclaimer of warranties would have had no effect and Nielsen would also be liable to May under the U.C.C. for supplying May with Generation V seed, which was not the seed for which May had contracted.

Streeks' cause of action is a tort claim based on fraud perpetrated by Nielsen. Streeks is not asserting any additional or better claim than that which would have been available to May. The trial court did not abuse its discretion in excluding the May-Nielsen contract as irrelevant. We find that based on the circumstances of this case, Nielsen's contract defenses were inapplicable against Streeks' fraud claim.

We find that Nielsen has asserted no error requiring reversal in this case. We now turn to Streeks' cross-appeal.

"A civil jury verdict will not be disturbed on appeal unless clearly wrong." "The amount of damages to be awarded is a determination solely for the fact finder, and its action in this respect will not be disturbed on appeal if it is supported by evidence and bears a reasonable relationship to the elements of the damages proved."

The jury verdict in this case was not clearly wrong. The jury awarded Streeks $25,000, which is approximately the amount Streeks paid May for the seed. The potatoes Streeks raised were still suitable for sale in other markets at a lower price. Streeks did not sell the potatoes immediately after harvest, but held them, hoping for an increase in price, which never materialized. A mitigation of damages instruction allowed the jury to reduce Streeks' damages by any amount that he could have received had he sold the potatoes sooner. Although the evidence could [**124] have supported a larger verdict, the amount awarded is not clearly wrong under all the evidence presented. Thus, the trial court did not abuse its discretion by denying Streeks' motion for new trial.

Having considered all assignments of error of both parties and finding them to be without merit, the judgment of the district court is affirmed.

DOUGLAS M. BLEVINS V. NEW HOLLAND NORTH AMERICA, INC.

97 F. Supp. 2d 747 (2000)

UNITED STATES DISTRICT COURT FOR THE WESTERN DISTRICT OF
VIRGINIA, ABINGDON DIVISION

JONES, DISTRICT JUDGE

Douglas M. Blevins filed this action against New Holland North America, Inc. ("New Holland") seeking damages as the result of an accident that occurred on July 3, 1997, when Blevins, while employed as a farm worker, was injured by a hay baler designed, manufactured, and sold by New Holland. Three counts of Blevins' complaint seek recovery due to New Holland's alleged negligence. Count IV of the complaint, the object of the present motion, seeks recovery for the claimed breach of the implied warranties of merchantability and fitness for intended use.

The plaintiff Blevins went to work for Vannoy Farms ("Vannoy") a few years after graduating from high school in 1984. He worked on Vannoy's several farms in Virginia and North Carolina, as well as for Vannoy's separate construction business. He was experienced in operating farm equipment.

At some point in time, Vannoy decided to purchase a new hay baler, the business having owned its only other hay baler for twelve years. Mark Vannoy, one of the owners of Vannoy, negotiated the purchase of a New Holland model 644 hay baler. It was delivered to the Vannoy farm premises in Galax, Virginia, on June 26, 1997, by Harold Porter, a salesman for Fowlkes Machinery Company, the local New Holland dealer. Present at the time of delivery were Mark Vannoy; Edward Dollinger, Blevins's stepfather, who was also employed by Vannoy; Blevins, the plaintiff; and perhaps James R. Vannoy, another owner.

Porter had with him a two-page (front and back) form document entitled "Warranty and Limitation of Liability - Agricultural Products." Among other things, this document described New Holland's express warranty applicable to the hay baler. In addition, it contained the following language:

LIMITATIONS, INCLUDING DISCLAIMER OF IMPLIED WARRANTIES AND CONSEQUENTIAL DAMAGES

This warranty gives you specific legal rights and you may also have other rights which vary, depending on state or provincial laws.

New Holland North America, Inc. or New Holland Canada, Ltd. does not authorize any person or dealer to create for it any other obligation or liability in connection with these products. TO THE EXTENT ALLOWED BY LAW, ANY IMPLIED WARRANTY OF MERCHANTABILITY OR FITNESS APPLICABLE TO THIS PRODUCT IS LIMITED TO THE STATED DURATION OF THIS WRITTEN WARRANTY. NEITHER COMPANY NOR THE SELLING DEALER SHALL BE LIABLE FOR LOSS OF THE USE OF THE PRODUCT, LOSS OF TIME, INCONVENIENCE, COMMERCIAL LOSS OR CONSEQUENTIAL DAMAGES.

Some states and provinces do not allow limitations on how long an implied warranty will last or the exclusion or limitation of incidental or consequential damages, so the above limitations or exclusions may not apply to you.

The remedy of repair or replacement of a defective part during the warranty period herein specified shall be the purchaser's exclusive remedy.

The purchaser's name was filled in on the form by Porter as "Vannoy Farms" and Blevins signed his own name above the space marked "signature." There had been no prior negotiation of the terms of the document, other than perhaps a discussion of the length of the warranty obligation, which was twelve months.

A few days later, on July 3, 1997, while using the hay baler in the course of his employment, Blevins grabbed at some hay sticking out of the mechanism, and his arm was pulled by an operating belt into a "nip" point, causing serious injury.

The parties are in agreement as to the general legal framework surrounding the present motion. The Uniform Commercial Code allows foreseeable users of goods a remedy against the seller, without regard to privity of contract. A seller may by contract limit the remedies for breach of warranty, and in particular, may exclude consequential damages, unless the exclusion is unconscionable. Personal injuries, such as those claimed here, are a type of consequential damages.

The issue is thus whether New Holland's exclusion of consequential damages is unconscionable. If it is, the plaintiff's breach of warranty claim is not barred. If the exclusion is not unconscionable, the motion for summary judgment must be granted.

The parties are also agreed that the plaintiff has the ultimate burden of proof on this issue. Section 8.2-719 provides that "limitation of consequential damages for injury to the person in the case of consumer goods is prima facie unconscionable but limitation of damages where the loss is commercial is not." Consumer goods are goods "used or bought for use primarily for personal, family or household purposes." Since the hay baler was purchased and used in a commercial enterprise and thus is not consumer goods, the exclusion is not prima facie unconscionable, and the plaintiff here bears the burden of proving that it is unconscionable.

Rule 56 "mandates the entry of summary judgment, after adequate time for discovery and upon motion, against a party who fails to make a showing sufficient to establish the existence of an element essential to that party's case, and on which that party will bear the burden of proof at trial." Celotex Corp. v. Catrett, 477 U.S. 317, 322, 91 L. Ed. 2d 265, 106 S. Ct. 2548 (1986); see Fed. R. Civ. P. 56(c). Thus, in order to avoid summary judgment against him on this issue, Blevins must produce sufficient factual evidence that the exclusion of consequential damages is unconscionable.

Unconscionability is a matter of law for decision by the court, even in the absence of a motion for summary judgment. The parties should be allowed adequate opportunity to present all relevant evidence on the issue, since it is decided on the entire circumstances.. Here the parties have agreed that the court has been presented with all of the facts necessary to determine the issue.

The essence of unconscionability in this context is "an absence of meaningful choice on the part of one of the parties together with contract terms which are unreasonably favorable to the other party." The court must consider all of the relevant circumstances in order to determine whether the exclusion of remedies is unconscionable. Naturally enough, the plaintiff contends that the determination should be made from his point of view, emphasizing his lack of opportunity to participate in any negotiation of the exclusion. On the other side, the defendant contends that the issue of unconscionability must be determined from the four corners of the written warranty, or at least solely as to its fairness as to Vannoy, the contracting party.

Contrary to the plaintiff's argument, it is settled that a sales contract that is not unconscionable as to the parties themselves cannot be unconscionable as to one of the parties' employees. Otherwise, the abolition of the defense of privity of contract would allow the noncontracting party to have greater rights under the contract then those persons actually parties to it, which would be an anomaly. No agreement can possibly be unconscionable with regard to a third party who may benefit from the agreement but who was not a party to the agreement in the first place.

In the present case, there is no showing that Vannoy did not have the business sophistication sufficient to give it meaningful choice as to the provisions of the contract. Vannoy was experienced in purchasing equipment used in its business and in dealing with equipment suppliers. Of course, Vannoy did not actually negotiate the terms of the exclusion, but that is beside the point-the question is whether Vannoy was compelled to accept it by lack of meaningful choice. While Harold Porter described the warranty as not negotiable from New Holland's point of view, there is evidence that Vannoy had the opportunity to purchase a hay baler from other suppliers. There is no evidence that Vannoy's free choice to reject the [**10] remedy exclusion was foreclosed.

Moreover, there has been no showing that the exclusion was unreasonably unfair as to Vannoy. There is no evidence that such an exclusion is uncommon or unexpected in farm equipment sales.

The plaintiff argues that the fact that the exclusion of remedies was contained in a paper delivered with the machine, after the sale itself had been negotiated, shows its unconscionability. However, the limitations on warranty here were expressly acknowledged in writing by Vannoy's agent and were not unilaterally submitted by the seller.

While Blevins himself may not have appreciated the significance of the document that he signed on behalf of his employer, it is clear that he had the apparent, if not the actual, authority to bind Vannoy. The defendant has presented evidence that Blevins signed numerous documents for Vannoy relating to farm equipment and supplies during his employment. There is no evidence that the document was misrepresented, or that if Blevins had had any doubt as to his authority to agree on behalf of his employer, he could not have declined to accept delivery of the hay baler until there had been opportunity for further consideration of the document.

Based on these considerations, I hold that the plaintiff has not shown that the exclusion of consequential damages was unconscionable.

For the forgoing reasons, defendant's motion for summary judgment is granted

MATTHEW H. FLEEGER, v. STEWART L.
BELL, Clark County District Attorney; SCOTT DOYLE, Douglas
County District Attorney; and DESERT PALACE, INC. dba
CAESARS PALACE, a corporation, Defendants.

95 F. Supp. 2d 1126 (2000)

UNITED STATES DISTRICT COURT FOR THE DISTRICT OF NEVADA

PRO. Judge

Defendant Desert Palace, Inc., dba Caesars Palace (hereinafter referred to as "Desert Palace") is a well-known provider of resort hotel and casino amenities. In order to better serve its gaming patrons, Desert Palace extends lines of gambling credit to those who fill out a pre-printed application form. This form requires specific information, such as a patron's name, home address, business address, telephone numbers, social security number, bank and bank account number. Upon approval of this credit application by Desert Palace, a patron may request the issuance of certain instruments commonly known as casino "markers."

The markers, if signed by the patron, may in turn be used to obtain casino chips with which to gamble at a Desert Palace establishment. Each marker identifies its value in United States dollars and bears the instruction "PAY TO THE ORDER OF." The markers also bear the following stipulation:

> I authorize the payee to complete any of the following items on this negotiable instrument: (1) any missing amounts; (2) a date; (3) the name, account number and/or address and branch of any bank or financial institution; and (4) any electronic encoding of the above items. This information can be for any account from which I may in the future have the right to withdraw funds, regardless of whether that account now exists, of whether I provided the information on the account to the payee. I acknowledge that I incurred the debt evidenced by this instrument in Nevada. I agree that any dispute regarding or involving this instrument, the debt, or the payee shall be brought only in a court, state or federal, in Nevada. I hereby submit to the jurisdiction of any court, state or federal, in Nevada.

According to Plaintiff Matthew Fleeger ("Fleeger"), spaces for information such as account number, bank address and bank branch are left blank on the marker at the time of execution. When a patron is finished gambling, he either cashes out the markers (i.e., pays them off) or leaves the casino with the markers outstanding as a debt owed to Desert Palace.

On at least two occasions in November 1997 and January 1998, Fleeger executed several such markers with Desert Palace. By April 1998, Fleeger had accumulated a debt of approximately $183,856.00 as reflected in unpaid markers owed to Desert Palace. When Desert Palace attempted to deposit some of the markers reflecting this -- outstanding debt, however, they were returned by Fleeger's banks with the notations "NSF" and "Returned Not Paid." After sending a payment demand letter to Fleeger, Desert Palace requested Clark County District Attorney Stewart L. Bell and Douglas County District Attorney Scott Doyle ("the District Attorneys") to collect the debt as a "bad check" under Nev. Rev. Stat. § 205.130. The District Attorneys each filed criminal charges against Fleeger. Arrest warrants were issued therefrom in both Nevada and Texas, leading to Fleeger's eventual arrest and detention in both Dallas, Texas and Colin, Texas.

Nevada Revised Statute § 205.130 Issuance of check or draft without sufficient money or credit: Penalties.

1. Except as otherwise provided in this subsection and subsections 2 and 3, a person who willfully, with an intent to defraud, draws or passes a check or draft to obtain:

(a) Money;

(b) Delivery of other valuable property;

(c) Services;

(d) The use of property; or

(e) Credit extended by any licensed gaming establishment, drawn upon any real or fictitious person, bank, firm, partnership, corporation or depositary, when the person has insufficient money, property or credit with the drawee of the instrument to pay it in full upon its presentation, is guilty of a misdemeanor. If that instrument, or a series of instruments passed in the state during a period of 90 days, is in the amount of $250 or more, the person is guilty of a category D felony and shall be punished as provided in [Nev. Rev. Stat. §] 193.130. In addition to any other penalty, the court shall order the person to pay restitution.

2. A person who was previously convicted three times of a misdemeanor under the provisions of this section, or of an offense of a similar nature, in this state or any other state, or in a federal jurisdiction, who violates this section is guilty of a category D felony and shall be punished as provided in [Nev. Rev. Stat. §] 193.130. In addition to any other penalty, the court shall order the person to pay restitution.

3. A person who willfully issues any check or draft for the payment of wages in excess of $250, when the person knows he has insufficient money or credit with the drawee of the instrument to pay the instrument in full upon presentation is guilty of a gross misdemeanor.

4. For the purposes of this section, "credit" means an arrangement or understanding with a person, firm, corporation, bank or depositary for the payment of a check or other instrument.

On November 4, 1999, Fleeger filed a Class Action Complaint on behalf of himself and other similarly situated plaintiffs. Desert Palace filed a Motion to Dismiss the Class Action Complaint for failure to state a claim on December 13, 1999.

While the Nevada criminal codes are silent as to what instruments may constitute a "check," this Court may reference sections of Nevada's commercial law code for interpretive aid. Under the Nevada Uniform Commercial Code, a "check" is defined as "[a] draft, other than a documentary draft, payable on demand and drawn on a bank." A draft is "payable on demand" when no time for payment is otherwise stated.

Here, the markers referenced within Fleeger's Amended Complaint specifically state that the payor empowers Desert Palace to fill in the amount, name, account number and address of any financial institution in which the payor holds funds. The markers also do not delineate any explicit dates for repayment, thereby subjecting the payor to a repayment obligation at the will of the payee. Thus, this Court finds the disputed casino markers to be negotiable "checks" for purposes of Nev. Rev. Stat. §§ 104.3104(6) and 205.130.

At least one other court characterizing casino markers under an analogous state commercial code has reached a similar conclusion. See TeleRecovery of Louisiana, Inc. v. Gaulon, 738 So. 2d 662, 666-67 (La. Ct. App. 1999) (applying Louisiana law).

IT IS THEREFORE ORDERED that Defendant Desert Palace, Inc.'s Motion to Dismiss is GRANTED. All causes of action asserted against Desert Palace, Inc. are DISMISSED.

COMMERCE BANK, N.A. V. BRUCE RICKETT, ET AL

329 N.J. Super. 379; 748 A.2d 111 (2000)

SUPERIOR COURT OF NEW JERSEY, APPELLATE DIVISION

NEWMAN, J.A.D.

On January 5, 1998, defendant, Bruce Rickett, individually and trading as Rick's Auto Sales, presented a check to Commerce Bank, N.A. (the Bank), issued to him on January 3, 1998 by DeSimone Auto, Inc, t/a Executive Auto Sales (DeSimone), in the amount of $12,000, for deposit into Rickett's checking account with the Bank. The Bank credited Rickett's account and shortly thereafter allowed him to draw against same.

The check, dated January 3, 1997, was drawn upon DeSimone's account at the Bank of Gloucester County for payment of a 1997 Buick LeSabre motor vehicle. The understanding between Rickett and DeSimone was that the check would not be presented for payment if the motor vehicle was damaged. Shortly after issuance of the check, DeSimone inspected the vehicle and found frame damage. DeSimone telephoned Rickett, advising him to pick up the vehicle and return the check. DeSimone returned the vehicle to Rickett, who accepted it. Thereafter, DeSimone issued a "stop payment" on the check, although the record does not reveal when the "stop payment" was requested. Contrary to their agreement, Rickett had already presented the check for payment on January 5, 1998, and drawn against it. The check was returned by the Bank of Gloucester County to the Bank as unpaid on January 13, 1998. The amount charged back to Rickett's account by the Bank was $11,016.48.

The Bank filed a complaint against both Rickett and DeSimone, seeking the amount charged back to Rickett's account. Rickett could not be located by the Bank. As to DeSimone, the Bank asserted that it was a "holder in due course" and, therefore, entitled to payment from DeSimone. DeSimone contended that the erroneous date of "January 3, 1997" placed the Bank on notice that the check may be overdue, and, accordingly, the Bank cannot be a holder in due course because "holder-in-due-course" status attaches at the time the transaction is made.

In support of its motion for summary judgment, the Bank submitted the certification of its assistant vice president, which states, in relevant part:

I have been employed by Commerce Bank, N.A. for approximately 17 years and have 11 years of branch experience. It has been my experience that checks presented for negotiation are often misdated in the first few days of a new year with the prior year still being written on the check.

In granting summary judgment in favor of the Bank in the amount of $11,016.48, Judge Supnick found that the Bank was a holder in due course, largely relying on the fact that DeSimone had admitted that the check was actually issued on January 3, 1998, not January 3, 1997, and on the Bank's proof that "checks presented for negotiation are often misdated in the first few days of a new year with the prior year still being written on the check." DeSimone moved for reconsideration. Judge Supnick denied the motion.

On appeal, DeSimone contends that the application of N.J.S.A. 12A:3-302a(2) negates the Bank's status as a holder in due course. That section reads as follows:

a. Subject to subsection c. of this section and subsection d. of 12A:3-106, "holder in due course" means the holder of an instrument if:

(2) the holder took the instrument for value, in good faith, without notice that the instrument is overdue or has been dishonored or that there is an uncured default with respect to payment of another instrument issued as part of the same series, without notice that the instrument contains an unauthorized signature or has been altered, without notice of any claim to the instrument described in 12A:3-306, and without notice that any party has a defense or claim in recoupment described in subsection a. of 12A:3-305.

DeSimone asserts that the "January 3, 1997" date on the face of the check made it "overdue." N.J.S.A. 12A:3-304 provides, in relevant part:

a. An instrument payable on demand becomes overdue at the earliest of the following times:

(2) if the instrument is a check, 90 days after its date[.]

DeSimone also cites to N.J.S.A. 12A:3-113, which provides, in pertinent part:

a. An instrument may be antedated or postdated. The date stated determines the time of payment if the instrument is payable at a fixed period after date.

DeSimone reasons that, because the check was dated January 3, 1997, and deposited in early January 1998, the Bank had actual notice that the check was overdue, as defined by the ninety-day period for checks set forth in N.J.S.A. 12A:3-304a(2), and was therefore not a holder in due course under N.J.S.A. 12A- 3:302a(2). DeSimone also construes N.J.S.A. 12A:3-113a to mean that the fact that the check was dated January 3, 1997, establishes the check's "date" as January 3, 1997, automatically rendering the check overdue when it was deposited on January 5, 1998.

DeSimone's reliance on N.J.S.A. 12A:3-113a to support its argument that January 3, 1997 must be viewed as the check's "date" for purposes of determining whether the instrument was overdue under N.J.S.A. 12A:3-304a(2) is misplaced. N.J.S.A. 12A:3-113a refers to an instrument payable at a fixed period of time. A check does not fit within that definition, but rather is a demand instrument.

The issue presented is whether, pursuant to N.J.S.A. 12A:3- 304a(2), a check becomes overdue ninety days after the date on the face of the check or ninety days after its date of issue. We construe N.J.S.A. 12A:3-304 a(2) to mean that a check becomes overdue ninety days after the date it is actually issued. To interpret N.J.S.A. 12A:3-304a(2) otherwise is impractical and inconsistent with other provisions in the Code.

The Bank has offered incontrovertible evidence, namely DeSimone's very admission, that the check was not in fact overdue at the time it was deposited.

DeSimone is correct that the Bank did not conclusively learn that the check was really made in 1998 until months after deposit. Had the check actually been made out in 1997, there is little question that the Bank would have had notice that the check was overdue and would not be able to lay claim to holder in due course status. To that extent, the Bank was taking a calculated risk.

Here, however, the check was not overdue. It is impossible for the Bank to have had notice of a circumstance which simply did not exist. While DeSimone was the victim of Rickett's breach, there is no doubt that, had the check been correctly dated, DeSimone would be liable for payment on it. To adopt DeSimone's reasoning would create a perverse incentive for drawers to intentionally misdate checks with knowledge that recourse could be sought in the courts should the transaction break down.

Moreover, the goal of the overdue provision is to prevent drawers from being indefinitely liable for payment on checks, not to prevent the type of fraud or breach of contract of which DeSimone was apparently the victim.

Affirmed.

THREE FEATHERS INC. V JAMES W. ROEMER JR., ET AL

704 N.Y.S.2d 746 (2000)

SUPREME COURT OF NEW YORK, APPELLATE DIVISION, THIRD
DEPARTMENT

CREW III, JUDGE

Defendant James W. Roemer Jr. and third-party defendant James D. Featherstonhaugh were partners in a law firm established in 1976. In 1984, they converted the partnership to a professional corporation, defendant Roemer and Featherstonhaugh P.C. (hereinafter R & F). In January 1993, Roemer executed an agreement that guaranteed Chemical Bank payment of any and all liabilities then existing or thereafter incurred by R & F. In August 1994, Chemical Bank granted a revolving credit loan to R & F secured by a promissory note. The credit loan agreement was signed by Roemer and Featherstonhaugh and provided for an absolute unconditional guarantee, which waived any legal or equitable defenses. Finally, in February 1995, Roemer executed another guarantee, again guaranteeing payment to Chemical Bank of any and all liabilities then existing or thereafter incurred and, again, waiving any and all defenses.

Shortly before Roemer signed the second guarantee, Featherstonhaugh announced his resignation from R & F to take effect in June 1995. Thereafter, on February 12, 1996, plaintiff, a subchapter S corporation owned by Featherstonhaugh and his wife, purchased R & F's promissory note and revolving credit agreement from Chemical Bank. On February 16, 1996, plaintiff declared R & F to be in default and demanded the entire amount due on the promissory note. When payment was not forthcoming, plaintiff commenced this action by way of a summons and notice of motion for summary judgment in lieu of complaint against Roemer, based upon his guarantees. Thereafter, Roemer commenced a third-party action against Featherstonhaugh by service of a summons and motion for summary judgment in lieu of third-party complaint. Featherstonhaugh then cross-moved for summary judgment dismissing the third-party complaint and R & F moved to intervene as a party defendant. Supreme Court granted R & F's motion to intervene and denied plaintiff's and Roemer's motions for summary judgment, as well as Featherstonhaugh's cross motion to dismiss the third-party complaint. These appeals by plaintiff and Featherstonhaugh ensued.

As a starting point, we agree that plaintiff made out a prima facie case for summary judgment based upon Roemer's guarantee as it established the existence of the underlying promissory note, the guarantee and R & F's failure to pay after demand for payment Equally persuasive is plaintiff's and Featherstonhaugh's contention that Supreme Court erred in finding the existence of questions of fact as to whether plaintiff is subject to the defenses of fraud in the inducement, misappropriation and diversion of income and bad-faith impairment of collateral. Nothing in the record before us reveals that plaintiff took the instruments in question with notice of any defense or claim against them, and the assertion that Featherstonhaugh fraudulently induced Roemer to enter into the various agreements with Chemical Bank does not constitute a defense against Chemical Bank from whom plaintiff took the instruments. Accordingly, plaintiff is a holder in due course of those negotiable instruments free of the foregoing defenses raised by Roemer and R & F. Furthermore, contrary to the contentions of Roemer and R & F, such defenses are not so intertwined with the promissory note and guarantees as to render a grant of summary judgment premature

We arrive at a different conclusion, however, with regard to the defense of champerty. Judiciary Law § 489 prohibits a corporation from taking a "promissory note * * * or other thing in action * * * with the intent and for the purpose of bringing an action or proceeding thereon", and the intent and purpose of a purchaser usually is a question of fact. Here, there clearly is a question of fact as to whether plaintiff purchased the instruments in question for the sole purpose of bringing an action thereon against Roemer and, as such, plaintiff's motion for summary judgment was properly denied. As a final matter, we note that R & F has raised a material issue of fact with regard to the alleged default on the promissory note. We have considered the remaining contentions of plaintiff and Featherstonhaugh and find them to be without merit.

ORDERED that the order and amended order are affirmed.

F. JAVIER MONREAL, M.D V. FLEET BANK

2000 N.Y. LEXIS 885 (2000)

COURT OF APPEALS OF NEW YORK

ROSENBLATT, JUDGE

Plaintiff, a physician, maintained a checking account with Fleet Bank. From 1988 through May 10, 1995, his bookkeeper purportedly embezzled money by forging plaintiff's name on his checks or altering the names of payees. During this period, the bank regularly furnished plaintiff with statements of account and canceled checks. Plaintiff reported the embezzlement to the bank on May 18, 1995, the day after he discovered it. He then sued the bank, alleging that it was negligent in paying the forged or altered checks.

In its defense, the bank asserted that UCC 4-406(4)'s one-year period had expired in 1989, thus barring all of plaintiff's claims. Supreme Court disagreed and held that each statement of account that the bank sent to plaintiff carried its own one-year period, thereby sustaining the claims arising within one year prior to May 18, 1995. Agreeing with the bank, the Appellate Division modified Supreme Court's order and dismissed all of plaintiff's claims.

The Uniform Commercial Code fastens strict liability on a bank that charges against its customer's account any "item" that is not "properly payable" (see, UCC 4-401). A check bearing a forgery of the customer's signature is an "item" not "properly payable" and therefore may not be charged against the customer's account (see, UCC 3-404[1], 4-104[g], 4-401[1]).

The Uniform Commercial Code goes on, however, to impose certain reciprocal duties on the customer, which limits the bank's strict liability exposure. Pursuant to UCC 4-406(1), a customer must (i) "exercise reasonable care and promptness to examine" statements of account and included items to discover his or her "unauthorized signature or any alteration on an item" and (ii) "notify the bank promptly after discovery thereof." A customer who fails to comply with these duties, with respect to an item appearing in a statement of account, is precluded from raising certain allegations against a bank (see, UCC 4-406[2]).

This preclusion, however, is not absolute. Even a customer failing in these duties may bring a claim against the bank if the customer can establish that the bank lacked ordinary care in paying the check (see, UCC 4-406[3]). In this context, UCC 4-406(4) provides that a customer whose claim is not precluded by UCC 4-406 (2) has "one year from the time the statement and items are made available to the customer" for asserting claims against a bank for an unauthorized signature of the customer or an alteration to the face or back of a check (see, UCC 4-406[4]).

In the case before us, the items purportedly forged or altered by the bookkeeper appear in successive statements of account over a seven-year period. Although the Uniform Commercial Code sets the one-year statutory limit to run from the time "the statement" becomes available to the customer, UCC 4-406(4) does not state when the one-year period begins to run in situations where forged or altered items by the same wrongdoer appear in successive statements of account.

Plaintiff argues that each successive statement of account carries its own one-year period. If so, plaintiff may still assert claims for forged or altered checks reported in statements made available to him between May 18, 1994 and May 18, 1995 -- assuming, of course, he can also establish that the bank failed to exercise ordinary care in paying the checks during that period (see, UCC 4-406[3]).

The bank, by contrast, argues that UCC 4-406(4)'s one-year period begins to run when a customer receives the first statement of account containing an unauthorized signature of the customer or an altered item. Under this interpretation plaintiff would be barred from asserting claims against the bank for any of his bookkeeper's forgeries or alterations, because plaintiff's statements of account reflected these forgeries or alterations as early as 1988.

The bank relies upon a portion of Official Comment 5 to UCC 4-406, which states that "there is little excuse for a customer not detecting an alteration of his own check or a forgery of his own signature." This phrase, however, must be read in its broader context, which is to explain the difference between the time limit for reporting altered checks or forgeries of a customer's own signature and the time limit for reporting unauthorized indorsements. The Comment emphasizes that it is far easier for customers to spot -- and therefore more promptly report -- alterations on their checks or forgeries of their own signatures, as opposed to unauthorized indorsements, which involve signatures [*7] of third parties. Accordingly, the period for reporting the former is one year, the latter, three (UCC 4- 406[4]).

The bank also relies on Official Comment 3 to UCC 4- 406, which states, in relevant part, that "one of the best ways to keep down losses in this type of situation is for the customer to promptly examine his statement and notify the bank of an unauthorized signature or alteration so that the bank will be alerted to stop paying further items."

Although this language aptly describes the importance of attentiveness generally, it does not support the bank's argument as to when the one-year period commences. Comment 3 relates to UCC 4-406(2), a subsection that applies when the bank has exercised ordinary care in paying the checks. Here, however, plaintiff's claim is based on the bank's alleged failure to exercise ordinary care under UCC 4-406(3) and (4). Indeed, a comparison of UCC 4-406(2) and UCC 4-406(4) provides the key to our determination. The 14-day period under UCC 4-406(2)(b) runs from the point at which [*8] "the first item and statement was available to the customer" (emphasis added). By way of contrast, UCC 4-406(4) conspicuously omits the word "first," stating merely that the one year period runs from "the statement and items." We are satisfied that this distinction was legislatively willed and that each statement therefore carries its own one-year period.

One of the Uniform Commercial Code's basic purposes is to "make uniform the law among the various jurisdictions." In that context we note that our decision is in accord with other courts that have treated the issue.

Accordingly, the order of the Appellate Division should be reversed, with costs, and the order of Supreme Court reinstated.

IN THE MATTER OF: CONSTANCE P. MERCER.

211 F.3d 214 (2000)

UNITED STATES COURT OF APPEALS FOR THE FIFTH CIRCUIT

DUHE, CIRCUIT JUDGE:

On November 10, 1995, AT&T opened Mercer's credit card account pursuant to a pre-approved credit application mailed to Mercer and signed by her. Although Mercer's credit limit on this AT&T account was $3,000, within a month she had exceeded this limit by $186.82 through charges and cash advances at automated teller machines ("ATM").

AT&T relies on third party credit agencies to screen potential applicants. A [*216] credit bureau makes an initial screening. These names are then matched against AT&T's own internal risk and scoring models to determine creditworthiness. The names that make this cut are then returned to the credit bureau for a second screening to review any change in credit standing or credit history. These credit bureaus place a risk or FICO score on each name to determine the probability of an account becoming delinquent. AT&T requires a minimum FICO score of 680 before sending out a solicitation offer to a prospective customer. The credit bureau assigned Mercer a FICO score of 735. Under the Fair Credit Reporting Act, AT&T must make a bonafide offer of credit to anyone who passed the screening process.

In September 1995, AT&T mailed Mercer and offer to open a credit card account. Mercer completed, signed, and returned her acceptance. Mercer provided AT&T an income figure of $24,500, a social security number, a date of birth, a home and business phone number, and a maiden name. AT&T then conducted a further review of Mercer's ability to service a credit line of $3,000. AT&T then sent Mercer on November 10, 1995 a card and a cardmember agreement. Mercer then used the account to obtain fourteen cash advances from ATMs, some in casinos. By early December, she had exceeded her credit limit, and AT&T barred her from further use of the account. In all, Mercer carried seven credit cards between March and December 1995.

The agreement became effective when Mercer used the card or the account. The agreement states that a card holder is "responsible for all amounts owned on [the card holder's] [a]ccount . . . and [the card holder] agree[s] to pay such amounts according to the terms of the [a]greement."

Regarding purchases and cash advances, the agreement says a card holder may use the card to "obtain a loan from [the card holder's] [a]ccount, by presenting it to any institution that accepts the [c]ard for that purpose, or to make a withdrawal of cash at an automated teller machine (ATM). Both of these transactions are treated as 'Cash Advance' on [the card holder's] [a]ccount." AT&T also may limit these cash advances.

Mercer filed a petition for bankruptcy relief under Chapter Seven of the Bankruptcy Code. AT&T challenged the dischargeability of the debt under Section 523(a)(2)(A). The bankruptcy court concluded that the debt was dischargeable. The court determined that Mercer did not make any representations to AT&T regarding her creditworthiness. Because she had made no representations, AT&T could not meet the reliance requirement to challenge dischargeability under Section 523(a)(2)(A). The district court affirmed the bankruptcy court's decision.

We review the bankruptcy court's factual findings for clear error and its conclusions of law de novo.

Section 523(a)(2)(A) of the Bankruptcy Code provides:

> A discharge under section 727 . . . of this title does not discharge an individual from any debt . . . for money, property, services, or an extension, renewal, or refinancing of credit, to the extent obtained by false pretense, a false representation, or actual fraud, other than a statement respecting the debtor's or an insider's financial condition. . . .

A creditor must prove its claim of nondischargeability by a preponderance of the evidence. In order for a debtor's representation to be a false representation or pretense, a creditor must show that the debtor (1) made a knowing and fraudulent falsehood; (2) describing past or current facts; (3) that was relied upon by the creditor; (4) who thereby suffered a loss. The creditor must show that it actually and justifiably relied on the debtor's representations.

The bankruptcy court concluded that AT&T did not actually rely on representations by Mercer because Mercer made no representations. AT&T pre-approved the card based solely on its own screening process. The court said, "Mercer never solicited the credit card from AT&T; never knew of nor gave her permission for the investigations; and was never asked about her debts, gambling losses, financial condition, or other credit cards being used by her or the balances thereon. . . . AT&T solely relied on its own agents and investigative processes to makes its decision."

The bankruptcy court's determination is correct. Because AT&T provided Mercer a pre-approved credit card with a pre-approved credit limit, Mercer could not make any false representations AT&T could rely on. The information Mercer returned to AT&T with her acceptance does not amount to any sort of false representation regarding her intent to pay. AT&T correctly points out that it has no duty to investigate the debtor to show justifiable reliance. However, justifiable reliance pre-supposes that the debtor has made a representation. Here Mercer made no representation. Therefore, AT&T neither could have actually nor justifiably relied.

AT&T also contends that the bankruptcy court erroneously concluded that because AT&T did not rely on the debtor's representations when the card was issued AT&T could not subsequently rely on implied representations made by the debtor with her use of the card. AT&T argues that we should adopt the implied representation theory. Under this theory, the card holder makes a representation that he or she intends to pay each time he or she receives money at an ATM. The money received amounts to a loan from the bank.

This Circuit has not adopted the implied representation theory, and we decline to do so in the pre-approved credit card context. First, although the debtor has borrowed money, the primary decision to extend credit was made before the implied representation. AT&T assumes the risk of any future lending by the debtor. Second, adoption of this theory would improperly shift the burden of proof in Section 523(a)(2)(A) actions. The debtor would essentially become the guarantor of his or her financial condition, and the theory would offend the balance of bankruptcy policy struck by Section 523. We conclude that we should apply a rule that favors the debtor instead of the creditor at least in the pre-approved credit card context, and we decline to apply the implied representation theory

Finally, the dissent argues that this holding will only encourage "irresponsible and dishonest debtors to go on unrestrained spending sprees" leading to more consumer bankruptcies and greater costs passed on to all credit card users through higher interest rates. The credit card issuers' irresponsible lending practices are another part of this problem. In this case, AT&T issued Mercer a pre-approved credit card based on a minimal third-party credit check. If AT&T had merely asked Mercer for information regarding her credit card usage, AT&T may have been more prudent in its lending practices, but AT&T did not.

This holding properly places a greater responsibility on credit card issuers for their lending practices, which have become increasingly irresponsible. According to a recent newspaper article, credit card issuers are "paying more attention to high-risk groups, such as households with proven debt problems and younger consumers. Some issuers are even targeting high-school students." This holding properly favors the debtor instead of the creditor, and will hopefully encourage more responsible lending practices by credit card issuers.

For these reasons, we affirm.

GENERAL MOTORS ACCEPTANCE CORPORATION V. LINCOLN NATIONAL BANK

2000 Ky. LEXIS 2; 40 U.C.C. Rep. Serv. 2d (Callaghan) 610 (2000)

SUPREME COURT OF KENTUCKY

LAMBERT, CHIEF JUSTICE

From 1976 through 1991, General Motors Acceptance Corporation ("GMAC") provided floor plan financing to Donohue Ferrill Motor Company, Inc., ("Donohue Ferrill"), a Chevrolet dealer in Hodgenville. Under the floor plan agreement, GMAC lent funds to Donohue Ferrill to purchase new vehicle inventory. Donohue Ferrill granted GMAC a security interest in all of its vehicle inventory and all of the proceeds of that inventory. The security agreements and financing statements were executed by A.G. Back, Jr., the founder of Donohue Ferrill and its president from 1966 through August 1990. Back was also a longtime officer of Lincoln National and chairman of its board of directors. Back was board chairman of Lincoln National when he, as president of Donohue Ferrill, signed the security agreement in favor of GMAC on September 26, 1983.

Routinely, Lincoln National's president, Robert D. Haynes, dealt with customer overdrafts. The established procedure when an account was overdrawn was for Haynes to contact the customer, inquire about the problem, and decide whether to authorize payment of the overdraft or return the check. However, this procedure was not followed when Donohue Ferrill's account was overdrawn. All of Donohue Ferrill's overdrafts were handled by Back personally, not by Haynes. For 38 of the 62 business days of September, October, and November 1991, Donohue Ferrill's account was overdrawn. Lincoln National honored 133 overdrafts during these three months and charged Donohue Ferrill a total of $1,995 in fees. The total amount of the overdrawn balances for those 38 days was $1,943,306.25.

In December 1991, Donohue Ferrill failed as a business and defaulted on its obligations to GMAC. After liquidation of its assets, Donohue Ferrill remained indebted to GMAC in the amount of $308,088.22. Prior to Donohue Ferrill's business failure, in September, October, and November 1991, Donohue Ferrill sold six trucks that were covered by GMAC's perfected security interest. The proceeds from these sales were deposited in a demand deposit (or checking) account Donohue Ferrill maintained at Lincoln National. The proceeds, along with other funds in the checking account, were applied to Donohue Ferrill overdrafts at Lincoln National. Donohue Ferrill never paid GMAC for the six trucks, even though the security agreement specifically required Donohue Ferrill to "faithfully and promptly remit" from the proceeds of the vehicles the amounts loaned by GMAC.

GMAC sued Lincoln National [*4] in Larue Circuit Court for $124,610.80 in proceeds from the sale of these six vehicles. GMAC argued that these proceeds were identifiable upon their deposit to the checking account and the trial court so found. Thus, GMAC argues, the bank's application of those funds to Donohue Ferrill's overdrafts constituted a conversion of its monies by the bank. GMAC based its claim upon KRS 355.9-306(2), which states;

> Except where this article otherwise provides, a security interest continues in collateral notwithstanding sale, exchange or other disposition thereof unless the disposition was authorized by the secured party in the security agreement or otherwise, and also continues in any identifiable proceeds including collections received by the debtor.

The bank sought dismissal of the complaint, contending that it took the funds free of any security interest because the funds were used to cover the overdrafts in the ordinary course of the bank's business with Donohue Ferrill. The bank also argued that GMAC's complaint should fail because GMAC acquiesced in the bank's possession and use of the proceeds.

The trial court granted the bank's motion for summary judgment. In reaching this result, the trial court found that the funds in question, upon deposit with other funds in the Donohue Ferrill account, lost their identifiable security cloak because the funds were credited by the bank against the account overdrafts in the ordinary course of its business with Donohue Ferrill. See UCC § 9-306(2), Official Comment 2(c), infra. Furthermore, the trial court believed GMAC was aware of the bank's custom of covering Donohue Ferrill's overdrafts, and, under the floor plan agreement, GMAC had access to Donohue Ferrill's bank records, which clearly revealed the pattern of overdrafts. Moreover, despite GMAC's manifest knowledge of Donohue Ferrill's financial difficulties, GMAC did not request that the bank separate or otherwise treat differently the funds generated by Donohue Ferrill from the sale of the floor plan vehicles. Finally, the trial court concluded that even if the subject transfers were not legitimized by the "ordinary course of business" principle, GMAC's claims would be barred because of GMAC's acquiescence in the banking relationship between Donohue Ferrill and Lincoln [*6] National.

The Court of Appeals affirmed, holding that Lincoln National's actions did not exceed the scope of its "ordinary course of business." For its interpretation of KRS 355.9-306(2), the Court of Appeals relied upon the official commentary to the UCC as follows:

Where cash proceeds are covered into the debtor's checking account and paid out in the operation of the debtor's business, recipients of the funds of course take free of any claim which the secured party may have in them as proceeds. What has been said relates to payments and transfers in ordinary course. The law of fraudulent conveyances would no doubt in appropriate cases support recovery of proceeds by a secured party from a transferee out of ordinary course or otherwise in collusion with the debtor to defraud the secured party.

The Court of Appeals also noted that KRS 355.4-401(1) specifically permits a bank to honor an overdraft if it is "authorized by the customer and is in accordance with any agreement between the customer and the bank."

Payment of an overdraft by a bank is of the nature of a loan to the account owner and is premised upon the condition of repayment. Thus, Lincoln National made loans to Donahue Ferrill in the amount of the overdrafts paid. Since the bank had no security for such loans, it was an unsecured creditor of Donahue Ferrill.

KRS 355.9-201 n5 gives a secured party priority over all others in the collateral or its proceeds, except as provided elsewhere by Article 9. Under KRS 355.9-306, a security interest continues in the identifiable proceeds of collateral. Thus, as an unsecured creditor, Lincoln National was without any right to take or retain assets of Donohue Ferrill that were subject to the perfected security interest of GMAC, unless allowed by an exception to KRS 355.9-306.

KRS 355.9-201 states: "Except as otherwise provided by this chapter, a security agreement is effective according to its terms between the parties, against purchasers of the collateral and against creditors."

The trial court and the Court of Appeals found such an exception in holding that the proceeds of the collateral used to cover prior overdrafts were transferred out of Donohue Ferrill's account in the ordinary course of business. We disagree with this interpretation. Although the commentary provides an exception for proceeds from the debtor's checking account and paid in the ordinary course of the operation of the debtor's business, this exception does not apply when a bank seizes funds deposited in a customer's account and applies such funds to payment of overdrafts or antecedent debts. Such an interpretation would eviscerate the security interest in proceeds of collateral contrary to KRS 355.9-306(2) and permit a bank that had made an unsecured loan to leapfrog secured creditors.

We have considered the Bank's contention that GMAC's claim of conversion should fail due to acquiescence in the relationship between Donahue Ferrill and the Bank. We believe this contention is sufficiently answered by our analysis of the law contained hereinabove and the paucity of evidence that GMAC knew of the Bank's practice of allowing such overdrafts. The evidence was woefully inadequate to establish that GMAC voluntarily relinquished a known right effectively waiving the provisions of KRS 355.9-306(2) and subordinating its priority as a creditor to that of the Bank. In any event, mere acquiescence is insufficient to constitute an equitable estoppel.

For the foregoing reasons, the decision of the Court of Appeals is reversed, and this cause is remanded to the trial court for entry of judgment consistent herewith.

PHYLLIS JASKEY JONES, ET AL V. CHEMETRON CORPORATION

212 F.3d 199 (2000)

UNITED STATES COURT OF APPEALS FOR THE THIRD CIRCUIT

ROSENN, CIRCUIT JUDGE.

Beginning in 1965, appellee Chemetron Corporation ("Chemetron") owned and operated a manufacturing facility on Harvard Avenue in Cuyahoga Heights, Ohio, as well as a nearby landfill on Bert Avenue in Newburgh Heights, Ohio. From 1965 to 1972, Chemetron employed a manufacturing process at the Harvard Avenue facility that utilized depleted uranium. After Chemetron ceased to use this process, it demolished a portion of its Harvard Avenue facility and placed a quantity of rubble from the demolition in the Bert Avenue landfill. This rubble was apparently contaminated due to radiation exposure.

Later in 1975, Chemetron sold both sites to McGean Chemical Company. McGean Chemical Co. subsequently merged with Rohco, Inc., to become McGean-Rohco, Inc., the current owner of both sites.

Between 1980 and 1988, Chemetron was involved in periodic clean-up efforts at both the Harvard Avenue and Bert Avenue sites at the direction of the Nuclear Regulatory Commission ("NRC"), with some involvement by the federal and Ohio Environmental Protection Agencies. The presence of hazardous materials at the Bert Avenue dump and these efforts to clean up the area received considerable local attention beginning shortly after its discovery in 1980. The local press reported on these cleanup efforts for the next decade. Town meetings were held in which environmental officials explained the situation to area residents. A community watchdog group formed that distributed a questionnaire to everyone in the neighborhood requesting information about contact with the dump and medical conditions suffered. The mayor's office sent out a newsletter in 1980 noting concern about the contamination. As early as 1980, another resident in the area filed a lawsuit against Chemetron charging that the presence of hazardous materials at the Bert Avenue dump was responsible for her daughter's health problems.

On February 20, 1988, Chemetron filed a petition for reorganization under Chapter 11 of the Bankruptcy Code. Following Bankruptcy Rule 3003(c)(3), the bankruptcy court issued a bar date order, fixing the claims bar date at May 31, 1988. Under bankruptcy law, the bar date is the last day on which existing claims can be filed against the debtor. The bar date order required

that actual notice be provided to all persons known to have claims against the debtors. The order required notice to all other claimants by publication in the national editions of the New York Times and Wall Street Journal. Chemetron complied with the order and, in addition, voluntarily published notice in seven other newspapers in areas where it was doing business at the time of the filing. On July 12, 1990, the bankruptcy court confirmed Chemetron's reorganization plan.

Nevertheless, Jones and the other plaintiffs assert in affidavits that they were unaware of the degree of risk posed to their health and safety by the contaminated site until after reading about a 1991 federal lawsuit filed against Chemetron in Cleveland by other local residents. Only then, the plaintiffs assert, did they contact lawyers, who proceeded to gather their medical records, have these records analyzed by physicians, and subsequently report to the plaintiffs that their health problems resulted from the contamination.

In March 1992, almost four years after the claims bar date and twelve years after the first newspaper articles reported on contamination at the sites, Phyllis Jones and ultimately twenty other individuals brought suit against Chemetron, McGean Chemical Co., and McGean-Rohco, Inc., in the Court of Common Pleas of Cuyahoga County, Ohio. The gravamen of the complaint alleged injury from exposure to toxic chemicals as a result of time spent living in or visiting the Bert Avenue area.

Of the twenty-one plaintiffs, one, Ivan Schaffer, was born on August 27, 1992, more than two years after the bankruptcy court confirmed Chemetron's plan of reorganization.

On remand from this court's decision in Chemetron I, the plaintiffs argued that the bankruptcy court should permit them to file their claims late because their failure to file prior to the May 31, 1998 bar date was attributable to excusable neglect. The district court affirmed the bankruptcy court's ruling that the plaintiffs failed to demonstrate excusable neglect. It concluded that to allow the plaintiffs to proceed with claims potentially amounting to $36 million four years after Chemetron's bankruptcy petition was filed and two years after its reorganization plan was confirmed "would cause disruption to the bankruptcy process that has already taken place," and therefore would cause extreme prejudice to the debtor." It further noted that "the length of delay in this case was significant," and that the plaintiffs did not contest this. The court also concluded that there is no evidence of bad faith on the part of the plaintiffs. Finally, the court rejected the plaintiffs' arguments (1) that Chemetron's prepetition actions contributed to their delay in filing their claim, by Chemetron's misrepresentation of the danger present at the Bert Avenue dump to the relevant government agencies and to the public; (2) that the investigating agencies failed to adequately investigate or independently follow up with Chemetron's clean-up efforts; and (3) that newspaper accounts inaccurately reported the extent of the contamination, and failed to warn the community that residents could suffer physical harm from the exposure.

Federal Rule of Bankruptcy Procedure 9006(b)(1) provides:

When an act is required or allowed to be done at or within a specified period by these rules or by a notice given thereunder or by order of court, the court for cause shown may at any time in its discretion . . . on motion made after the expiration of the specified period permit the act to be done where the failure to act was the result of excusable neglect.

Under this test, to show "excusable neglect" sufficient to waive the requirement that all bankruptcy claims be filed by the bar date, a bankruptcy court must make an equitable inquiry into the totality of the relevant circumstances. Relevant circumstances to be considered include (1) the danger of prejudice to the debtor, (2) the length of the delay and its potential impact on judicial proceedings, (3) the reason for the delay, including whether it was within the reasonable control of the movant, and (4) whether the movant acted in good faith.

The bankruptcy court made the following pertinent findings:

[Chemetron's cleanup] efforts were not satisfactory according to reports by the NRC. However, in the summer and early fall of 1980, several newspaper articles were published in the Cleveland Plain Dealer and Cleveland Press regarding the contamination and the concerns expressed by the residents of the area.

Specifically, articles appeared in the Cleveland Plain Dealer on 7/9/80, 9/5/80, 9/10/80, 9/12/80, 11/21/80 and 11/21/80. The Cleveland Press also had an article on July 8, 1980. In particular, one article reported on a town meeting held in September of 1980 to address residents concerns about the levels of radiation in the area. The article indicated that six members of the Nuclear Regulatory Commission as well as approximately 80 people from the community were in attendance. The residents were informed that while levels of radiation were present on the Chemetron and McGean properties, the levels were not high enough to cause harm.

In addition to the potential dangers being reported in the newspapers, members of the community organized and formed the Concerned Citizens of Newburgh Heights. This association prepared and distributed a community health survey which stated that the citizens were working to remove the danger of hazardous waste from the community.

Several investigative and administrative agencies were involved in the assessment and cleanup efforts in conjunction with the NRC including the U.S. Environmental Protection Agency ("EPA"), the Ohio Environmental Protection Agency and the Ohio Health Department. A Congresswoman made inquiry and follow up inquiry to the federal EPA in the fall of 1980 into 1981. There was awareness of the site and attention focused on it by at least 1980. This level of awareness and inquiry does not support plaintiffs contention that misrepresentations by Chemetron hindered them from learning the necessary information.

Moreover, the court found that even assuming Chemetron did mislead or provide inadequate information regarding the contamination to the community, the plaintiffs failed to adequately investigate the situation themselves, a factor wholly within their control. Specifically, the court noted that "not one of [the plaintiffs'] affidavits indicates what efforts had been made through the course of plaintiffs' medical history to determine the cause of their injuries until they learned of the class action suit filed by the other residents . . . [,] despite the fact that certain affidavits state that the families had serious health problems." Moreover, the court noted that "nothing in the record[ ] . . . suggests that plaintiffs sought information from Chemetron which may have assisted them in their determination which was denied."

We must accept the bankruptcy court's factual determinations unless clearly erroneous. Our review of issues of pure law, or mixed questions of law and fact, is plenary. We review the bankruptcy court's ultimate determination regarding the existence of excusable neglect for abuse of discretion.

On appeal, the plaintiffs contend that the bankruptcy court imposed an "unreasonable burden" on them because they had no way of knowing that they had a claim against Chemetron prior to the 1988 bar date, and therefore the delay was beyond their control. The burden of proving excusable neglect lies with the late-claimant. Moreover, "ignorance of one's own claim does not constitute excusable neglect."

The plaintiffs, relying on cases involving motions for summary judgment, suggest that the bankruptcy court should have viewed the facts in a light more favorable to them. This case does not involve summary judgment, however, and therefore the bankruptcy court properly placed the burden on the plaintiffs.

We conclude that the determinations of the bankruptcy court that contamination generally was known in the community in the early 1980's, and that some residents publicly expressed concern about the health effects of these toxins in press accounts and at public meetings, are supported by the record. Moreover, the record supports the court's observation that the plaintiffs introduced no evidence to show what measures they took to specifically investigate the cause of their medical problems. Therefore, these findings are not clearly erroneous.

The plaintiffs also filed a motion for an adversarial proceeding requesting a determination by the bankruptcy court that even absent excusable neglect, their claims arose after the confirmation of Chemetron's bankruptcy reorganization plan. Therefore, their Cleveland Action was unaffected by the earlier bankruptcy proceeding.

The parties dispute the correct standard for determining when the plaintiffs' claims arose. Chemetron contends that the question of when the plaintiffs' claims arose is not governed by state law dictating when a cause of action accrues, but rather by a federal common law of bankruptcy. Although significant authority supporting this proposition exists in other circuits, this circuit has held the reverse. [T]his court held that in most circumstances a "claim" arises for bankruptcy purposes at the same time the underlying state law cause of action accrues.

[T]he bankruptcy court found that the plaintiffs had failed to present evidence to show that they satisfied their duty to investigate the cause of their manifest injuries. Specifically, the court noted that the record amply demonstrated that other residents in the Newburgh Heights community were aware of the existence of harmful substances at the Bert Avenue dump prior to 1990. The bankruptcy court also found it significant that one neighborhood resident, Barbara Looby, had made inquiry into a connection between medical conditions and exposure to toxins present at the dump as early as 1980. The court found that there was no reason that competent medical authority was unable to make the appropriate diagnosis. There is nothing to suggest that the medical community at the time did not have the knowledge or necessary scientific evidence to determine medical conditions resulting from toxic exposure.

Accordingly, the bankruptcy court determined that had the plaintiffs undertaken a reasonable investigation of the cause of their manifest injuries, they would have discovered this potential cause, and their causes of action would have arisen prior to the filing of Chemetron's bankruptcy petition. Consequently, the court held their claims were discharged by the 1990 confirmation order.

Accordingly, with regard to twenty of the twenty-one plaintiffs, the bankruptcy court's finding that these plaintiffs failed to diligently investigate the cause of their injuries is not clearly erroneous. Its holding that these plaintiffs' claims were discharged by the 1990 confirmation order is therefore affirmed.

We note, however, that one of the plaintiffs, Ivan Schaffer, was not born until August 27, 1992, more than two years after the bankruptcy court confirmed Chemetron's plan of reorganization. We believe his situation merits separate discussion.

Under Chapter 11 of the Bankruptcy Code, "the confirmation of a plan . . . discharges the debtor from any debt that arose before the date of such confirmation." Thus, in most circumstances, "confirmation of the debtor's reorganization plan discharges all prior claims against the debtor." However, if a potential claimant lacks sufficient notice of a bankruptcy proceeding, due process considerations dictate that his or her claim cannot be discharged by a confirmation order.

Such due process considerations are often addressed by the appointment of a representative to receive notice for and represent the interests of a group of unknown creditors. [T]his court held that a representative could be appointed to represent the interests of future unknown asbestos claimants in bankruptcy reorganization proceedings because such claimants are "sufficiently affected by the reorganization proceedings" as to require some voice in them and therefore qualify as "parties in interest. Ivan Schaffer cannot be deemed to have received adequate notice of Chemetron's Chapter 11 bankruptcy proceeding, because no effort was made to address his potential claims in that proceeding.

Where no action is taken to address the interests of unborn future claimants in a Chapter 11 bankruptcy reorganization proceeding, the reorganized former debtor cannot later avoid liability to such claimants by arguing that their claims were discharged in bankruptcy. Under fundamental notions of procedural due process, a claimant who has no appropriate notice of a bankruptcy reorganization cannot have his claim extinguished in a settlement pursuant thereto. Here, Ivan Schaffer had no notice of or participation in the Chemetron reorganization plan. No effort was made during the course of the bankruptcy proceeding to have a representative appointed to receive notice for and represent the interests of future claimants. Therefore, whatever claim Ivan Schaffer may now have was not subject to the bankruptcy court's bar date order, and was not discharged by that court's confirmation order.

Chemetron contends that as a future claimant, Ivan Schaffer had sufficient notice of the bankruptcy proceeding because his mother, also a plaintiff to this action, had notice of the proceeding and was qualified to act as guardian for her unborn children. Although we do not dispute that a parent can represent the interests of her minor children, because of the imponderables involved, we do not believe the law imposes a duty upon a parent to take action to protect a potential claim of a child not yet conceived or born. Nor do we believe that in a

Chapter 11 reorganization, a bankruptcy court is obligated sua sponte to appoint a representative to deal with future interests if no request is made. Such a duty would impose an enormous and unreasonable responsibility of prescience on the courts. Accordingly, we hold that the potential claim of an unborn child not represented in bankruptcy reorganization proceedings is not discharged by a confirmation order.

For the foregoing reasons, the judgment of the district court will be affirmed except as to plaintiff Ivan Schaffer. As to Ivan Schaffer, the May 18, 1999 order of the district court will be reversed and the case remanded with instructions to direct the bankruptcy court to issue a declaration that his potential claim was not discharged by the July 12, 1990 confirmation order.

SHEILA JONES, INDIV. AND AS MOTHER AND NEXT FRIEND OF
SHAWNDALE JONES, A MINOR, V. CHICAGO HMO LTD. OF ILLINOIS

2000 Ill. LEXIS 656 (2000)

SUPREME COURT OF ILLINOIS

BILANDIC, JUSTICE

On January 18, 1991, Jones' three-month-old daughter Shawndale was ill. Jones called Dr. Jordan's office, as she had been instructed to do by Chicago HMO. Jones related Shawndale's symptoms, specifically that she was sick, was constipated, was crying a lot and felt very warm. An assistant advised Jones to give Shawndale some castor oil. When Jones insisted on speaking with Dr. Jordan, the assistant stated that Dr. Jordan was not available but would return her call. Dr. Jordan returned Jones' call late that evening. After Jones described the same symptoms to Dr. Jordan, he also advised Jones to give castor oil to Shawndale.

On January 19, 1991, Jones took Shawndale to a hospital emergency room because her condition had not improved. Chicago HMO authorized Shawndale's admission. Shawndale was diagnosed with bacterial meningitis, secondary to bilateral otitis media, an ear infection. As a result of the meningitis, Shawndale is permanently disabled.

The medical expert for the plaintiff, Dr. Richard Pawl, stated in his affidavit and deposition testimony that Dr. Jordan had deviated from the standard of care. In Dr. Pawl's opinion, upon being advised of a three-month-old infant who is warm, irritable and constipated, the standard of care requires a physician to schedule an immediate appointment to see the infant or, alternatively, to instruct the parent to obtain immediate medical care for the infant through another physician. Dr. Pawl gave no opinion regarding whether Chicago HMO was negligent.

Although Jones filed this action against Chicago HMO, Dr. Jordan and another party, this appeal concerns only counts I and III of Jones' second amended complaint, which are directed against Chicago HMO. Count I charges Chicago HMO with institutional negligence for, inter alia, (1) negligently assigning Dr. Jordan as Shawndale's primary care physician while he was serving an overloaded patient population, and (2) negligently adopting procedures that required Jones to call first for an appointment before visiting the doctor's office or obtaining emergency care. Count III charges Chicago HMO with breach of contract and is based solely on Chicago HMO's contract with the Department of Public Aid.

Chicago HMO is a for-profit corporation. During all pertinent times, Chicago HMO was organized as an independent practice association model HMO under the Illinois Health Maintenance Organization Act

In her deposition testimony, Jones described how she first enrolled in Chicago HMO while living in Park Forest. A Chicago HMO representative visited her home. According to Jones, he "was telling me what it was all about, that HMO is better than a regular medical card and everything so I am just listening to him and signing my name and stuff on the papers. *** I asked him what kind of benefits you get out of it and stuff, and he was telling me that it is better than a regular card."

The "HMO ENROLLMENT UNDERSTANDING" form signed by Jones in 1987 stated: "I understand that all my medical care will be provided through the Health Plan once my application becomes effective." Jones remembered that, at the time she signed this form, the Chicago HMO representative told her "you have got to call your doctor and stuff before you see your doctor; and before you go to the hospital, you have got to call."

Jones testified that when she later moved to Chicago Heights another Chicago HMO representative visited her home. This meeting was not arranged in advance. It occurred because the representative was "in the building knocking from door to door." Jones informed the representative that she was already a member.

When Jones moved to Chicago Heights, she did not select Dr. Jordan as Shawndale's primary care physician. Rather, Chicago HMO assigned Dr. Jordan to her. Jones explained:

"They gave me *** Dr. Jordan. They didn't ask me if I wanted a doctor. They gave me him.

*** They told me that he was a good doctor *** for the kids because I didn't know what doctor to take my kids to because I was staying in Chicago Heights so they gave me him so I started taking my kids there to him."

Dr. Mitchell J. Trubitt, Chicago HMO's medical director, testified at his deposition that Dr. Jordan was under contract with Chicago HMO for two sites, Homewood and Chicago Heights.

Dr. Trubitt also explained that Dr. Jordan was Chicago HMO's only physician who was willing to serve the public aid membership in Chicago Heights. Dr. Trubitt characterized this lack of physicians as "a problem" for Chicago HMO.

Dr. Jordan testified at his deposition that, in January of 1991, he was a solo practitioner. He divided his time equally between his offices in Homewood and Chicago Heights. Dr. Jordan was under contract with Chicago HMO for both sites. In addition, Dr. Jordan was under contract with 20 other HMOs, and he maintained his own private practice of non-HMO patients. Dr. Jordan estimated that he was designated the primary care physician of 3,000 Chicago HMO members and 1,500 members of other HMOs. In contrast to Dr. Jordan's estimate, Chicago HMO's own "Provider Capitation Summary Reports" listed Dr. Jordan as being the primary care provider of 4,527 Chicago HMO patients as of December 1, 1990.

The record also contains evidence concerning Chicago HMO procedures for obtaining health care. Chicago HMO's "Member Handbook" told members in need of medical care to "Call your Chicago HMO doctor first when you experience an emergency or begin to feel sick." (Emphasis in original.) Also, Chicago HMO gave its contract physicians a "Provider Manual." The manual contains certain provisions with which the providers are expected to comply. The manual contains a section entitled, "The Appointment System/Afterhours Care," which states that all HMO sites are statutorily required to maintain an appointment system for their patients.

Dr. Trubitt testified that Chicago HMO encouraged its providers to maintain an appointment system and also "to retain open spaces on their schedules so that patients who came in as walk-ins could be seen." Retaining space on the schedule for walk-ins was recommended because it offers quicker access to care, keeping patients out of the emergency room with its increased costs, and because, historically, the Medicaid patient population often did not make or keep appointments.

Dr. Jordan related that his office worked on an appointment system and had its own written procedures and forms for handling patient calls and appointments. When a patient called and Dr. Jordan was not in the office, written forms were used by his staff or his answering service to relay the information to him.

Regarding appointments, this agreement stated that Chicago HMO "shall encourage members to be seen by appointment, except in emergencies." The agreement also stated that "members with more serious or urgent problems not deemed emergencies shall be triaged and provided same day service, if necessary," and that "emergency treatment shall be available on an immediate basis, seven days a week, 24-hours a day." Finally, the agreement directed that Chicago HMO "shall have an established policy that scheduled patients shall not routinely wait for more than one hour to be seen by a provider and no more than six appointments shall be made for each primary care physician per hour."

Institutional negligence is also known as direct corporate negligence. Since the landmark decision of Darling v. Charleston Community Memorial Hospital, 33 Ill. 2d 326, 211 N.E.2d 253 (1965), Illinois has recognized that hospitals may be held liable for institutional negligence. Darling acknowledged an independent duty of hospitals to assume responsibility for the care of their patients. Ordinarily, this duty is administrative or managerial in character.

Underlying the tort of institutional negligence is a recognition of the comprehensive nature of hospital operations today. The hospital's expanded role in providing health care services to patients brings with it increased corporate responsibilities. As Darling explained: "Present-day hospitals, as their manner of operation plainly demonstrates, do far more than furnish facilities for treatment. They regularly employ on a salary basis a large staff of physicians, nurses and internes, as well as administrative and manual workers, and they charge patients for medical care and treatment, collecting for such services, if necessary, by legal action." Expounding on the point, this court later stated: "[A] modern hospital *** is an amalgam of many individuals not all of whom are licensed medical practitioners. Moreover, it is clear that at times a hospital functions far beyond the narrow sphere of medical practice." Thus, in recognizing hospital institutional negligence as a cause of action, Darling merely applied principles of common law negligence to hospitals in a manner that comports with the true scope of their operations.

In accordance with the preceding rationale, we now hold that the doctrine of institutional negligence may be applied to HMOs. Moreover, because HMOs undertake an expansive role in arranging for and providing health care services to their members, they have corresponding corporate responsibilities as well. Our nationwide research has revealed no decision expressing a contrary view, and Chicago HMO makes no argument against extending the doctrine of institutional negligence to HMOs. Hence, we conclude that the law imposes a duty upon HMOs to conform to the legal standard of reasonable conduct in light of the apparent risk. To fulfill this duty, an HMO must act as would a "reasonably careful" HMO under the circumstances.

Having determined that institutional negligence is a valid claim against HMOs, we turn to the parties' arguments in this case. Jones contends that Chicago HMO is not entitled to summary judgment on her claim of institutional negligence. She asserts that genuine issues of material fact exist as to whether Chicago HMO (1) negligently assigned more enrollees to Dr. Jordan than he was capable of serving, and (2) negligently adopted procedures requiring Jones to call first for an appointment before visiting the doctor's office.

Chicago HMO argues that Jones' claim of institutional negligence cannot proceed because she failed to provide sufficient evidence delineating the standard of care required of an HMO in these circumstances. In particular, Chicago HMO contends that Jones should have presented expert testimony on the standard of care required of an HMO.

Jones responds that she has provided sufficient evidence showing the standard of care required of an HMO in these circumstances. She argues further that her claim does not require expert testimony on this point. In support, Jones relies on Darling, where a claim of institutional negligence was allowed against a hospital without expert testimony because other evidence established the hospital's standard of care.

Given that the parties' dispute centers on standard of care evidence and the need for expert testimony, we briefly review the roles of the standard of care and expert testimony in negligence cases.

The elements of a negligence cause of action are a duty owed by the defendant to the plaintiff, a breach of that duty, and an injury proximately caused by the breach. The standard of care, also known as the standard of conduct, falls within the duty element.

A duty, in negligence cases, may be defined as an obligation, to which the law will give recognition and effect, to conform to a particular standard of conduct toward another.

In an ordinary negligence case, the standard of care required of a defendant is to act as would an " 'ordinarily careful person' " or a " 'reasonably prudent' person." No expert testimony is required in a case of ordinary negligence.

In contrast, in a professional negligence case, the standard of care required of a defendant is to act as would an "ordinarily careful professional." Pursuant to this standard of care, professionals are expected to use the same degree of knowledge, skill and ability as an ordinarily careful professional would exercise under similar circumstances. Expert testimony is usually required in a case of professional negligence. Expert testimony is necessary to establish both (1) the standard of care expected of the professional and (2) the professional's deviation from the standard. The rationale for requiring expert testimony is that a lay juror is not skilled in the profession and thus is not equipped to determine what constitutes reasonable care in professional conduct without the help of expert testimony.

The foregoing principles of law establish that the crucial difference between ordinary negligence and professional malpractice actions is the necessity of expert testimony to establish the standard of care and that its breach was the cause of the plaintiff's injury. Although not applicable to this case, there are exceptions to the requirement of expert testimony in professional negligence cases. For example, in instances where the professional's conduct is so grossly negligent or the treatment so common that a lay juror could readily appraise it, no expert testimony or other such relevant evidence is required

We first consider Jones' assertion that Chicago HMO negligently assigned more patients to Dr. Jordan than he was capable of serving. Parenthetically, we note that this assertion involves an administrative or managerial action by Chicago HMO, not the professional conduct of its physicians. Therefore, this claim properly falls within the purview of HMO institutional negligence.

To determine whether a duty exists in a certain instance, a court considers the following factors: (1) the reasonable foreseeability of injury, (2) the likelihood of injury, (3) the magnitude of the burden of guarding against the injury, and (4) the consequences of placing that burden upon the defendant. Lastly, the existence of a duty turns in large part on public policy considerations. Whether a duty exists is a question of law to be determined by the court.

Here, given the circumstances of this case, we hold that Chicago HMO had a duty to its enrollees to refrain from assigning an excessive number of patients to Dr. Jordan. HMOs contract with primary care physicians in order to provide and arrange for medical care for their enrollees. It is thus reasonably foreseeable that assigning an excessive number of patients to a primary care physician could result in injury, as that care may not be provided. For the same reason, the likelihood of injury is great. Nor would imposing this duty on HMOs be overly burdensome. Here, for example, Chicago HMO needed only to review its "Provider Capitation Summary Reports" to obtain the number of patients that it had assigned to Dr. Jordan. This information is likely to be available to all HMOs, as they must know the number of patients that a physician is serving in order [*39] to compute the physician's monthly capitation payments. The HMO may also simply ask the physician how many patients the physician is serving. Finally, the remaining factors favor placing this burden on HMOs as well. Public policy would not be well served by allowing HMOs to assign an excessive number of patients to a primary care physician and then "wash their hands" of the matter.

The central consequence of placing this burden on

In conclusion, Chicago HMO is not entitled to summary judgment on Jones' claim of institutional negligence for assigning too many patients to Dr. Jordan.

We next consider Jones' assertion that Chicago HMO negligently adopted procedures requiring Jones to call first for an appointment before visiting the doctor's office or obtaining emergency care. Jones fails to develop this argument in her brief. In particular, she points to no evidence in the record as providing the standard of care required of an HMO in developing appointment procedures. This claim cannot proceed without standard of care evidence. Chicago HMO is therefore entitled to summary judgment with respect to this portion of Jones' claim of institutional negligence.

Jones argues that Chicago HMO is not entitled to summary judgment on her breach of contract claim. This claim, set forth in count III of Jones' complaint, is based solely on the contract between Chicago HMO and the Department of Public Aid. Jones is not a signatory to this contract, but rather a beneficiary. Jones, however, expressly disclaims any reliance on a third-party beneficiary theory of liability. Instead, Jones insists that she may maintain an action for damages against Chicago HMO as if she were a party to the agreement.

The appellate court held that summary judgment was properly awarded to Chicago HMO on this claim

HMOs is HMO accountability for their own actions. because Jones is not a party to the contract at issue. The appellate court also noted that Jones' theory of liability in this regard was "murky at best."

We hold that Chicago HMO is entitled to summary judgment on count III. The record discloses that Jones is not a party to the contract that she seeks to enforce. Rather, the contracting parties are Chicago HMO and the Department. Nonetheless, Jones insists that she may maintain a cause of action on that contract, while also disclaiming any reliance on a third-party beneficiary theory of liability. Jones' position is not correct as a matter of law. We also agree with the appellate court that the theory presented by Jones on this point is not clear.

An HMO may be held liable for institutional negligence. Chicago HMO is not entitled to summary judgment on Jones' claim charging Chicago HMO with institutional negligence for assigning more enrollees to Dr. Jordan than he was capable of serving. We therefore reverse the award of summary judgment to Chicago HMO on count I of Jones' second amended complaint and remand that claim to the circuit court for further proceedings. As to count III, we affirm the award of summary judgment to Chicago HMO.

The judgments of the appellate and circuit courts are affirmed in part and reversed in part and the cause is remanded to the circuit court.

RONALD LYNN CLARK V. JOSE R. PANGAN,

2000 UT 37; 998 P.2d 268 (2000)

SUPREME COURT OF UTAH

RUSSON, ASSOCIATE CHIEF JUSTICE:

In July 1996, Clark and Pangan were working for the United States Postal Service. At that time, Pangan was a part-time supervisor, and his duties included supervising Clark. On July 17, Clark and Pangan had a disagreement regarding instructions that Pangan had given to Clark on how to conduct an inspection and complete the required paperwork. Pangan claims that he twice tried to escort Clark into an office to avoid arguing in front of the other employees. Pangan claims that the second time, he told Clark to clock out and go home but that Clark refused once again and tried to walk away. Pangan maintains that at that point, he opened one hand to block Clark and pointed toward his office with the other hand. Clark alleges, however, that Pangan hit or shoved him.

Clark filed charges in Utah state court alleging assault and battery, negligence, intentional infliction of emotional distress, and negligent infliction of emotional distress. After the complaint was filed, the United States certified that Pangan was acting within the scope of employment at the time of the incident. This allowed the United States to substitute itself as party defendant under the Westfall Act, and the action was removed to federal court.

Clark argues that battery should be considered outside the scope of employment as a matter of law but that exceptions should be made if the use of force is foreseeable by the employer. Pangan asserts that it is possible for the intentional tort of battery to have occurred within the scope of a person's employment and, therefore, battery should not be held to lie outside the scope of employment as a matter of law. He also argues that the question of whether an employee acted within the scope of employment should be decided by the trier of fact.

Holding an employer vicariously liable for the tortious acts of an employee has been justified under the theory of respondeat superior. The policy objectives given for implementing vicarious liability under this theory "are to prevent the recurrence of tortious conduct, to give greater assurance of compensation for the victim, and to ensure that the victim's losses will be equitably borne by those who benefit from the enterprise that gave rise to the injury. It is also generally believed that an employer is best able to control the conduct of an employee.

This court has long recognized that an employer can be vicariously liable for the intentional tortious acts of employees under the theory of respondeat superior if those acts are conducted within the scope of employment. We have considered scope of employment in determining the liability of an employer in numerous cases involving intentional torts.

It has been noted that in all states, an employer may be held vicariously liable for the intentional and tortious use of force by an employee if the conduct is within the scope of employment. See Restatement (Second) of Agency: Specific Torts of Servants § 245 cmt. b (1958).

Moreover, as a general rule, whether one is acting within the scope of employment is a question to be determined by the finder of fact. Only when the conduct in question is so clearly either within or outside the scope of employment that reasonable minds could not differ as to the finding is the court permitted the discretion to decide as a matter of law.

In D.D.Z., the court of appeals reviewed whether an employer was vicariously liable for the sexual assault and battery committed by an employee. See D.D.Z., 880 P.2d at 4-5. In its review, the D.D.Z. court recognized that under Utah law, an employer is vicariously liable for the acts of its employees when those acts are committed within the scope of employment and that the determination of scope of employment is generally a question of fact. The D.D.Z. court also stated the three criteria on which Utah cases focus to determine whether an employee is acting within the scope of employment.. Additionally, the D.D.Z. court recognized the general rule that some conduct is so clearly outside the scope of employment that the trial court may decide the question as a matter of law.

In applying all of these rules to the facts of D.D.Z., the court of appeals ruled that the trial court could decide the issue as a matter of law because the sexual assault and battery were clearly outside the scope of the employee's employment. However, the D.D.Z. court continued its review by applying the third factor of the scope of employment test to find that the employee was not motivated by the purpose of serving his employer's interest and that his actions were purely self-serving and motivated by personal impulses.

The court of appeals did not rule in D.D.Z. that assault and battery are outside the scope of employment as a matter of law. Instead, the D.D.Z. court ruled that in light of the facts of that case, reasonable minds could not disagree that the sexual assault and battery were outside the scope of this employee's employment and, therefore, the sexual assault and battery were outside the scope of employment as a matter of law.

It is important to note that D.D.Z. involved sexual assault and battery rather than assault and battery. It has been noted in dicta of other cases that other jurisdictions do hold that an employee's sexual misconduct falls outside the scope of employment as a matter of law. However, this is not the question that we have been asked to rule upon, and therefore, we do not address the issue of whether sexual assault and battery are outside the scope of employment as a matter of law.

[E]ach case concerning scope of employment is very complex and must be carefully analyzed in light of the facts present. Intentional torts, including battery, must be subjected to a fact-finding analysis of the employee's conduct in relation to the employment. No justification can be found to separate the intentional tort of battery outside the scope of employment when this court has analyzed scope of employment for sexual battery, sexual abuse, alienation of affections, and fraud. Therefore, the intentional tort of battery is not outside the scope of employment as a matter of law.

This court has already established a three-part test for determining whether an employee was acting within the scope of employment. See Birkner v. Salt Lake County, 771 P.2d 1053, 1056-57 (Utah 1989). In that case, we examined Utah law and other legal authorities. The analysis resulted in three basic criteria for determining whether an employee's conduct lies within the scope of employment. These three criteria are that the employee's conduct must (1) "be of the general kind the employee is employed to perform," (2) "occur within the hours of the employee's work and the ordinary spatial boundaries of the employment," and (3) "be motivated, at least in part, by the purpose of serving the employer's interest."

[I]f the employee acts 'from purely personal motives . . . in no way connected with the employer's interests' or if the conduct is 'unprovoked, highly unusual, and quite outrageous,'" the conduct should be considered outside the scope of employment. Birkner, 771 P.2d at 1057

We believe that "expectability" is already taken into account by applying the three elements of the Birkner test while considering that conduct that is "unprovoked, highly unusual, and quite outrageous" should be outside the scope of employment. We can see no justification for deviating from the Birkner test. We believe that by applying the test on a case-by-case basis, its flexibility will allow a fair evaluation of whether an employee's conduct can be considered within the scope of employment. Therefore, we hold that the three-part Birkner test, as stated above, should be used to determine whether the intentional tort of battery is within the scope of employment.

We conclude that under Utah law, it is possible for the intentional tort of battery to be within the scope of a person's employment. Further, in analyzing whether a battery is within or outside the scope of employment, the three-part test set out in Birkner should be applied.

BEST CELLARS INC V. GRAPE FINDS AT DUPONT, INC. ET AL

90 F. Supp. 2d 431 (2000)

UNITED STATES DISTRICT COURT FOR THE SOUTHERN DISTRICT OF NEW YORK

SWEET, JUSTICE

Best Cellars operates retail wine stores in New York, New York, Brookline, Massachusetts, and Seattle, Washington. The company was founded by Joshua Wesson ("Wesson"), Green, and Richard Marmet ("Marmet").

Wesson is an internationally recognized wine expert who has worked in the field since 1979. He has received national and international awards as a sommelier. Throughout this period, he also wrote numerous articles on wine. In 1989, he co-authored, with David Rosengarten, an award-winning book entitled "Red Wine With Fish," which discussed the concept of "wine by style," i.e., categorizing wine by taste and weight, rather than by grape type or place of origin.

Wesson continued to promote the "wine by style" concept through additional writings and frequent speaking engagements. In the early 1990's, he began to think about developing a new kind of retail wine store where people who knew little or nothing about wine could feel as comfortable when shopping as wine connoisseurs, and in which the "wine by style" concept could be implemented. The name "Best Cellars" came to him in 1993.

In 1994 or 1995, Wesson began to include Green, who at the time was working at Acker Merrall & Condit, an upscale New York retail wine store, in the discussions for the new store. In 1995, Wesson met Marmet, a practicing lawyer who had written all of the wine sections for Food and Wine magazine's cookbooks. Wesson, Green, and Marmet then set out to make the Best Cellars concept a reality.

Wesson, with the input of Marmet and Green, spent considerable time before and during the design phase of the first Best Cellars store refining the "wine by style" concept. Wesson eventually reduced the "world of wine" to eight taste categories: sparkling wines, light-, medium-, and full-bodied white wines, light-, medium-, and full-bodied red wines, and dessert wines. For each category, he selected, after a long winnowing process, a single word to serve as a "primary descriptor." Words which were "runners-up" for each

category became "secondary descriptors." The eight primary descriptors are: "fizzy" (for sparkling wine), "fresh" (light-bodied white), "soft" (medium-bodied white), "luscious" (full-bodied white), "juicy" (light-bodied red), "smooth" (medium-bodied red), "big" (full-bodied red), and "sweet" (dessert wine). This conceptual reduction is the heart of the Best Cellars "system."

A principal reason Wesson reduced the world of wine to eight taste categories was in order to demystify wine for casual, non-connoiseur purchasers who might be intimidated purchasing wine in a traditional wine store, where wines are customarily organized by grape type and place of origin.

The co-founders consulted John Alison, an intellectual property attorney at Finnegan Henderson, a Washington, D.C. firm, for advice on how to protect what they were developing. The lead architect from Rockwell for the Best Cellars project was Samuel Houston Trimble ("Trimble"). Trimble was asked to create an "anti-wine store," or, ideally, "not a wine store at all," as part of the effort to "reinvent the way that wine was retailed." The partners also searched for a graphic design firm and ultimately settled on Hornall Anderson, after the bulk of Trimble's design work had been completed.

Hornall Anderson and Rockwell were provided with copies of Best Cellars' marketing and business plans. Hornall Anderson also signed a confidentiality agreement with Best Cellars.

> There was testimony at the hearing that everyone involved on the Best Cellars project had to sign confidentiality agreements. Presumably this included Rockwell.

Wesson and Trimble visited many wine stores in order to get ideas "about what not to do". Trimble and other architects from Rockwell then developed between six and eight different architectural interpretations of the ideas supplied to them by Wesson, Marmet, and Green. The co-founders met with Rockwell on a regular basis and eventually settled on the final design. Rockwell also consulted on the Seattle and Brookline stores.

The Rockwell architectural design is simple, elegant, and striking. The wines are primarily displayed along the perimeter walls of the store. A display bottle for each wine stands upright on a stainless-steel wire pedestal slightly above eye-level, so that the label on the bottle may be viewed by the customer. Under each display bottle, at eye-level, is a "shelf-talker": a 4"x4" info card, designed by Hornall Anderson, providing the name of the wine, its vintage, a five- or six-line description of its taste, the type of grape from which it is made, its place of origin, a "FYI" blurb (often mentioning foods which the wine would complement), and its price. The top third of the shelf-talker has a color strip corresponding to the Best Cellars taste category to which the wine belongs.

Although the design and layout of the shelf-talker was done by Hornall Anderson, the text itself is created by Best Cellars. Using a computer program, Best Cellars employees can create new shelf-talkers as the store rotates through different selections of wines.

The racking system, which is patented by Marmet, Wesson, and Trimble, is lit from behind, which causes the bottles to glow but does not harm the wine. The bottles can be placed in the tubes so that either the cork end or the bottom of the bottle is visible. Both methods of display are utilized, although the bottom method is more prevalent. The overall effect, which is quite striking, is of rows and rows of glowing bottles in the walls of the store. The wine is thus a decorative element.

Above the wall racks are large signs, designed by Hornall Anderson, with the name of each taste category, together with its assigned color and icon-identifier. The categories are arranged in the following order as one moves clockwise around the store from the doorway: fizzy, fresh, soft, luscious, juicy, smooth, big, and sweet (corresponding to sparkling, light-, medium-, and full-bodied white, light-, medium-, and full-bodied red, and dessert wine, respectively). The wines displayed beneath each individual sign belong to the category identified by the sign. Also, affixed to each bottle of wine is a label with the Best Cellars name and logo, and the color, icon-identifier, and name of the category into which the wine has been classified.

Of course, the perimeter fixtures -- the wine racks, the signs, and the storage drawers -- while dominant in the design, are not its only elements. There is a plaster ceiling with track lighting, and a poured concrete floor. The wall behind the cash wrap is a burgundy-colored plaster with copper powder mixed in. The store has no fixed aisles, but in the floor space is a wooden table with benches, used for displays and wine tastings, and a mobile cart, designed by Rockwell, with a stove and cook top for food preparation to accompany the wine tastings.

The dominant architectural material in the store is light wood. Stainless steel is used as a highlight: in the wire pedestals holding the display bottles, in the rings circling the holes in the racking system, and as trim on the cash wrap.

Certain aspects of the Seattle and Brookline stores differ from the New York store. Of these aspects, some were deliberate changes by Best Cellars, i.e., improvements. Others were dictated by the idiosyncracies of the store locations, lease terms, and local zoning laws.

Among the "improvements": the category signs posted around the store were doubled in size, changed in shape from square to rectangular and given a three-dimensional concave look in which the sign bows out from the wall, the texture was removed from the back of the signs, the typography was modified, and the colors were changed slightly in appearance (possibly due to the use of a different material); the category order was slightly adjusted by placing "fizzy" wines at the end rather than at the beginning, and the layout of the categories in the stores was reversed so that it runs in counter-clockwise fashion to reflect market research suggesting that customers normally travel in a counter-clockwise pattern in a retail store environment; a refrigerator was placed in one wall in order that certain wines could be kept chilled, with the added sign "cool" placed above the refrigerator, although that sign was subsequently removed, and the "fizzy" sign shifted so it is now over the refrigerator in the Seattle store; the cook's table in the Seattle store is different and was not designed by Rockwell; and the cash wrap is in an "island" in the center of the store.

Many of the design elements described above are not found in any other retail wine store, with the exception of Grape Finds. On average, a retail wine store in the U.S. carries about 500 different kinds of wine, displayed not only along the perimeter but throughout the floor space by the use of freestanding or built-in shelves. Although many wine stores use shelf talkers, apparently only one other store, Nancy's, in New York, has a shelf-talker for each type of wine displayed, and even the shelf-talkers at Nancy's differ significantly from those at Best Cellars: they are handwritten, and the formatting of the information (and even the nature of the information) changes from shelf-talker to shelf-talker. No other store has a uniform display of shelf-talkers at eye level. No store arranges wine by taste category, along the perimeter, backlit in vertical arrays of nine, with storage cabinets underneath.

The concept of categorizing wine by taste and style, while it had not previously been utilized in any retail wine store, has been utilized by various writers of books on wine. These writers use differing numbers of categories. For example, Serena Sutcliffe, author of "The Wine Handbook," uses 14 categories. Fiona

Beckett uses 12 categories in one book and 13 in another.

The Manhattan Best Cellars store opened in November 1996. It has received local, national, and international press coverage from a wide variety of general interest and wine industry publications, including Harper's, BusinessWeek, the Wall Street Journal, Food and Wine, and Wine and Spirits. The store has also been highlighted on local and national television programs, during which Wesson or other Best Cellars employees have been interviewed. An article in Wine Business Monthly, a publication serving the wine industry, stated that " Best Cellars is unlike any wine store that ever existed on Main Street, in cyberspace, or anywhere else."

Rockwell won numerous awards for its architectural design of the store, including one for Best Retail Environment of the Year. Hornall Anderson won numerous awards as well. Wesson won the Golden Grape Award, for retail innovator of the year, from the wine industry.

Green, who had signed a confidentiality agreement with Best Cellars, was, in addition to being a co-founder, responsible for managing the New York store. However, his employment was terminated in February 1997, shortly after the store opened.

As part of its plan for expansion, Best Cellars looked for a Washington, D.C. location for over two years. It was notified by Bruce Frankel, its D.C. real estate broker, that a "knock-off" store (Grape Finds) was moving into a space at Dupont Circle. It was also notified regarding Grape Finds by Andrew Stenzler, CEO of Xando, a licensee of the Best Cellars' classification system. Best Cellars has a license permitting Xando to sell wine under the Best Cellars system, but the written license is limited to Xando's stores in New York. A verbal agreement was in place to extend the use to Xando's stores nationally. Use of the Best Cellars system in Xando's Washington D.C. store began on December 7, 1999, i.e., four days after the opening of the Grape Finds store.

At some point prior to October 14, 1998, Best Cellars terminated Hornall Anderson (before the opening of the Brookline store, in October 1998) due to disagreement over how to improve Best Cellars' trade dress.

The Grape Finds story begins with Mazur, who attended Columbia Business School in New York from 1996 through May 1998, when he received an M.B.A. Mazur wanted to run his own business, and he had an interest in wine. While at Columbia, he discovered the Best Cellars New York store, which he has visited at least ten times. Mazur has also visited the Best Cellars web site between 100 and 200 times, and has downloaded hundreds of articles about Best Cellars from the LEXIS-NEXIS database.

Mazur had studied and admired Starbucks' phenomenally successful remerchandising of coffee retailing and saw in the Best Cellars model a way to do a similar remerchandising of wine retailing. Seeking to capitalize on Best Cellars' innovations, Mazur began to draft a business plan, cutting and pasting descriptions of the Best Cellars concept and design from the articles downloaded from LEXIS-NEXIS and substituting "Grape Finds" for "Best Cellars."

After graduation, Mazur moved to the Washington, D.C. metropolitan area and began to implement a plan to open a Grape Finds retail wine store using the Best Cellars conceptual model. Mazur was assisted in his enterprise by his father, Jack Mazur, from whom at least some business advice and some funding came. Jack Mazur is a former attorney who surrendered his license to practice law in conjunction with a lawsuit initiated against him for fraud.

On March 15, 1999, GFI was incorporated, and on March 24, 1999, GFI executed a contract to purchase a liquor store in the Dupont Circle area of Washington, D.C. Also during mid-March, Mazur contacted Theodore Adamstein ("Adamstein"), a principal at the architectural firm of Adamstein and Demietrou ("A&D"), to discuss the possibility of A&D designing the store. At the first meeting, when Mazur described his concept for Grape Finds, Adamstein remarked that the concept was similar to Best Cellars. Adamstein testified that "it was an easy leap" from Mazur's description of Grape Finds to the thought of Best Cellars, "as easy as [if] they were describing hamburgers and I thought of McDonald's." Adamstein was familiar with the Best Cellars design because he had seen photographs of it in numerous design publications.

A&D was subsequently hired to design the store, and Jack Mazur participated in the hiring negotiations. As part of the design research, Adamstein was paid to go to New York and visit the Best Cellars store on April 20, 1999. Adamstein testified that he visited many wine stores in New York on that trip. He did not, however, identify any other than Best Cellars, and he acknowledged that he took the train to New York, arrived at Penn Station, visited Ruby Foo's, a restaurant on the Upper West Side also designed by Trimble and Rockwell, and then went to Best Cellars, which is on the Upper East Side. For the trip, Adamstein only turned in for reimbursement three taxi receipts. Three cab rides would take him from Penn Station to Ruby Foo's, then to Best Cellars, then back to Penn Station. Adamstein testified that he misplaced the other receipts and that he regularly does so, but this testimony is not entirely credible. Mazur testified that he directed Adamstein to visit the Best Cellars New York store, while Adamstein testified that he proposed the trip to Mazur. Adamstein did not make trips to any cities other than New York to look at retail wine stores. While he did look at stores in Washington, D.C., the logical inference from the testimony is that Grape Finds sent Adamstein to New York in order to copy elements of the Best Cellars design.

Notwithstanding their self-serving and less-than-credible testimony, Mazur, Jack Mazur (and through them, Grape Finds), and Adamstein had a "meeting of the minds" in March 1999 at which it was decided that Grape Finds would seek to appropriate the look and feel of Best Cellars' stores. In furtherance of this conspiracy, Adamstein was sent to New York to view the Best Cellars store in order to copy elements of the trade dress.

Adamstein became an investor in Grape Finds. He is currently a five percent owner, though plans are to give him options which would increase his percentage, ultimately, to ten percent.

A&D presented its design to Grape Finds on May 12, 1999. The design incorporated images from "the world of wine": the vineyards where the grapes are grown, the production process, the cellars used in the aging process, and the enjoyment of drinking wine.

Mazur began to search for a wine buyer in April, 1999. In May, 1999, Mazur called Green in New York, inviting him to come to Washington at Mazur's expense, which Green did on May 27. On July 20, 1999, Mazur formally offered Green a job. Green accepted the offer to become an employee and principal of Grape Finds. Although Green had not been an employee of Best Cellars since February, 1997, he still held shares in Best Cellars. In 1999, Wesson and Marmet held unsuccessful negotiations with Green to repurchase those shares. Also in 1999, Green attempted to be released from his confidentiality agreement. Wesson and Marmet through a letter issued on September 30, 1999, refused to do so. On June 6, 1999, Green faxed Mazur a copy of his Best Cellars' employment agreement and an outline of the initial distribution of shares in Best Cellars. Also included were materials from the Best Cellars private placement memorandum describing pricing and valuation, material which Wesson and Marmet regarded as confidential. Green also faxed to Mazur a copy of Best Cellars' New York liquor license application.

Mazur contacted Campbell toward the end of April 1999. Campbell had also received an M.B.A. from Columbia at the same time as Mazur. Campbell had previously told Mazur that he was interested in the wine business. On May 20, 1999, Mazur and Campbell met in Baltimore and agreed to go into Grape Finds together. From that point forward, Campbell was involved, although he was not brought in as a partner until July 1999.

Hornall Anderson was engaged to do the graphic design work for Grape Finds. Mazur had been impressed with their work for Best Cellars, Starbucks, Jamba Juice, and other retailers. At the initial meeting in Seattle on June 1, 1999, at which Mazur, Jack Mazur, and Adamstein were in attendance, Jack Anderson stated that Hornall Anderson had no conflict of interest working for Grape Finds, notwithstanding its prior work for Best Cellars. Anderson did not mention that Hornall Anderson had signed a confidentiality agreement with Best Cellars.

At the July 3, 1999 Four Seasons meeting, thirty minutes was scheduled for a presentation by Green entitled, "The Best Cellars Model and Lessons Learned," although Mazur testified that the presentation never took place, the meeting having taken a less formal turn from the beginning, i.e., they didn't stick to the agenda.

Green and Campbell worked on the Grape Finds website, which contains material substantially similar to material on the Best Cellars website and in the Best Cellars promotional materials, including its brochure. Campbell has visited the Best Cellars New York store at least three times, including after beginning to work for Grape Finds.

Design work continued on the Grape Finds store through September 1999. The store opened on December 3, 1999.

The leased space is narrow and deep, with one large window looking out onto the street. The exterior of the store has a curved awning above the window, which echoes the vaulted ceiling inside the store. The echo is continued with a long, curved door handle. A purple blade sign "slices" through the awning. The Grape Finds logo bears no resemblance to the Best Cellars logo.

Inside, there are many marked similarities to the Best Cellars store. First, the display is organized according to eight taste categories: CRISPfinds, MELLOWfinds, RICHfinds, FRUITYfinds, SMOOTHfinds, BOLDfinds, BUBBLYfinds, and SWEETfinds, corresponding to light-, medium-, and full-bodied whites, light-, medium-, and full-bodied reds, sparkling, and dessert wines (i.e., the same eight categories in the Best Cellars classification system).

Mazur admitted that he copied the Best Cellars category system. Moreover, many of the Grape Finds primary and secondary descriptors, although purportedly created by Davey, were copied from the primary and secondary descriptors used by Best Cellars, although the words were rearranged slightly. In many cases, words among the Best Cellars secondary descriptors appear as primary descriptors in the Grape

Finds system, while Best Cellars' primary descriptors appear among Grape Finds' secondary descriptors.

As with Best Cellars, Grape Finds has assigned to each taste category a corresponding color and icon-identifier, likewise designed by Hornall Anderson. The categories are likewise arranged in the store in systematic order. There are approximately 100 value-priced wines displayed around the perimeter of the store. Most significantly, each display wine is placed slightly above eye-level, on a stainless steel pedestal held in place by stainless steel wire. At eye-level, directly underneath the display bottle, is a square shelf-talker, formatted, once again, by Hornall Anderson, containing almost the identical set of information as the Best Cellars shelf talkers. Under each Grape Finds shelf-talker, nine bottles are horizontally stored in a stainless steel rack. The bottles are held in stainless-steel cradles lined with cork to protect the bottles. There is no "wall" concealing the bottles as there is in the Best Cellars stores, yet the effect of the nine-bottle vertical array wrapping around the perimeter of the store gives the same design feel of a "wall of wine." Moreover, lights above the racks are directed down; much of this light bounces against the wall behind the racks, thereby indirectly backlighting the bottles and causing them to glow. As in Best Cellars, beneath the racks are storage cabinets, creating the same visual look of an equivalent to baseboard molding or wainscotting.

On the walls above the bottle racks, around the perimeter of the store, as in Best Cellars' stores, are large signs denoting the categories. While the signs were created as a continuous thirty-foot-long computer-enhanced photographic mural, the presence of vertical stainless-steel blades (which divide the category sections), and the need to chop the mural into at least three sections (one continuous section along the left wall (from the perspective of a customer looking into the store from the doorway), and two sections along the right wall, broken up by the cash wrap, above which is a color-coded placard explaining the Grape Finds system) reduces the sense of a continuous mural and makes it more similar to the Best Cellars wall signs.

The combination of these visual elements -- color-coded, iconographic wall signs identifying taste categories, single display bottles on stainless-steel wire pedestals along the store perimeter, identical color-coded textually formatted square shelf talkers below the display bottles, vertical arrays of nine glowing bottles stacked horizontally, and a strip of cabinets or drawers between the wine racks and the floor -- dominates the overall look of both the Best Cellars and the Grape Finds stores.

There are differences between the two stores. The Grape Finds store has a vaulted ceiling, meant to evoke a wine cellar. It is a prominent design feature. The floor of the store is cork. There are eleven mobile boxes in the store which can be used as seats, for display, and for storage of additional cases of wine. The boxes are arranged in varying ways on the store floor.

There is an alcove space at the back of the store where a wooden table and several chairs are located for wine tastings. In the alcove there is also traditional shelving with smoked glass panels. Grape Finds does not have a mobile cart for food preparation.

Stainless steel is more prominent in the Grape Finds design. As mentioned, there are stainless steel blades running from floor to ceiling, dividing the categories. On each blade is written the primary and the secondary descriptors for the Grape Finds category marked off by that blade.

The layout of the Grape Finds store resembles a wine bottle, though Adamstein testified that this was more happenstance based on the configuration of the lease space than deliberate design.

Mazur, Campbell, and Green worked on the Grape Finds web site, and created the in-store brochure. The original brochure has since been replaced by a new brochure. Many descriptive phrases on the web site and in the original brochure are substantially similar to the Best Cellars in-store brochure, although the phrases do not appear in the same order or layout in the Grape Finds materials as they are found in the Best Cellars brochure. For example, the Best Cellars brochure states, "Welcome to Best Cellars, a completely new kind of wine store," while the Grape Finds web site states "Grape Finds is a completely new type of wine-store," and the Grape Finds in-store brochure states "Welcome to Grape Finds, a completely new way to shop for wine!" Again, the Best Cellars brochure states "We've tried to remove any obstacles that could stand between you and your enjoyment of wine," while the Grape Finds web site states "Grape Finds . . . aims to remove many of the obstacles between people and their enjoyment of wine." There are numerous other examples of virtual word-for-word similarity.

Although Mazur testified that he did not intend to copy the Best Cellars trade dress or brochure, Mazur is not a credible witness. Among the incidents which came to light at the hearing giving credence to this conclusion are:

(1) Mazur sent an e-mail to Best Cellars on November 29, 1999, to congratulate them on the opening of the Seattle store in October 1999. He represented that he was from New York, although at the time he had been living in Washington, D.C. for a year and a half.

(2) Mazur admitted in his testimony at the hearing that much of the material on the Grape Finds web site was substantially similar to material on the Best Cellars

web site and in other writings on Best Cellars. Mazur denied, however, that he directly copied anything, stating instead that because he had seen the Best Cellars' materials so many times he could essentially sit down and compose from memory.

(3) Mazur admitted that the section of the Grape Finds private placement memorandum entitled "Store Design" was almost entirely created by cutting and pasting sentences from articles written about Best Cellars.

(4) Mazur, in a deposition taken prior to the hearing, testified that he downloaded materials from the Best Cellars website. At the hearing, however, he denied that he ever downloaded materials until confronted with his deposition testimony, at which point he attempted to clarify his answer by stating that he "printed out" materials.

(5) Mazur also testified that the design for the store was unique, and that one of the things he did to make sure it was unique was to consult with counsel. However, the opinion of counsel, Blank Rome, was dated November 1, 1999, after the designs for the store were complete.

In a case involving allegations of infringement of trade dress under the Lanham Act, irreparable harm is presumed if the plaintiff can demonstrate a likelihood of success on the merits of the infringement claim. In such actions, a finding of likelihood of confusion between the trade dresses in question generally provides sufficient grounds for issuance of a preliminary injunction, without further evidence of actual injury.

Best Cellars Has Demonstrated A Likelihood of Success on the Merits of Its Trade Dress and Unfair Competition Claims

Section 43(a) of the Lanham Act provides in pertinent part:

(1) Any person who, on or in connection with any goods or services, or any container for goods, uses in commerce any word, term, name, symbol, or device, or any combination thereof, or any false designation of origin, false or misleading description of fact, or false or misleading representation of fact, which--

(A) is likely to cause confusion, or to cause mistake, or to deceive as to the affiliation, connection, or association of such person with another person, or as to the origin, sponsorship, or approval of his or her goods, services, or commercial activities by another person...shall be liable in a civil action by any person who believes that he or she is or is likely to be damaged by such act.

Section 43(a) . . . 'though enacted as part of the Trademark Act, . . . functions as a federal law of unfair competition for unregistered goods . . . [and] extends protection to a product's "trade dress.

Trade dress has a broad meaning, and includes "all elements making up the total visual image by which [a] product is presented to customers, . . . 'as defined by its overall composition and design, including size, shape, color, texture, and graphics.'"

Protection of trade dress, no less than of trademarks, serves the [Lanham] Act's purpose to "secure to the owner of the mark the goodwill of his business and to protect the ability of consumers to distinguish among competing producers. National protection of trademarks is desirable, Congress concluded, because trademarks foster competition and the maintenance of quality by securing to the producer the benefits of good reputation."

Adding a secondary meaning requirement could have anticompetitive effects, creating particular burdens on the startup of small companies. It would present special difficulties for a business ... that seeks to start a new product in a limited area and then expand into new markets. [It] would allow a competitor, which has not adopted a distinctive trade dress of its own, to appropriate the originator's dress in other markets and to deter the originator from expanding into and competing in these areas.

To establish a claim of trade dress infringement under § 43(a), a plaintiff must demonstrate (1) "that its trade dress is either inherently distinctive or that it has acquired distinctiveness through a secondary meaning," (2) "that there is a likelihood of confusion between defendant's trade dress and plaintiff's,", and (3) where, as here, the dress has not been registered, that the design is non-functional.

The inherent distinctiveness of a trademark or trade dress is evaluated under the test set forth by Judge Friendly in Abercrombie & Fitch Co. v. Hunting World, Inc., 537 F.2d 4, 9 (2d Cir. 1976). Under the Abercrombie test, trade dress is classified on a spectrum of increasing distinctiveness as generic, descriptive, suggestive, or arbitrary/fanciful. Suggestive and arbitrary or fanciful trade dress are deemed inherently distinctive and thus always satisfy the first prong of the test for protection. A descriptive trade dress may be found inherently distinctive if the plaintiff establishes that its mark has acquired secondary meaning giving it distinctiveness to the consumer. A generic trade dress receives no Lanham Act protection.

On the other hand, an idea, a concept, or a generalized type of appearance" cannot be protected under trade dress law, although "the concrete expression of an idea in a trade dress has received protection. This can be a difficult distinction to draw, and in doing so "a helpful consideration will be the purpose of trade dress law: to protect an owner of a dress in informing the public of the source of its products, without permitting the owner to exclude competition from functionally similar products."

Best Cellars has met its burden under the standard for a preliminary injunction, set forth above, of establishing the inherent distinctiveness of its trade dress. Under the Abercrombie analysis, the trade dress of Best Cellars is arbitrary. This arbitrary trade dress consists of the total visual image which a customer entering a Best Cellars store encounters -- an image that was acknowledged as unique by both Mazur and Adamstein in their testimony. As described above in the "Facts" section of this opinion, a huge number of articles written about the Best Cellars stores have focused on the distinctiveness of their look. The unique design -- both the architectural component and the graphical component -- has been further acknowledged in numerous awards. The point does not need to be belabored; the Best Cellars stores look like no other wine stores. Best Cellars achieved its goal of designing an "anti-wine store." As such, the trade dress is not suggestive of the product being sold, let alone descriptive or generic.

Courts in this Circuit apply an eight-factor test, drawn from Polaroid Corp. v. Polarad Electronics Corp., 287 F.2d 492 (2d Cir. 1961), to determine the likelihood of confusion between the trade dress of two competitors:

(1) the strength of the plaintiff's trade dress, [**66] (2) the similarity between the two trade dress, (3) the proximity of the products in the marketplace, (4) the likelihood that the prior owner will bridge the gap between the products, (5) evidence of actual confusion, (6) the defendant's bad faith, (7) the quality of defendant's product, and (8) the sophistication of the relevant consumer group.

While the factors are meant to be a guide, the inquiry ultimately hinges on whether an ordinarily prudent person would be confused as to the source of the allegedly infringing product. Here, that inquiry can be put as follows: is there a substantial likelihood that an ordinarily prudent consumer would, when standing in the Grape Finds store, think he was standing in a Best Cellars store?

1. The Strength of the Trade Dress

The strength of a trade dress or trademark is measured in terms of its distinctiveness, "or more precisely, [by] its tendency to identify the goods sold . . . as emanating from a particular . . . source."

Arbitrary dress is by its very nature distinctive and strong.

A secondary meaning is acquired when "it [is] shown that the primary significance of the term in the minds of the consuming public is not the product but the producer." Factors relevant for assessing secondary meaning include "'(1) advertising expenditures, (2)

consumer studies linking the mark to a source, (3) unsolicited media coverage of the product, (4) sales success, (5) attempts to plagiarize the mark, and, (6) length and exclusivity of the mark's use.'" Under this standard, Best Cellars' trade dress is quite strong.

2. Similarity Between The Trade Dresses

The degree of similarity factor looks to whether it is probable that the similarity of the dresses will cause confusion among numerous customers who are ordinarily prudent. "The presence and prominence of markings tending to dispel confusion as to the origin, sponsorship or approval of the goods in question is highly relevant to an inquiry concerning the similarity of the two dresses. When prominently displayed it can go far towards . . . countering any suggestion of consumer confusion arising from any of the other Polaroid factors.

As described above, the dominant visual element of both the Best Cellars and the Grape Finds store is the wall of wine. Neither the vaulted ceiling, nor the exterior, nor the cork floor, nor the multi-purpose cubes, nor the steel racking system, nor any other difference in the Grape Finds store, significantly modifies the overall visual effect achieved by merchandising the eight categories of wines almost exclusively along the perimeter walls of the store, with display bottles set at a uniform height, identical shelf talkers, nine bottles lying on their side in a vertical array, wall signs above and cabinets below. While the Grape Finds trade name is displayed both outside and inside the store, the name is not recognizable and thus carries less weight. In sum, the evidence demonstrates a significant probability that numerous ordinarily prudent customers in the Grape Finds store will be confused as to whether they are, in fact, in a Best Cellars store.

3. The Proximity of the Products

The 'proximity-of-the-products' inquiry concerns whether and to what extent the two products compete with each other. The court must consider "'the nature of the products themselves and the structure of the relevant market,'" including "the class of customers to whom the goods are sold, the manner in which the products are advertised, and the channels through which the goods are sold."

The products here are indisputably similar: value-priced bottles of wine. As for the structure of the relevant market, there are also similarities. The class of customers is nearly identical. Both stores target consumers who are not necessarily wine connoisseurs. No evidence has been presented about advertising. The channels through which the goods are sold are the stores themselves, as well as mail-order sales through the respective web sites.

In sum, there is considerable proximity between the products.

4. Bridging the Gap

The issue here is whether the two companies are likely to compete directly in the same market. This factor applies when the first user sells its products in one field and the second user sells its products in a closely related field, into which the first user might expand, thereby "bridging the gap." Here, there is no gap to bridge: Best Cellars and Grape Finds sell the same products in the same field. This factor, therefore, also favors Best Cellars.

5. Evidence of Actual Confusion

Best Cellars has presented some evidence of actual confusion. Several individuals who know Wesson and Marmet informed them that a "copycat" or "knock off" store was opening in Washington, and several customers were overheard outside the Grape Finds store remarking that it looked like a store in Brookline, while a customer inside the store asked whether Grape Finds had a sister store in New York and Boston. Because no survey or other type of systematic research was conducted, however, too much weight cannot be attached to this evidence. The comments are anecdotal, and it is possible that confusion arose because the concepts -- selling wine by taste -- are similar.

6. Grape Finds' Bad Faith

This factor 'looks to whether the defendant adopted its [dress] with the intention of capitalizing on plaintiff's reputation and goodwill and any confusion between his and the senior user's product.

Given the overwhelming evidence of copying by Mazur of so many aspects of the Best Cellars business, it strains credulity to think that the reproduction of the trade dress -- in particular, the "wall of wine" -- in the Grape Finds store was not meant to capitalize on the reputation, goodwill, and any confusion between Grape Finds and Best Cellars.

7. The Quality of Grape Finds' Products

No evidence has been presented that Grape Finds' products are inferior to those of Best Cellars. This factor therefore favors Grape Finds.

8. Sophistication of Purchasers

This factor requires consideration of the general impression of the ordinary purchaser, buying under the normally prevalent conditions of the market and giving the attention such purchasers usually give in buying that class of goods. . .

This factor also favors Best Cellars. Both stores are specifically targeting non-sophisticated wine purchasers, and the overwhelming majority of wines sold in each store are priced at the lower end of the spectrum.

As set forth above, in this case seven of the eight factors weigh in favor of Best Cellars. This is not a case requiring a careful balancing of the factors. Some factors weigh more strongly than others, but there is no doubt that, taken together, Best Cellars has made a substantial showing of a likelihood of confusion between its trade dress and that of Grape Finds.

For the reasons set forth above, a preliminary injunction will issue.

IN RE: TAYLOR & ASSOCIATES, L.P., et al, v. DUDLEY W. TAYLOR,

2000 U.S. App. LEXIS 8418 (2000)

UNITED STATES COURT OF APPEALS FOR THE SIXTH CIRCUIT

NELSON, Circuit Judge

The appellants in this case are investors who entrusted funds to Joseph Taylor, a stockbroker, now deceased. The funds were deposited in an account opened in the name of Taylor and Associates, L.P. ("TALP") and were used by Mr. Taylor for his own purposes. The issue on appeal is whether TALP was shown to have been a partnership under Tennessee law, and thus a "person" eligible for bankruptcy as a "debtor."

A bankruptcy court dismissed an involuntary petition in bankruptcy filed against TALP by the appellants, and the district court affirmed the dismissal.

Joseph Taylor committed suicide after a Ponzi scheme that he was operating collapsed in November of 1995. Mr. Taylor had been employing various business names, one of which was "Taylor and Associates, L.P.," or TALP. A partnership of that name was originally to have been formed as the entity through which Mr. Taylor and another man, John Buchheit, would invest in a medical equipment company. After determining that a limited partnership would be the best vehicle for the investment, Dudley Taylor -- an attorney representing Joseph Taylor -- drafted a limited partnership agreement, filed a certificate of limited partnership, and obtained a federal employer identification number in TALP's name. Mr. Buchheit decided, however, that he did not wish to make the investment. He never signed the partnership agreement, and TALP was never formed as originally intended.

Joseph Taylor nevertheless began to use the TALP name for his own purposes. He made the originally planned investment (without Buchheit's participation) as "TALP." He opened bank accounts in that name, used the accounts to hold funds received from various investors, and wrote checks on the accounts. He also had his accountant issue tax reporting information to investors on I.R.S. forms used to report partnership income. The name "TALP" was used on the forms, and investors were referred to as limited partners.

In the summer of 1995 a financial planning corporation with which Joseph Taylor was associated inquired into the nature of TALP. Joseph Taylor hired an attorney, David Andrew, to represent him in connection with that inquiry. Dudley Taylor told Mr. Andrew that TALP was a partnership consisting of persons who jointly invested in real estate and other ventures. Dudley Taylor described TALP as an "investment club" that he controlled with his law partner, Lori Fleishman. Through this vehicle Dudley Taylor and Ms. Fleishman entrusted their own funds, as well as funds belonging to several of their friends and family members, to Joseph Taylor.

The appellants similarly entrusted funds to Joseph Taylor for the purpose of making investments. The funds were deposited in a TALP bank account, and some of the appellants received payments from that account. Mr. Taylor did not invest the appellants' money, however.

After Mr. Taylor committed suicide, the appellants filed an involuntary petition in bankruptcy against TALP. Dudley Taylor, alleged by the appellants to be a general partner of TALP, moved to dismiss the involuntary petition on the ground that TALP is not a "debtor" eligible for bankruptcy under 11 U.S.C. § 109(b).

After a hearing on the merits of the petition, the bankruptcy court granted relief to the appellants. Dudley Taylor appealed to the district court. That court vacated the bankruptcy court's order and remanded the case for further proceedings on the ground that genuine issues of fact remained as to whether TALP was a partnership.

The bankruptcy court held a trial on the partnership issue, concluded that TALP was not a limited or general partnership under Tennessee law, and dismissed the petition. The district court affirmed, and this appeal followed.

Although some Tennessee lower courts have applied a "preponderance" or "greater weight of the evidence" standard in determining whether an oral partnership exists, they have done so without analyzing the appropriateness of such a standard. The question was explicitly addressed by the Tennessee Supreme Court in Tidwell v. Walden, 205 Tenn. 705, 330 S.W.2d 317 (Tenn. 1959). There the Supreme Court declared that "the authorities clearly support" the plaintiffs' contention that an "alleged partnership, being based upon an oral agreement, should be established 'by clear and convincing' evidence." We take Tidwell to be an authoritative pronouncement of Tennessee's highest court, and we conclude that the bankruptcy court properly applied the "clear and convincing evidence" standard in determining whether TALP was a Tennessee partnership.

The bankruptcy court did not commit clear error in finding, under the standard identified above, that the appellants had failed to prove the existence of a partnership. Tennessee law defines a partnership as an association of two or more persons to carry on a business for profit, and to do so as "co-owners." A "contract of partnership, either express or implied, is essential to the creation of partnership status . . . ." Bass v. Bass, 814 S.W.2d 38, 41 (Tenn. 1991). Partners need not have entered into an express partnership agreement, but in the absence of such an agreement they must at least have agreed impliedly to operate as a partnership -- i.e., to combine their property, labor, skill, experience, or money in a joint business undertaking the profits of which will be shared.. We are not persuaded that Joseph Taylor was a party to any such agreement, express or implied.

Although both Joseph Taylor and Dudley Taylor held out TALP as a partnership and referred to themselves and to various investors as partners, the existence of a partnership does not turn on the words used to describe the parties' relationship. On the critical question of whether Joseph Taylor and his investors agreed to combine their money, labor, or property in a business venture and to share the resulting profits, there is no substantial evidence to support the existence of a partnership. Nothing in the record reflects a mutual understanding as to which specific investors were partners in TALP, let alone an agreement as to how profits and losses would be shared among the partners. In fact, three investors testified that they never agreed to share profits with Joseph Taylor or anyone else; their intent was to make individual investments, with Mr. Taylor acting as a broker. No investor testified to a contrary intent.

There is evidence that Dudley Taylor and Lori Fleishman agreed to pool their own funds and funds of their friends and family members for the purpose of making shared investments through Joseph Taylor. The name "TALP" was used in connection with this "investment club." Joseph Taylor had no control over the enterprise, however, and there is no evidence that he was a party to the agreement or that he participated in any way other than as a broker. If there was an investment club partnership that used the name "TALP," Joseph Taylor was not one of its partners -- and that partnership is not the entity against which the appellants filed their involuntary petition.

The appellants were clearly not members of any investment club partnership; they did not invest jointly with Dudley Taylor, Lori Fleishman, et al. On the contrary, the appellants entrusted funds directly to Joseph Taylor for individual investment. As far as Joseph Taylor was concerned, and setting aside the investment club to which neither he nor the appellants belonged, TALP was nothing more than a name used on bank accounts and tax forms. There is no evidence of any agreement with Joseph Taylor to combine resources and share profits; the investors regarded him as a broker, not as a partner. AFFIRMED.

EVELYN HUNTER ISAMINGER, v. DAN GIBBS

2000 Tex. App. LEXIS 4525 (2000)

COURT OF APPEALS OF TEXAS, FIFTH DISTRICT, DALLAS

WRIGHT, Justice

Dan Gibbs sued Jack S. Isaminger seeking reimbursement for one-half of a tax liability incurred by a travel agency business which they operated. Following a bench trial, the trial court ordered Isaminger to reimburse Gibbs. In four points of error, Isaminger contends generally that the trial court erred by making certain findings regarding the business entities at issue in the case and by denying him recovery on his requests for contribution and an accounting.

Gibbs testified that he and Isaminger purchased a franchise travel agency, "Travel With Us," in 1988. They intended to set up a limited partnership with a corporation, Magical Tours, Inc., as the general partner and themselves, together with friends and spouses, as the limited partners. Gibbs arranged for a service in Austin to incorporate Magical Tours, and the charter from the Secretary of State's Office issued in April 1988. Isaminger and Gibbs each owned fifty percent of the corporation's stock. They also served as the directors and officers of the corporation. Later, the corporation filed an assumed name certificate showing Magical Tours, Inc. would conduct business as Travel With Us. Isaminger and Gibbs then contacted friends and organized contributions to the limited partnership.

Ultimately, a number of couples, including the Isamingers and the Gibbs, invested in the travel agency. Thereafter, Isaminger's daughter, an attorney, and Gibbs drafted a limited partnership agreement and each limited partner executed an agreement. Gibbs then prepared and signed a certificate of limited partnership for Isaminger's daughter to file with the Secretary of State's office. However, during the course of this lawsuit, Gibbs became aware that the certificate was never filed with the secretary of state.

The travel agency was not profitable, and both Isaminger and Gibbs loaned money to the business. In the summer of 1992, Gibbs sent a letter to the limited partners requesting that they contribute more money to the limited partnership and notifying them that without an additional contribution to capital, the limited partnership could "no longer survive. Sometime thereafter, a handwritten letter was sent to the limited partners informing them that "Magical Tours, Inc., as General Partner, will withdraw from the Agreement on August 3, 1992" and that, pursuant to "Article XI, Paragraph Ill. 2d of the Partnership Agreement, the withdrawal of the General Partner dissolves the partnership 'unless all Limited Partners agree upon a new General Partner.'" On August 29, 1992, Gibbs sent a final letter informing the limited partners that Magical Tours had withdrawn as general partner, no action had been taken to select a new general partner, and the "agency [was] a ship without a rudder." The letter also indicated the agency was being advertised for sale and the limited partners would be given a final financial report once it was sold.

Attempts to sell the travel agency were unsuccessful. Gibbs and Isaminger then took over the assets and assumed the obligations of the limited partnership and continued to do business "through the corporation." Both men continued to loan money to the business, although it is undisputed that Isaminger loaned a considerably larger amount. They hired Joan Lyons to manage the day-to-day operations of the business. A short time later, they became aware they owed withholding taxes to the Internal Revenue Service (IRS). Isaminger and Gibbs agreed to pay the delinquent taxes by using the proceeds from two $10,000 certificates of deposit (CDs). When Gibbs received the funds and interest from his CD, he deposited it into his bank account. A short time later, the IRS seized the account, containing approximately $30,000. Gibbs contacted Isaminger to ask him about his CD, and Isaminger said he was unable to contribute the CD proceeds towards the tax liability because he was broke. Ultimately, each of the two men contributed an additional $4,000 to settle the tax debt.

Gibbs sued Isaminger to recover one-half of the money that was levied out of his account for payment of the tax liability. He alleged he was entitled to the money under the theory of contribution, or, in the alternative, pursuant to an oral agreement that each would pay half of the tax liability. Isaminger counterclaimed, alleging that he and Gibbs operated the travel agency as a partnership, not a corporation, and Isaminger was therefore entitled to an accounting. According to Isaminger, any amount he owed Gibbs for the tax debt was offset by Isaminger's contributions to operate the travel agency. Isaminger calculated that, even after the tax liability, Gibbs owed Isaminger at least $77,500.

After hearing the evidence and argument of counsel, the trial court awarded Gibbs $13,672.24 together with interest and attorney's fees as reimbursement of the tax payment. The trial court denied Isaminger recovery on his counterclaim for an accounting and offset. Subsequently, the trial court entered findings of fact and conclusions of law. This appeal followed.

Isaminger brings four issues for our consideration, complaining that the trial court erred by making certain findings of fact and conclusions of law. Generally, Isaminger complains of the trial court's determinations about the business entity formed by Isaminger and Gibbs and its denial of his request for an offset and an accounting. Isaminger concedes that he and Gibbs were jointly and severally liable for the tax debt. The crux of Isaminger's complaint is that the trial court should not have carved out a single transaction (the tax liability) to determine his liability to Gibbs, but should have ordered a general accounting of the entire business relationship and offset his liability on the tax debt accordingly.

At issue in this appeal are the following findings and conclusions of the trial court: (1) Travel With Us was formed as a limited partnership, with Magical Tours as the general partner and Isaminger and Gibbs as limited partners; (2) the limited partners in Travel With Us forfeited their interest in Travel With Us, leaving Magical Tours as the sole surviving partnership interest; (3) because Magical Tours and Travel With Us "were owned by the same people and there were no corporate formalities observed," a general partnership consisting of Magical Tours, Isaminger, and Gibbs remained; and (4) Isaminger was not entitled to recovery on his counterclaim for an accounting and offset

In his first issue, Isaminger contends that the trial court erred by finding that Travel With Us was formed as a limited partnership. According to Isaminger, because a certificate of limited partnership was never filed with the secretary of state, a limited partnership was never formed and Travel With Us was therefore a general partnership.

Article 6132a-1 of the Texas Revised Limited Partnership Act (the Act), the statute governing formation of limited partnerships at the time Travel With Us was formed, provided as follows:

Sec. 201 (a) To form a limited partnership, the partners must enter into a partnership agreement and one or more partners, including all of the general partners, must execute a certificate of limited partnership.

(b) A limited partnership is formed at the time of the filing of the initial certificate of limited partnership with the secretary of state or at a later date or time specified in the certificate if there has been substantial compliance with the requirements of this section.

Section 2.01(b) states that the partnership is formed when there has been substantial compliance with the requirements for filing a certificate

It is undisputed that Isaminger and Gibbs incorporated Magical Tours in April 1988. Magical Tours, as the sole general partner, together with the other limited partners, executed a limited partnership agreement. Gibbs, together with Isaminger's daughter, drafted a certificate of limited partnership, which he executed and forwarded to Isaminger for his signature with the understanding that Isaminger's daughter would file it with the secretary of state. The certificate, however, was never filed.

Thus, with the exception of filing the certificate of limited partnership, the partners completed all of the statutory requirements for formation of a limited partnership. Under these circumstances, we conclude they substantially complied with the statutory requirements for formation of a limited partnership. Consequently, we conclude that there is some evidence to support the trial court's determination that Travel With Us was formed as a limited partnership, with Magical Tours as the general partner and Isaminger and Gibbs, among others, as limited partners. Further, after examining the entire record, we conclude that the trial court's determination is not so contrary to the overwhelming weight and preponderance of the evidence that it is clearly wrong and manifestly unjust.

In issue two, Isaminger argues that because Magical Tours "failed to observe and maintain corporate formalities," Isaminger and Gibbs should be treated as general partners. In finding of fact seven, the trial court found:

that the limited partners in [Travel With Us] forfeited their interest in [Travel With Us], leaving [Magical Tours] as the sole surviving partnership interest even though it had already left the limited partnership. The fact that both of these entities were owned by the same people and that there were no corporate formalities observed makes [Magical Tours] effectively the remaining general partner as well as the two individuals.

Thus, it appears the trial court had two reasons to disregard the corporate entity: (1) both Magical Tours and Travel With Us were owned and operated by Gibbs and Isaminger; and (2) corporate formalities were not observed.

[W]e conclude the evidence establishes that the travel agency was operated by Magical Tours. Gibbs testified that after unsuccessfully attempting to sell the travel agency, he and Isaminger took over the assets and assumed the obligations of the limited partnership and continued to do business "through the corporation." Craig Boyer, a certified public accountant, testified that he worked for Travel With Us. Boyer testified that he prepared a tax return in 1992 for the limited partnership, and after that point, he prepared tax returns for a corporation Magical Tours, Inc. d/b/a Travel With Us. The trial court found, and neither party challenges, that Isaminger held out to third persons that Magical Tours had taken over the assets and liabilities of Travel With Us. Although the record does not contain documentary evidence that the corporation assumed ownership of the travel agency, as previously stated, it is not unexpected that business would be conducted somewhat informally with only two stockholders.

In reaching this conclusion, we necessarily reject Isaminger's contention that Magical Tours could not have taken over the travel agency because it did not "hold the sole surviving partnership interest after the limited partnership was dissolved" as the trial court found. Isaminger assumes in his brief that the trial court found the limited partners, "exclusive of [Gibbs] and [Isaminger]," forfeited their interests, leaving Magical Tours, as well as Gibbs and Isaminger, as shareholders of the travel agency. However, the trial court found that "the limited partners in [Travel With Us] forfeited their interest in [Travel With Us]" upon dissolution of the limited partnership. We interpret this finding to be that all of the limited partners, inclusive of Isaminger and Gibbs, forfeited their partnership interests, and Isaminger does not challenge this finding.

At the time Magical Tours withdrew from the partnership, the Act provided that a person ceased to be a general partner of a limited partnership if he withdrew as provided by section 6.02 of the Act. Section 6.02 provided that a general partner could withdraw at any time from a limited partnership and cease to be a general partner by giving written notice to the other partners. Thus, Magical Tours ceased to be a general partner, at the latest, as of August 29, 1992, when Gibbs notified the limited partners, in writing, that Magical Tours, Inc. had withdrawn as general partner.

The handwritten letter originally notifying the limited partners that Magical Tours, Inc. had withdrawn as general partner is not dated. However, the record also contains a letter, dated August 29, 1992 and signed by Gibbs, stating "as you were informed by letter of recent date, Magical Tours Inc. is no longer the General Partner and no action has been taken by the Limited Partners to obtain a new General Partner as provided by the Partnership Agreement."

However, when Magical Tours withdrew from the limited partnership, it did not, as Isaminger suggests, forfeit its partnership interest. Rather, under the Act, the partnership interest held by the withdrawn general partner could either be converted to that of a limited partner, or "cashed out" by the remaining partners. In this case, there were no remaining partners, all of the limited partners having forfeited their partnership interests. Because there were no remaining partners, Magical Tours partnership interest was never converted to that of a limited partner nor cashed out. Notwithstanding this fact, Magical Tours retained a partnership interest in some form. Thus, the trial court correctly found that Magical Tours was left "as the sole surviving partnership interest even though it had already left the limited partnership."

In conclusion, the evidence in this case shows that in 1988, Travel With Us was formed as a limited partnership, with Magical Tours as the sole general partner and Isaminger and Gibbs, among others, as limited partners. In the summer of 1992, the limited partners forfeited their interests in the partnership and Magical Tours withdrew as general partner. At that time, the limited partnership was dissolved. Magical Tours retained the only surviving partnership interest, and it assumed the obligations of the travel agency and continued to do business. Although the record contains evidence that Isaminger and Gibbs operated the corporation informally, they were the sole shareholders and officers of a closely-held corporation. Therefore, the evidence is insufficient to disregard the corporate entity and find that Isaminger and Gibbs operated the business as a partnership consisting of Magical Tours and the two men individually. We overrule issue two. Having determined that the travel agency was operated by the corporation after the limited partnership dissolved, we need not address issues three and four.

Accordingly, we affirm the trial court's judgment.

GEBHARDT FAMILY INVESTMENT, L.L.C., et al. v. NATIONS TITLE
INSURANCE OF NEW YORK, INC.

132 Md. App. 457; 752 A.2d 1222 (2000)

COURT OF SPECIAL APPEALS OF MARYLAND

SMITH, Judge

The Gebhardts purchased 31.6707 acres of land in Prince George's County on September 1, 1987. They simultaneously purchased title insurance from Nations Title Insurance of New York, Inc. The policy named Joseph and Faye Gebhardt as the insureds.

In 1995, the Gebhardts learned that someone else was paying property taxes on 4.75 acres of the property. They reported to Nations that there was a cloud on the title as to the 4.75 acres, and demanded that Nations correct the situation by "negotiating a purchase from the alleged owner (who also has a cloud on title) . . . and obtaining a quitclaim in favor of [the Gebhardts]."

On December 18, 1996, before the matter was resolved, and apparently to facilitate their estate planning, the Gebhardts executed a special warranty deed conveying all 31.6707 acres in fee simple to Gebhardt Family Investment, L.L.C., a limited liability company created under Virginia law. The Gebhardts were the sole members of the L.L.C. The deed stated that the L.L.C. paid consideration of $160,990.00 for the property.

On November 13, 1997, the Gebhardts and the L.L.C sued Nations for breach of contract for failing to resolve the cloud on title. Trial was held on July 22, 1999, and the sole issue before the court was whether the Gebhardts and/or the L.L.C. were insured under the title insurance policy.

Joseph Gebhardt was the only witness called. He testified to the effect that he and his wife formed the L.L.C. and conveyed the property in question to it as part of their estate planning. Mr. Gebhardt stated that "not a penny" of consideration was paid for the conveyance, and that consideration of $160,990.00 was recited on the deed so that the State could "assess the transfer taxes from the individual to the L.L.C." Mr. Gebhardt added that he and his wife still own "one hundred percent" of the property and pay all of the taxes thereon.

Counsel for the Gebhardts and the L.L.C. argued that, despite the conveyance to the L.L.C.,

> we've clearly shown there's no purchase here, that the Gebhardts are still the owners and maintain the ownership interest which the

policy says, in the land, and therefore they're covered under this policy as well as the L.L.C., they're both covered under this policy.

The trial court disagreed, however. It explained that the "conveyance from Joseph M. Gebhardt and Faye W. Gebhardt to Gebhardt Family Investment, Limited Liability Company, was a conveyance to an entity distinct as a matter of law from Joseph M. Gebhardt and Faye W. Gebhardt." The court acknowledged that the consideration of 160,990.00 recited in the deed might have been recited merely to allow the calculation of transfer taxes, and that the money might not actually have changed hands. It nevertheless concluded that the transfer or the conveyance was one for consideration. The consideration has been the benefit of the limited liability accorded by the State of Virginia for limited liability companies. And also, the acquisition of an ownership interest in the Limited Liability Company and there was consideration by virtue of receiving certain estate planning benefits.

The court thus determined that the L.L.C. was not insured under the policy because it obtained the property by way of purchase rather than by operation of law. It determined that the Gebhardts' coverage terminated when they conveyed the property to a separate entity. The court directed that judgment be entered in favor of Nations.

The title insurance policy issued by Nations to the Gebhardts in 1987 states, in pertinent part:

> The coverage of this policy shall continue in force as of Date of Policy in favor of an insured so long as such insured retains an estate or interest in the land, or holds an indebtedness secured by a purchase money mortgage given by a purchaser from such insured, or so long as such insured shall have liability by reason of covenants of warranty made by such insured in any transfer or conveyance of such estate or interest, provided, however, this policy shall not continue in force in favor of any purchaser from such insured of either said estate or interest or the indebtedness secured by a purchase money mortgage given to such insured.

Paragraph 2(a) of Conditions and Stipulations to Policy of Title Insurance. The policy defines "insured" as the insured named [in the policy] and, subject to any rights or defenses the Company may have had against the named insured, those who succeed to the interest of such insured by operation of law as distinguished from purchase including, but not limited to, heirs, distributees, devisees, survivors, personal representatives, next of kin, or corporate or fiduciary successors.

The trial court determined, and the appellants conceded at oral argument, that the L.L.C. did not acquire the property by operation of law. The appellants thus tacitly concede that the L.L.C. is not an insured under the policy. The argument on appeal is that the Gebhardts remain insured despite the conveyance to the L.L.C. There is no dispute that the Gebhardts do not remain insured by virtue of a purchase money mortgage or covenants of warranty. The appellants argue that because the Gebhardts are the sole members of the L.L.C. the conveyance was, in effect, to themselves and they still retain an interest in the property within the meaning of Paragraph 2(a) of the policy's Conditions and Stipulations.

The argument is based on a misunderstanding of the nature of limited liability companies. It is widely recognized that the allure of the limited liability company is its unique ability to bring together in a single business organization the best features of all other business forms -- properly structured, its owners obtain both a corporate-styled liability shield and the pass-through tax benefits of a partnership. General and limited partnerships do not offer their partners a corporate-styled liability shield. Corporations, including those having made a Subchapter S election, do not offer their shareholders all the pass-through tax benefits of a partnership. All state limited liability company acts contain provisions for a liability shield and partnership tax status.

As we have indicated, the L.L.C. in question was formed under the laws of Virginia. While the record extract does not reveal whether the L.L.C. is registered to do business in Maryland, "the failure of a foreign limited liability company to register in this State does not impair the validity of a contract or act of the foreign limited liability company . . . ." Maryland law thus recognizes the conveyance from the Gebhardts to the L.L.C.

The Supreme Court of Virginia has explained that,

> under the Virginia Limited Liability Company Act, Code §§ 13.1-1002 through 12.1-1073, a limited liability company is an unincorporated association with a registered agent and office. . . . It is an independent entity which can sue and be sued and its members are not personally liable for the debt or actions of the company. . . . In contrast to a partnership, a limited liability company in Virginia is an entity separate from its members and, thus, the transfer of property from a member to the

> limited liability company is more than a change in the form of ownership; it is a transfer from one entity or person to another.

Hagan v. Adams Property Assocs., Inc., 253 Va. 217, 220, 482 S.E.2d 805, 807 (1997) (emphasis added; citations omitted). Indeed, under § 13.1-1009 of the Virginia Limited Liability Company Act, a limited liability company has the power, inter alia:

> 1. To sue and be sued, complain and defend in its name.

> 2. To purchase, receive, lease or otherwise acquire, and own, hold, improve, use and otherwise deal with, real or personal property, or any legal or equitable interest in property, wherever located.

The Virginia Code further provides that, with certain exceptions not relevant here, "[a] member of a limited liability company is not a proper party to a proceeding by or against a limited liability company . . ." "A membership interest in a limited liability company is personal property."

As the trial court recognized, when the Gebhardts' conveyed their interest in the property to the L.L.C., they effected a "transfer from one entity or person to another." Hagan, 482 S.E.2d at 807. The Gebhardts and the L.L.C. are separate entities. The Gebhardts may not file suit in their own names on behalf of the L.L.C. Nor may they be held individually liable for wrongful conduct of the L.L.C. While the Gebhardts have an interest in the L.L.C., they no longer have an interest in the property. Rather, it is the L.L.C. that has the interest in the property. To hold otherwise would be to disregard the nature and viability of limited liability companies.

Appellants's suggestion that there was no real conveyance from the Gebhardts to the L.L.C. because the L.L.C. paid no consideration for the property is utterly without merit. As the trial court pointed out, in exchange for the property the L.L.C. provided the Gebhardts with all of the benefits conferred by a Virginia limited liability company, including limited liability and certain estate planning benefits. By conveying the property under special warranty deed, moreover, the Gebhardts covenanted to protect the L.L.C. only against claims made "by, through, or under" the Gebhardts, as grantors. They did not warrant title against a claim of superior title made by someone else. There is no suggestion that the alleged cloud on title was created by any action or inaction on the part of the Gebhardts while the property was titled in their names. The Gebhardts thus transferred from themselves to the L.L.C. the problem of the cloud on title as to the 4.75 acres. Should the other persons claiming title to the 4.75 acres bring an action to quiet title, the L.L.C, rather than the Gebhardts, would be required to defend and the Gebhardts could not be held personally liable.

The deed recites that the L.L.C. paid $160,990.00 for the property. The appellants now argue that no money actually changed hands and that the figure was included on the deed only for the purpose of calculating transfer taxes. The argument is circular, however, in that a transfer tax is "a tax imposed on the transferring of property." Black's Law Dictionary 1472 (7th ed. 1999). If there had been no conveyance, there would have been no tax. In any event, upon executing the deed to the L.L.C., the Gebhardts reaped the limited liability and estate planning benefits conferred by the Virginia Limited   Liability Company Act. Having accepted those benefits, it is disingenuous for the Gebhardts to now deny that the conveyance ever took place.

As we have explained, the L.L.C. is a separate entity. The problem of the cloud on title is now the problem of the L.L.C. and not the Gebhardts. If any loss is suffered because of the cloud on title, it will be suffered by the L.L.C., which was not an insured under the policy either before or after the conveyance.

JUDGMENT AFFIRMED

CHARLES B. JONES V. GNC FRANCHISING,
INC., A PENNSYLVANIA CORPORATION; AND DOES 1 THROUGH 50,

211 F.3d 495 (2000)

UNITED STATES COURT OF APPEALS FOR THE NINTH CIRCUIT

POLITZ, CIRCUIT JUDGE:

GNC, a subsidiary of General Nutrition Companies, Inc., is franchisor of General Nutrition Stores throughout the United States. The company's principal place of business is Pittsburgh, Pennsylvania. Jones is the franchisee of a GNC store in LaVerne, California.

In January 1995 and August 1996, the parties entered into written agreements, including an Option Agreement and a Franchise Agreement, for Jones' store. Each agreement contains a choice of law clause requiring that it be "interpreted and construed under the laws of the Commonwealth of Pennsylvania, which laws shall prevail in the event of any conflict of law." Both agreements also contain a forum selection clause providing that any action instituted by a franchisee against GNC "in any court, whether federal or state, shall be brought only within the Commonwealth of Pennsylvania in the judicial district in which Franchisor has its principal place of business; and the parties waive all questions of personal jurisdiction or venue for the purpose of carrying out this provision."

A dispute about the agreements arose and Jones filed suit in California state court alleging multiple causes of action. GNC timely removed the litigation to federal court, invoking diversity jurisdiction. The company subsequently moved to either dismiss or transfer venue to the Western District of Pennsylvania.

Jones' claims include: (1) breach of written contract, (2) negligence, (3) breach of the covenant of good faith and fair dealing, (4) selling franchises by means of untrue or misleading statements, (5) intentional misrepresentation of fact, (6) negligent misrepresentation of fact, and (7) intentional interference with contractual relations.

[T]he Supreme Court held that a forum selection clause is presumptively valid and should not be set aside unless the party challenging the clause "clearly shows that enforcement would be unreasonable and unjust, or that the clause was invalid for such reasons as fraud or overreaching." The court added, however, that a contractual forum selection clause is "unenforceable if enforcement would contravene a strong public policy of the forum in which suit is brought, whether declared by statute or by judicial decision." Moreover, even though a clause is the product of a full and free bargaining process, and contravenes no public policy of the forum, it "may nevertheless be 'unreasonable' and unenforceable if the chosen forum is seriously inconvenient for the trial of the action." The party challenging the forum selection clause bears a "heavy burden" of establishing the existence of one of the aforementioned grounds for rejecting its enforcement.

The district court declined to enforce the parties' contractual forum selection clause, concluding that it contravened California's strong public policy against enforcing such clauses in franchise agreements, as expressed in § 20040.5 of the California Business and Professions Code. Section 20040.5 provides that "[a] provision in a franchise agreement restricting venue to a forum outside this state is void with respect to any claim arising under or relating to a franchise agreement involving a franchise business operating within this state." The forum selection clause at bar would restrict venue to Pennsylvania courts. It is apparent that § 20040.5 is intended to void this clause with respect to any claim arising under or relating to the agreement involving the franchise located in LaVerne, California. GNC, however, contends that the district court erred in concluding that the California statute embodies a strong public policy interest precluding enforcement of the clause under federal law.

We find this contention to be without merit. By voiding any clause in a franchise agreement limiting venue to a non-California forum for claims arising under or relating to a franchise located in the state, § 20040.5 ensures that California franchisees may litigate disputes regarding their franchise agreement in California courts. We conclude and hold that § 20040.5 expresses a strong public policy of the State of California to protect California franchisees from the expense, inconvenience, and possible prejudice of litigating in a non-California venue. A provision, therefore, that requires a California franchisee to resolve claims related to the franchise agreement in a non-California court directly contravenes this strong public policy and is unenforceable. Accordingly, we affirm the district court's order denying GNC's motion to dismiss or transfer the action under § 1406(a).

Under § 1404(a), the district court has discretion "to adjudicate motions for transfer according to an 'individualized, case-by-case consideration of convenience and fairness.'" A motion to transfer venue under § 1404(a) requires the court to weigh multiple factors in its determination whether transfer is appropriate in a particular case. For example, the court may consider: (1) the location where the relevant agreements were negotiated and executed, (2) the state that is most familiar with the governing law, (3) the plaintiff's choice of forum, (4) the respective parties' contacts with the forum, (5) the contacts relating to the plaintiff's cause of action in the chosen forum, (6) the differences in the costs of litigation in the two forums, (7) the availability of compulsory process to compel attendance of unwilling non-party witnesses, and (8) the ease of access to sources of proof. Additionally, the presence of a forum selection clause is a "significant factor" in the court's § 1404(a) analysis. We also conclude that the relevant public policy of the forum state, if any, is at least as significant a factor in the § 1404(a) balancing.

The district court weighed each of the aforementioned factors and concluded that GNC failed to meet its burden of showing that Pennsylvania was the more appropriate forum for the action. Although the forum selection clause designates Pennsylvania as the exclusive forum, the court determined that other factors "clearly" demonstrated that California was more appropriate. For example, the court found that the vast majority of the other agreements underlying Jones' claims were negotiated and executed in California. The court noted that Jones chose California as the forum for his lawsuit, and his choice is supported by California's strong public policy to provide a protective local forum for local franchisees. The court further found that the extent of the parties' contacts with Pennsylvania and California clearly favored California, and that Jones' claims arose out of the construction and initial operation of the store located in LaVerne, California. The court also concluded that the relative financial burdens of litigating in each of the forums favored California. Finally, the court noted that more of the relevant witnesses and other sources of proof were located in California. Review of the relevant law and record on appeal persuades us that the trial court did not abuse its discretion in denying the motion to transfer venue under § 1404(a).

Under the doctrine of forum non conveniens, GNC bears the burden of proving that an adequate alternative forum exists.

The judgment appealed is, in all respects, AFFIRMED.

UNITED STATES, ET AL. v. PLAYBOY ENTERTAINMENT GROUP, INC.

120 S. Ct. 1878 (2000)

SUPREME COURT OF THE UNITED STATES

KENNEDY, JUSTICE

This case presents a challenge to § 505 of the Telecommunications Act of 1996. Section 505 requires cable television operators who provide channels "primarily dedicated to sexually-oriented programming" either to "fully scramble or otherwise fully block" those channels or to limit their transmission to hours when children are unlikely to be viewing, set by administrative regulation as the time between 10 p.m. and 6 a.m.. Even before enactment of the statute, signal scrambling was already in use. Cable operators used scrambling in the regular course of business, so that only paying customers had access to certain programs. Scrambling could be imprecise, however; and either or both audio and visual portions of the scrambled programs might be heard or seen, a phenomenon known as "signal bleed." The purpose of § 505 is to shield children from hearing or seeing images resulting from signal bleed.

To comply with the statute, the majority of cable operators adopted the second, or "time channeling," approach. The effect of the widespread adoption of time channeling was to eliminate altogether the transmission of the targeted programming outside the safe harbor period in affected cable service areas. In other words, for two-thirds of the day no household in those service areas could receive the programming, whether or not the household or the viewer wanted to do so.

Appellee Playboy Entertainment Group, Inc., challenged the statute as unnecessarily restrictive content-based legislation violative of the First Amendment. After a trial, a three-judge District Court concluded that a regime in which viewers could order signal blocking on a household-by-household basis presented an effective, less restrictive alternative to § 505.

Playboy Entertainment Group owns and prepares programs for adult television networks, including Playboy Television and Spice. Playboy transmits its programming to cable television operators, who retransmit it to their subscribers, either through monthly subscriptions to premium channels or on a so-called "pay-per-view" basis. Cable operators transmit Playboy's signal, like other premium channel signals, in scrambled form. The operators then provide paying subscribers with an "addressable converter," a box placed on the home television set. The converter permits the viewer to see and hear the descrambled signal. It is conceded that almost all of Playboy's programming consists of sexually explicit material as defined by the statute.

The statute was enacted because not all scrambling technology is perfect. Analog cable television systems may use either "RF" or "baseband" scrambling systems, which may not prevent signal bleed, so discernible pictures may appear from time to time on the scrambled screen. Furthermore, the listener might hear the audio portion of the program.

These imperfections are not inevitable. The problem is that at present it appears not to be economical to convert simpler RF or baseband scrambling systems to alternative scrambling technologies on a systemwide scale. Digital technology may one day provide another solution, as it presents no bleed problem at all. Indeed, digital systems are projected to become the technology of choice, which would eliminate the signal bleed problem. Digital technology is not yet in widespread use, however. With imperfect scrambling, viewers who have not paid to receive Playboy's channels may happen across discernible images of a sexually explicit nature. How many viewers, how discernible the scene or sound, and how often this may occur are at issue in this case.

Section 505 was enacted to address the signal bleed phenomenon. As noted, the statute and its implementing regulations require cable operators either to scramble a sexually explicit channel in full or to limit the channel's programming to the hours between 10 p.m. and 6 a.m. 47

On March 7, 1996, Playboy obtained a temporary restraining order (TRO) enjoining the enforcement of § 505. and brought this suit in a three-judge District Court pursuant to § 561. Playboy sought a declaration that § 505 violates the Constitution and an injunction prohibiting the law's enforcement. The District Court denied Playboy a preliminary injunction, and we summarily affirmed. The TRO was lifted, and the

Federal Communications Commission announced it would begin enforcing § 505 on May 18, 1997.

When the statute became operative, most cable operators had "no practical choice but to curtail [the targeted] programming during the [regulated] sixteen hours or risk the penalties imposed . . . if any audio or video signal bleed occurred during [those] times." The majority of operators -- "in one survey, 69%" -- complied with § 505 by time channeling the targeted programmers. Since "30 to 50% of all adult programming is viewed by households prior to 10 p.m.," the result was a significant restriction of communication, with a corresponding reduction in Playboy's revenues.

In March 1998, the District Court held a full trial and concluded that § 505 violates the First Amendment. The District Court observed that § 505 imposed a content-based restriction on speech. It agreed that the interests the statute advanced were compelling but concluded the Government might further those interests in less restrictive ways. One plausible, less restrictive alternative could be found in another section of the Act: § 504, which [**14] requires a cable operator, "upon request by a cable service subscriber . . . without charge, [to] fully scramble or otherwise fully block" any channel the subscriber does not wish to receive. As long as subscribers knew about this opportunity, the court reasoned, § 504 would provide as much protection against unwanted programming as would § 505. At the same time, § 504 was content neutral and would be less restrictive of Playboy's First Amendment rights.

The court described what "adequate notice" would include, suggesting

"[operators] should communicate to their subscribers the information that certain channels broadcast sexually-oriented programming; that signal bleed . . . may appear; that children may view signal bleed without their parents' knowledge or permission; that channel blocking devices . . . are available free of charge . . .;and that a request for a free device . . . can be made by a telephone call to the [operator]."

The means of providing this notice could include

"inserts in monthly billing statements, barker channels (preview channels of programming coming up on Pay-Per-View), and on-air advertisement on channels other than the one broadcasting the sexually explicit programming."

The court added that this notice could be "conveyed on a regular basis, at reasonable intervals," and could include notice of changes in channel alignments.

The District Court concluded that § 504 so supplemented would be an effective, less restrictive alternative to § 505, and consequently declared § 505 unconstitutional and enjoined its enforcement. The court also required Playboy to insist on these notice provisions in its contracts with cable operators.

Two essential points should be understood concerning the speech at issue here. First, we shall assume that many adults themselves would find the material highly offensive; and when we consider the further circumstance that the material comes unwanted into homes where children might see or hear it against parental wishes or consent, there are legitimate reasons for regulating it. Second, all parties bring the case to us on the premise that Playboy's programming has First Amendment protection. As this case has been litigated, it is not alleged to be obscene; adults have a constitutional right to view it; the Government disclaims any interest in preventing children from seeing or hearing it with the consent of their parents; and Playboy has concomitant rights under the First Amendment to transmit it. These points are undisputed.

The speech in question is defined by its content; and the statute which seeks to restrict it is content based. Section 505 applies only to channels primarily dedicated to "sexually explicit adult programming or other programming that is indecent." The statute is unconcerned with signal bleed from any other channels. [Section 505] does not apply when signal bleed occurs on other premium channel networks, like HBO or the Disney Channel. The overriding justification for the regulation is concern for the effect of the subject matter on young viewers. Section 505 is not "'justified without reference to the content of the regulated speech.'" It "focuses only on the content of the speech and the direct impact that speech has on its listeners. This is the essence of content-based regulation.

Not only does § 505 single out particular programming content for regulation, it also singles out particular programmers. The speech in question was not thought by Congress to be so harmful that all channels were subject to restriction. Instead, the statutory disability applies only to channels "primarily dedicated to sexually-oriented programming." One sponsor of the measure even identified appellee by name. (statement of Sen. Feinstein(noting the statute would apply to channels "such as the Playboy and Spice channels"). Laws designed or intended to suppress or restrict the expression of specific speakers contradict basic First Amendment principles. Section 505 limited Playboy's market as a penalty for its programming choice, though other channels capable of transmitting like material are altogether exempt.

The effect of the federal statute on the protected speech is now apparent. It is evident that the only reasonable way for a substantial number of cable operators to comply with the letter of § 505 is to time channel, which silences the protected speech for two-thirds of the day in every home in a cable service area, regardless of the presence or likely presence of children or of the wishes of the viewers. According to the District Court, "30 to 50% of all adult programming is viewed by households prior to 10 p.m.," when the safe-harbor period begins. To prohibit this much speech is a significant restriction of communication between speakers and willing adult listeners, communication which enjoys First Amendment protection. It is of no moment that the statute does not impose a complete prohibition. The distinction between laws burdening and laws banning speech is but a matter of degree. The Government's content-based burdens must satisfy the same rigorous scrutiny as its content-based bans.

Since § 505 is a content-based speech restriction, it can stand only if it satisfies strict scrutiny. If a statute regulates speech based on its content, it must be narrowly tailored to promote a compelling Government interest.. If a less restrictive alternative would serve the Government's purpose, the legislature must use that alternative. To do otherwise would be to restrict speech without an adequate justification, a course the First Amendment does not permit.

Our precedents teach these principles. Where the designed benefit of a content-based speech restriction is to shield the sensibilities of listeners, the general rule is that the right of expression prevails, even where no less restrictive alternative exists. We are expected to protect our own sensibilities "simply by averting [our] eyes." Here, of course, we consider images transmitted to some homes where they are not wanted and where parents often are not present to give immediate guidance. Cable television, like broadcast media, presents unique problems, which inform our assessment of the interests at stake, and which may justify restrictions that would be unacceptable in other contexts. No one suggests the Government must be indifferent to unwanted, indecent speech that comes into the home without parental consent. The speech here, all agree, is protected speech; and the question is what standard the Government must meet in order to restrict it. As we consider a content-based regulation, the answer should be clear: The standard is strict scrutiny. This case involves speech alone; and even where speech is indecent and enters the home, the objective of shielding children does not suffice to support a blanket ban if the protection can be accomplished by a less restrictive alternative.

When a plausible, less restrictive alternative is offered to a content-based speech restriction, it is the Government's obligation to prove that the alternative will be ineffective to achieve its goals. The Government has not met that burden here.

The District Court employed the proper approach. When the Government restricts speech, the Government bears the burden of proving the constitutionality of its actions.

This is for good reason. The line between speech unconditionally guaranteed and speech which may legitimately be regulated, suppressed, or punished is finely drawn. Error in marking that line exacts an extraordinary cost. It is through speech that our convictions and beliefs are influenced, expressed, and tested. It is through speech that we bring those beliefs to bear on Government and on society. It is through speech that our personalities are formed and expressed. The citizen is entitled to seek out or reject certain ideas or influences without Government interference or control.

Basic speech principles are at stake in this case. When the purpose and design of a statute is to regulate speech by reason of its content, special consideration or latitude is not accorded to the Government merely because the law can somehow be described as a burden rather than outright suppression. We cannot be influenced, moreover, by the perception that the regulation in question is not a major one because the speech is not very important. The history of the law of free expression is one of vindication in cases involving speech that many citizens may find shabby, offensive, or even ugly. It follows that all content-based restrictions on speech must give us more than a moment's pause. If television broadcasts can expose children to the real risk of harmful exposure to indecent materials, even in their own home and without parental consent, there is a problem the Government can address. It must do so, however, in a way consistent with First Amendment principles. Here the Government has not met the burden the First Amendment imposes.

The Government has failed to show that § 505 is the least restrictive means for addressing a real problem; and the District Court did not err in holding the statute violative of the First Amendment. In light of our ruling, it is unnecessary to address the second question presented: whether the District Court was divested of jurisdiction to consider the Government's postjudgment motions after the Government filed a notice of appeal in this Court. The judgment of the District Court is affirmed the less intrusive methods of discovery are unsatisfactory, insufficient or inadequate."

The court of appeals stated: "A party requesting an apex deposition must show that the corporate official to be deposed has an [sic] unique or superior personal knowledge that is unavailable through less intrusive means." That phrasing of the guidelines improperly collapses the two discrete inquiries into a single test. Under Crown Central, if the party seeking the deposition has "arguably shown that the official has any unique or superior personal knowledge of discoverable information," the trial court should deny the motion for protection and the party seeking discovery should be entitled to take the apex depositions. The party seeking the apex deposition is required to pursue less intrusive means of discovering the information only when that party cannot make the requisite showing concerning unique or superior knowledge.

In this case, when Samsung moved for the protective orders the parties had already engaged in significant discovery, including more than 300 hours of depositions. At this stage of discovery, nothing in Crown Central precluded the trial court from considering whether DSC had attempted to gain the information by less intrusive means and otherwise satisfied the second Crown Central test. The parties argued both Crown Central tests in the trial court, and both the discovery master and trial judge denied the requested protective orders without specifying the reasons. Accordingly, mandamus is not appropriate if the trial court's order can be sustained under either Crown Central test. We consider first whether DSC arguably showed that Lee or Kang have unique or superior personal knowledge of discoverable information.

The most comprehensive discussion of Kun-Hee Lee's knowledge as it relates to this lawsuit is found in a document submitted by DSC titled: "Kun-Hee Lee's Significance and Connection to This Lawsuit." In that document, DSC urges several reasons why Lee's deposition is necessary. First, under the heading "Kun-Hee Lee Sets Samsung's Course," DSC claims that (1) Lee is the leader of the Samsung Chaebol, (2) Lee sets the overall vision for the Samsung companies, and (3) Samsung's goal is to be one of the world's top five telecommunications companies by 2005. Second, under the heading "Kun-Hee Lee's Ties To The Lead Defendant, Samsung Electronics Co., Ltd.," DSC states that Lee (1) was the chief executive officer and president of SEC, (2) was a long-standing director of SEC, and (3) is the largest single owner of Samsung and its subsidiaries.

IN RE ALCATEL USA, INC. F/K/A DSC COMMUNICATIONS
INCORPORATED, RELATOR

11 S.W.3d 173 (2000)

SUPREME COURT OF TEXAS

ABBOTT, JUSTICE

The issue in this mandamus proceeding is whether the trial court abused its discretion by allowing DSC Communications to take the apex depositions of two high-level Samsung executives. The court of appeals conditionally granted mandamus relief, concluding that DSC failed to prove that the executives had "unique or superior knowledge that is unavailable through less intrusive means."

In September 1998, DSC Communications Corporation merged with and changed its name to Alcatel USA, Inc. We refer to Relator throughout this opinion as DSC, as it was referenced in the trial court and the court of appeals.

DSC filed this suit alleging that Samsung engaged in a plan to steal a new DSC telecommunication technology known as "intelligent network" and "next generation switching" systems. DSC asserts that Samsung identified and lured a team of engineers away from DSC and then specifically assigned them to develop the same type of product they had developed at DSC. DSC claims that Samsung's actions were the direct result of a plan engineered at the highest level of Samsung's executive structure, and that highest-level Samsung executives were involved in the plan's execution at all stages.

DSC noticed the depositions of two high-level Samsung executives, Jin-Ku Kang and Kun-Hee Lee. Kang served as Chairman of defendant Samsung Electronics Co., Ltd. (SEC) during the earliest events giving rise to this case and is currently Chairman Emeritus of that corporation. Lee is currently Chairman and CEO of SEC and formerly served as the Chairman of the Samsung Chaebol during the earliest events at issue in this case. DSC and Samsung agree, and therefore we assume, that the Kang and Lee depositions qualify as apex depositions.

A chaebol is a Korean conglomerate in which subordinates are extremely deferential to their hierarchical superiors.

Samsung moved to quash both depositions. At the first evidentiary hearing on the issue, the special discovery master assigned to the case deferred ruling until after the deposition of Mr. K. H. Kim, the former President and CEO of SEC at all times relevant to this matter. After Kim's deposition, DSC renewed its request for the Kang and Lee depositions and moved to compel both. After holding another evidentiary hearing, the special discovery master denied Samsung's motion to quash and ordered that both depositions proceed. Samsung appealed the special discovery master's order to the trial court. The trial court reviewed the transcripts of these hearings and conducted a third hearing. The trial judge denied Samsung's appeal and affirmed the special discovery master's order. Samsung moved for reconsideration. After a fourth hearing on Samsung's motion to reconsider, the trial judge denied the motion.

Samsung filed a petition for writ of mandamus with the court of appeals. [T]he court of appeals held that DSC had failed to prove that it was entitled to take the apex depositions and conditionally granted mandamus relief. DSC filed a petition for writ of mandamus in this Court, arguing that the court of appeals abused its discretion by granting the writ because the trial court did not abuse its discretion.

Mandamus relief is available only to correct a "clear abuse of discretion" when there is no other adequate remedy at law. When a party alleges that the court of appeals abused its discretion by granting mandamus relief, this Court focuses on whether the trial court's ruling was an abuse of discretion.

This Court first adopted the apex deposition guidelines in Crown Central Petroleum Corp. v. Garcia, 904 S.W.2d 125 (Tex. 1995). We held that the apex deposition guidelines apply "when a party seeks to depose a corporate president or other high level corporate official." A party initiates the Crown Central guideline proceedings by moving for protection and filing the corporate official's affidavit denying any knowledge of relevant facts. The trial court evaluates the motion first by deciding if the party seeking the deposition has "arguably shown that the official has any unique or superior personal knowledge of discoverable information." "If the party seeking the deposition cannot show that the official has any unique or superior personal knowledge of discoverable information, the trial court should" not allow the deposition to go forward without a showing, after a good faith effort to obtain the discovery through less intrusive means, "(1) that there is a reasonable that the less intrusive methods of discovery are unsatisfactory, insufficient or inadequate."

The court of appeals stated: "A party requesting an apex deposition must show that the corporate official to be deposed has an [sic] unique or superior personal knowledge that is unavailable through less intrusive means." That phrasing of the guidelines improperly collapses the two discrete inquiries into a single test. Under Crown Central, if the party seeking the deposition has "arguably shown that the official has any unique or superior personal knowledge of discoverable information," the trial court should deny the motion for protection and the party seeking discovery should be entitled to take the apex depositions. The party seeking the apex deposition is required to pursue less intrusive means of discovering the information only when that party cannot make the requisite showing concerning unique or superior knowledge.

In this case, when Samsung moved for the protective orders the parties had already engaged in significant discovery, including more than 300 hours of depositions. At this stage of discovery, nothing in Crown Central precluded the trial court from considering whether DSC had attempted to gain the information by less intrusive means and otherwise satisfied the second Crown Central test. The parties argued both Crown Central tests in the trial court, and both the discovery master and trial judge denied the requested protective orders without specifying the reasons. Accordingly, mandamus is not appropriate if the trial court's order can be sustained under either Crown Central test. We consider first whether DSC arguably showed that Lee or Kang have unique or superior personal knowledge of discoverable information.

The most comprehensive discussion of Kun-Hee Lee's knowledge as it relates to this lawsuit is found in a document submitted by DSC titled: "Kun-Hee Lee's Significance and Connection to This Lawsuit." In that document, DSC urges several reasons why Lee's deposition is necessary. First, under the heading "Kun-Hee Lee Sets Samsung's Course," DSC claims that (1) Lee is the leader of the Samsung Chaebol, (2) Lee sets the overall vision for the Samsung companies, and (3) Samsung's goal is to be one of the world's top five telecommunications companies by 2005. Second, under the heading "Kun-Hee Lee's Ties To The Lead Defendant, Samsung Electronics Co., Ltd.," DSC states that Lee (1) was the chief executive officer and president of SEC, (2) was a long-standing director of SEC, and (3) is the largest single owner of Samsung and its subsidiaries.

Evidence tending to support these allegations does not satisfy the first Crown Central test; it merely demonstrates that Lee is a long-time company leader who sets the company vision with lofty goals. Virtually every company's CEO has similar characteristics. Allowing apex depositions merely because a high-level corporate official possesses apex-level knowledge would eviscerate the very guidelines established in Crown Central. Such evidence is too general to arguably show the official's knowledge is unique or superior.

J. K. Kang served as Chairman of defendant SEC during the earliest events that gave rise to this case and is currently Chairman Emeritus of that corporation. DSC contends that Kang's unique or superior personal knowledge is arguably shown by the deposition testimony of Dr. Joo Hyung Lee, an SEC manager who personally oversaw the establishment of Samsung's Dallas laboratory. Contrary to DSC's contention, Joo Hyung Lee's deposition conveys that Kang may have been made aware of information contained in reports prepared by others, but still does not show why Kang's knowledge may be unique or superior.

In his deposition, Joo Hyung Lee testified that he prepared a status report of the next-generation switching system and presented it to, among others, Song, the Samsung executive in charge of telecommunications, and Kang. Joo Hyung Lee characterized the report as an overview that did not last very long -- it was "kind of a simple thing." He further testified that, other than that single presentation, he had no other communication with Kang concerning the next-generation switching system. Further probing by DSC during Joo Hyung Lee's deposition indicated that none of the project's details were conveyed to Kang by Joo Hyung Lee; instead, it was Joo Hyung Lee and Song who were involved in the details:

This evidence arguably shows that Kang may have discoverable information. But the first Crown Central guideline requires more; it requires that the person to be deposed arguably have "unique or superior personal knowledge of discoverable information." This requirement is not satisfied by merely showing that a high-level executive has some knowledge of discoverable information. If "some knowledge" were enough, the apex deposition guidelines would be meaningless; they would be virtually indistinguishable from the scope of general discovery. Although Crown Central did not elaborate on what character of knowledge makes it unique or superior, there must be some showing beyond mere relevance, such as evidence that a high-level executive is the only person with personal knowledge of the information sought or that the executive arguably possesses relevant knowledge greater in quality or quantity than other available sources.

Because DSC failed to arguably show that either Kang or Lee possesses unique or superior knowledge of discoverable information, the trial court's order cannot be supported under the first Crown Central test. Nevertheless, DSC argues that it has pursued less intrusive means and therefore is entitled to the depositions under Crown Central's second guideline:

If the party seeking the deposition cannot show that the official has any unique or superior personal knowledge of discoverable information, the trial court should grant the motion for protective order and first require the party seeking the deposition to attempt to obtain the discovery through less intrusive methods. . . . After making a good faith effort to obtain the discovery [**20] through less intrusive methods, the party seeking the deposition may attempt to show (1) that there is a reasonable indication that the official's deposition is calculated to lead to the discovery of admissible evidence, and (2) that the less intrusive methods of discovery are unsatisfactory, insufficient or inadequate. If the party seeking the deposition makes this showing, the trial court should modify or vacate the protective order as appropriate. . . . If the party seeking the deposition fails to make this showing, the trial court should leave the protective order in place.

From the record before us, DSC has not shown that it attempted to obtain the information it sought from Kang through less intrusive methods. DSC based its contention that Kang has unique or superior knowledge largely on his presence at a written and oral presentation concerning the next generation switching system. But, DSC was allowed to depose Joo-Hyung Lee, who presented the report to Kang and Song. Also, DSC deposed Song, the Samsung executive in charge of telecommunications, who also attended the presentation. Yet, DSC has failed to identify any relevant information that it seeks from Kang that it attempted and failed to obtain from either Joo-Hyung Lee or Song.

In addition, DSC failed to establish that it attempted to obtain the information that it sought from Lee through less intrusive methods. DSC argued that Lee has unique and superior knowledge regarding Samsung's policies. But the special master allowed DSC to depose Kim, the president and CEO of SEC during the relevant time. Yet, DSC failed to ask Kim any questions about Samsung's "vision" for telecommunications or any of the other issues DSC now contends justify an apex deposition of Lee. DSC also did not issue interrogatories, requests for admissions, or any other forms of discovery to Samsung regarding its corporate policies. The record simply does not show that the information sought from Lee was sought by less intrusive means or that the information sought was unobtainable from other sources.

Absent a showing that an executive arguably has unique or superior personal knowledge, a court has no discretion to allow an apex deposition unless the party seeking the deposition establishes that it has attempted to obtain the information through less intrusive methods. The special master provided DSC with the opportunity to depose other Samsung executives who at least arguably possessed the information DSC seeks. Yet, DSC either failed to take advantage of that opportunity or failed to preserve its attempts in the record. Thus, the trial court abused its discretion in overruling Samsung's motion to quash the depositions of Kang and Lee.

We agree with the court of appeals' conclusion that the trial court abused its discretion when it refused to quash the depositions of Kang and Lee because it failed to properly apply the guidelines set forth in Crown Central v. Garcia. Accordingly, we deny the mandamus relief requested by DSC.

HMO-W INCORPORATED V. SSM HEALTH CARE SYSTEM, ET AL

234 Wis. 2d 707; 611 N.W.2d 250 (2000)

SUPREME COURT OF WISCONSIN

BRADLEY, JUDGE

The appraisal action at the center of this review represents the culmination of a relationship between HMO-W and SSM that spanned more than a decade. In 1983, SSM and a number of other health care providers formed HMO-W as a provider-owned health care system. All shareholders assumed minority status in this closely held corporation. SSM and the Neillsville Clinic, another shareholder, together owned approximately twenty percent of HMO-W's shares.

By the early 1990's, competitive pressures from within the health care business led HMO-W to explore the possibility of merging with another health care system. SSM recommended DeanCare Health Plan (DeanCare), a company with which SSM had close connections, as a potential merger partner. HMO-W later eliminated DeanCare from consideration after having met with company representatives numerous times to discuss a partnership deal. HMO-W instead proposed a joint venture with United Wisconsin Services (United).

Before shareholder approval of the merger, HMO-W retained Valuation Research Corporation (VR) to value HMO-W's net assets both prior to and upon the merger. VR prepared a final valuation report that HMO-W accepted and which estimated the company's net value to fall within the range of $16.5 to $18 million.

Subsequently, HMO-W's board of directors voted to approve the proposed merger with United and to submit the merger to a shareholder vote. In addition to the VR report, the proxy materials sent to the shareholders informed them of their statutory right to dissent to the merger. At the shareholder meeting, both SSM and the Neillsville Clinic voted against the proposed merger. The merger was nevertheless approved.

Both SSM and the Neillsville Clinic then perfected a demand for the payment of their dissenting shares. Wis. Stat. § 180.1323 (1997-98). n2 Abandoning [*713] the VR report, HMO-W hired a new appraiser to value its assets. The appraiser arrived at a valuation of approximately $7.4 million, and based upon this valuation, HMO-W sent SSM a check for almost $1.5 million as the value of SSM's shares. Disputing HMO-W's valuation of the shares, SSM [***5] informed the

company that SSM's fair value calculation of its shares yielded a figure of approximately $4.7 million.

Pursuant to Wis. Stat. § 180.1330(1), HMO-W instituted a special proceeding to determine the fair value of the dissenting shares. In response, SSM asserted that HMO-W was estopped from claiming a company value that was lower than the $16.5 to $18 million value it had represented to the shareholders prior to the merger vote.

At trial, several experts testified as to the net value of HMO-W. HMO-W's expert testified that the company's value immediately prior to the merger was $10,544,000. SSM's expert submitted the value as $19,250,000. The circuit court accepted the valuation offered by HMO-W's expert, noting various flaws in the earlier VR report that called into question the accuracy of that report.

Upon accepting HMO-W's valuation and observing the dissenters' minority status, the circuit court applied a minority discount of 30% to the value of the dissenting shares but refrained from applying a lack of marketability discount. The circuit court concluded that it was required to apply the minority discount as a matter of law. The court then ordered SSM and the Neillsville Clinic to repay with interest the amount by which HMO-W's initial payment exceeded the court's fair value determination.

A minority discount addresses the lack of control over a business entity on the theory that non-controlling shares of stock are not worth their proportionate share of the firm's value because they lack voting power to control corporate actions. A lack of marketability discount adjusts for a lack of liquidity in one's interests in a firm, on the theory that there is a limited supply of potential buyers in closely held corporations. Id. The type of discount at issue in this case is the minority discount, and thus we do not address the applicability of a lack of marketability discount under the statute.

SSM filed a post-decision motion requesting the court to clarify whether it had considered SSM's argument that HMO-W be estopped from asserting at the appraisal proceeding a substantially lower value of its assets than the value set forth in the initial VR report. In response, the court issued an order stating that it had considered SSM's arguments and that it was affirming its prior decision in HMO-W's favor. SSM appealed.

The court of appeals affirmed in part and reversed in part, remanding the case for a fair value determination without the application of a minority discount. It held as a matter of law that the Wisconsin statutes governing dissenters' rights do not allow minority discounts to be applied in determining the fair value of a dissenter's shares.

The court reasoned that minority discounts frustrate the purpose of dissenters' rights statutes, which protect the rights of shareholders to voice objection to corporate actions and to receive an equitable value for their minority shares.

At common law, unanimous shareholder consent was required to achieve fundamental corporate changes. Courts and legislatures questioned the wisdom of allowing one shareholder to frustrate changes deemed desirable and profitable by the majority and thus modified tradition by authorizing majority consent.

Although permitting the majority to approve fundamental changes was viewed as a solution to the potential stalemate attendant to a requirement of corporate unanimity, majority consent nevertheless opened the door to victimization of the minority. In response, legislatures widely adopted statutes to address minority victimization by affording dissenters appraisal rights for their shares.

. The appraisal remedy has its roots in equity and serves as a quid pro quo: minority shareholders may dissent and receive a fair value for their shares in exchange for relinquishing their veto power. Appraisal thus grants protection to the minority from forced participation in corporate actions approved by the majority.

We turn now to address whether a minority discount may apply in determining the fair value of a dissenter's shares. This issue presents a question of statutory interpretation, and we examine first the statutory language to discern legislative intent. If the language is clear, we need not look beyond the statutory language to determine that intent. If the statute is ambiguous, however, we resort to such extrinsic aids as legislative history and statutory purpose for guidance.

The definition of fair value set forth in Wis. Stat. § 180.1301(4) provides:

"Fair value", with respect to a dissenter's shares other than in a business combination, means the value of the shares immediately before the effectuation of the corporate action to which the dissenter objects, excluding any appreciation or depreciation in anticipation of the corporate action unless exclusion would be inequitable. "Fair value", with respect to a dissenter's shares in a business combination, means market value.

HMO-W maintains that under the clear language of Wis. Stat. § 180.1301(4), the circuit court retains the discretion to apply a minority discount in appropriate circumstances by valuing the dissenter's shares as a minority block of shares. Because the language is silent

as to the applicability of a minority discount, there is no indication that the legislature aimed to curtail the court's discretion. HMO-W claims that the legislature would have so stated had it intended to impose a blanket prohibition against such a discount.

Although HMO-W advances a statutory interpretation permitting circuit court discretion, it fails, however, to offer a standard by which this discretion should be exercised. HMO-W does not definitively set forth any guidelines to contour the discretion it contends is inherent in the statute, including when a circuit court may apply a minority discount and how much of a discount the court should apply.

SSM also argues that Wis. Stat. § 180.1301(4) is unambiguous, yet maintains that the clear words of the statute reflect an opposite intent. It asserts that the legislature intended to prohibit the application of a minority discount by its chosen words. The juxtaposition of the term "fair value" in the first statutory sentence with "market value" as it relates to business combinations in the second sentence leads SSM to conclude that the legislature envisioned two distinct valuation approaches. Each approach is based on the type of shareholder asserting dissenters' rights in any particular corporate action.

According to SSM, the separate definition of fair value to mean market value in the context of business combinations reflects the legislative intent to define fair value for shares of non-business combinations without equating the term with fair market value. n5 Because a minority discount represents a market concept and is premised on the theory that controlling shares are worth more on the market than non-controlling shares, SSM contends that the legislature prohibited the application of a minority discount.

We agree with SSM that the legislature clearly did not intend to render fair value synonymous with fair market value when appraising dissenters' shares in a non-business combination.

Consistent with the statutory purpose in granting dissenters' rights, an involuntary corporate change approved by the majority requires as a matter of fairness that a dissenting shareholder be compensated for the loss of the shareholder's proportionate interest in the business as an entity. Otherwise, the majority may "squeeze out" minority shareholders to the economic advantage of the majority.

As the Delaware Supreme Court observed in the seminal case of Cavalier Oil Corp. v. Harnett, 564 A.2d 1137, 1145 (Del. 1989):

Where there is no objective market data available, the appraisal process is not intended to reconstruct a pro forma sale but to assume that the shareholder was willing to maintain his investment position, however slight, had the merger not occurred. . . . To fail to accord to a minority shareholder the full proportionate value of his shares imposes a penalty for lack of control, and unfairly enriches the majority shareholders who may reap a windfall from the appraisal process by cashing out a dissenting shareholder, a clearly undesirable result.

A minority discount based on valuing only the minority block of shares injects into the appraisal process speculation as to the myriad factors that may affect the market price of the block of shares. Examining the purpose of dissenters' rights statutes, we conclude that the application of a minority discount in determining the fair value of a dissenter's shares frustrates the equitable purpose to protect minority shareholders.

A dissenting stockholder is thus entitled to the proportionate interest of his or her minority shares in the going concern of the entire company. Although Wis. Stat. § 180.1301(4) defines "fair value" as "the value of the shares" immediately before the corporate action, the focus of fair valuation is not the stock as a commodity but rather the stock only as it represents a proportionate part of the enterprise as a whole.

The price of publicly traded shares generally rises upon the announcement of a proposed merger. This inflated price often serves to offset the implicit discount based on market value.

In rejecting the application of a minority discount, we join a significant number of jurisdictions that have likewise disavowed the minority discount. These courts have also concluded that a minority discount thwarts the purpose of dissenters' rights statutes to protect shareholders subjected to an involuntary corporate change.

Reasoning against a minority discount, courts have recognized that to apply such a discount inflicts a double penalty upon the minority shareholder and upsets the quid pro quo underlying dissenters' appraisal rights. The shareholder not only lacks control over corporate decision making, but also upon the application of a minority discount receives less than proportional value for loss of that control.

In sum, we conclude that Wis. Stat. § 180.1301(4) does not permit the application of a minority discount in determining the fair value of a dissenter's shares. A minority discount runs contrary to the protective purpose of the dissenters' rights statute by discounting a minority interest solely because it is the minority.

In this case, the circuit court properly considered SSM's evidence of unfair dealing and rendered a determination of HMO-W's net value that is supported by the record. Accordingly, we affirm the court of appeals.

The decision of the court of appeals is affirmed.

UNITED STATES SECURITIES AND EXCHANGE COMMISSION, v. THE
INFINITY GROUP COMPANY; ET AL

212 F.3d 180 (2000)

UNITED STATES COURT OF APPEALS FOR THE THIRD CIRCUIT

MCKEE, CIRCUIT JUDGE

In November 1995, defendants Geoffrey Benson and Geoffrey O'Connor formed the Infinity Group Company Trust (the "Trust" or "TIGC"). Thereafter, the Trust unveiled an "Asset Enhancement Program" that offered investors an opportunity to invest with the expectation of exceedingly high return and minimal risk. Investors in TIGC were asked to execute "property transfer contracts" pursuant to which the investors contributed substantial sums of money to the Trust for the Trust to invest. TIGC guaranteed investors that they would receive an annual rate of return ranging from 138% to 181% depending on the amount of the participant's principal investment. The guarantees were based upon the Trust's purported performance experience, financial connections, and the ability to pool large amounts of money. Participants were promised that their principal would be repaid upon demand. Once the property transfer contracts were executed, the transferred funds became assets of the Trust and were subject to investment at the sole discretion of the Board of TIGC.

Benson was the Executive Trustee Director of TIGC. O'Connor was also a trustee of TIGC. As Trustees of TIGC, Benson and O'Connor exercised sole discretion of the Trust's investment programs.

For property transfers of $1,200 to $50,000, the guaranteed rate of return was 138. For amounts greater than $50,000, the return rate was 181.

TIGC's solicitation was successful. It raised approximately $26.6 million from over 10,000 investors nationwide. However, TIGC only invested $12 million of the funds it received pursuant to the property transfer contracts, and it never earned a profit on the funds it did invest. Rather, the Trust sustained mounting loses that it failed to disclose to investors. The district court described what happened as follows:

TIGC also used over $2 million in so-called downline commissions to keep the engine of this enterprise humming like a new Mercedes on the autobahn. In the time-dishonored tradition of Charles Ponzi, TIGC substituted new investors' money for real investment return on old investors' funds.

The rest of TIGC's expenditures were even less investment-related. More than $816,000 was spent on real estate, a significant portion of which went to the purchase and development of a personal residence for Geoffrey and Susan Benson . . . the purchase or lease of cars for their garage, . . . a $6,133.46 spending spree at Circuit City; more than $2,000 spent at television retailers; over $50,000 in 'household expenses'; $5,000 to pay off a home mortgage; $10,000 to pay off personal credit card bills; $10,000 for school tuition for the Bensons' son; as well as hundreds for jewelry, bowling equipment and membership fees, [sic] groceries. In short, the Bensons used TIGC as their personal checking account.

In addition, Geoffrey Benson made an undisclosed donation of $1.265 million of investor funds to Lindsey K. Springer, d/b/a Bondage Breaker Ministries.

In addition to all this, defendants Geoffrey Benson and Geoffrey O'Connor paid themselves nearly $300,000 in cash from TIGC's funds, none of it reported to the Internal Revenue Service or even documented on TIGC's books-- which did not exist. Lastly, more than $1.9 million remains unaccounted for.

Defendants contend that the money that was not invested was used for "operating expenses" and charitable contributions or that it constituted "excess profits." The evidence at trial established that the money not invested was used to pay "dividends" to earlier investors and personal expenses of the Benson family.

The district court agreed with the SEC's claim that the operation of the Trust was "the classic modus operandi of Ponzi schemes."

On August 27, 1997, the SEC filed the instant complaint in the United States District Court for the Eastern District of Pennsylvania charging "an ongoing scheme, directed by Benson and O'Connor, to defraud public investors through the offer and sale of TIGC securities, in the form of investment contracts," The Commission sought a permanent injunction, a freeze of the assets of TIGC, appointment of a Trustee to manage the affairs of TIGC, and an order requiring defendants, and certain third parties (the "relief defendants") to disgorge assets of TIGC that had been improperly transferred.

On September 5, 1997, after a hearing, the district court issued an Order for Preliminary Injunction, Appointment of Trustee, and Freeze of Assets and Other Relief. On February 6, 1998, the district court entered a final judgment against the defendants enjoining them from further violations of the securities laws and ordering disgorgement of all amounts contributed to the Trust by the Trust participants. This appeal followed.

We must first address the defendants' claim that the district court lacked subject matter jurisdiction because the "property transfer contracts" were not "securities" under federal securities laws.

It is well established that federal securities laws only apply to the purchase or sale of "securities" as defined therein.

'Security' means any note, stock, treasury stock, bond, debenture, evidence of indebtedness, certificate of interest or participation in any profit-sharing agreement, collateral-trust certificate, . . . investment contract, voting-trust certificate, . . . any interest or instrument commonly known as a 'security', or any certificate of interest or participation in, . . . or right to subscribe to or purchase, any of the foregoing.

The property transfer agreements that TIGC's investors executed certainly appear to be "investment contracts," however the term investment contract has not been defined by Congress, nor does the legislative history to the 1933 and 1934 Acts illuminate what Congress intended by the term investment contract [and] the Supreme Court provided a framework for determining when such agreements are subject to federal law. The Court stated:

> An investment contract for purposes of the Securities Act means a contract, transaction or scheme whereby a person invests his money in a common enterprise and is led to expect profits solely from the efforts of the promoter or a third party, it being immaterial whether the shares in the enterprise are evidenced by formal certificates or by nominal interests in the physical assets employed in the enterprise. Howey, 328 U.S. at 298-99. Thus, the property transfer contracts between TIGC and its investors are securities if they were (1) "an investment of money," (2)"in a common enterprise," (3) "with profits to come solely from the efforts of others."

Defendants agree that the property transfer contracts satisfy the first and third prongs of the Howey test. Indeed, they can hardly deny it. There clearly was an investment of money because the contracts required and evidenced the monetary transfer solely for the purposes of receiving the "guaranteed" return of

between 138% and 181%. Similarly, the third prong is clearly satisfied here because the expected return was to be "with profits to come solely from the efforts of others."

The Infinity Group Company invests for profit by accepting amounts as low as [$1200] from thousands of people like you, and creating large blocks of funds that are in the millions of dollars. This gives the Trust a leverage position whereby we can command large profits, and have the security of never putting the principal at risk. This is very sophisticated investing that cannot be accomplished unless you have millions of dollars to deposit in a top world US bank.

However, TIGC argues that commonality is nevertheless lacking because the investors did not "share proportionately in the profits or losses of TIGC or the various investment programs," Appellant's Br. at 19 (emphasis omitted). Rather, TIGC asserts that each participant would execute an individual contract with TIGC providing for a fixed return, payable on demand (principal only) or on a specific date. . .

The property transfers were obligations of TIGC to repay the other party to the contract at a specific time, and did not represent a direct interest in TIGC, any other entity or a specific security or investment vehicle. . . . The property transfers were not earmarked for any particular purpose, or even any particular type of investment. . . . Under these contracts, the TIGC Board retained exclusive control over the investment decision and participants were not promised that their funds would be invested in any particular investment program.

However, TIGC's denial of horizontal commonality is contrary to the record. By the plan's very terms, the return on investment was to be apportioned according to the amounts committed by the investor. Each investor's apportionment of profits was represented by certain "capital units" obtained in exchange for executing a "property transfer agreement." The number of units an investor purchased was, of course, dependent upon the size of his or her investment and the investor's return was directly proportional to the amount of that investment. TIGC's solicitation materials stated:

TIGC seeks to negate the obvious import of its structure by arguing that there are technical characteristics that distinguish the instruments involved here from those that are "securities." We are not persuaded. The defendants' claim that the property transfer contracts do not constitute "investment contracts" because the investors were to receive a fixed rate of return rather than a rate dependent on the success of the investments. The defendants argue:

If the aggregate value of the investments increased, each contract holder would not share in the appreciation. Rather, they would receive only their fixed, contractually agreed-upon return. . . . Similarly, if the value of TIGC investments decreased, the contract holder would still be entitled to the agreed-upon, fixed return on his or her property transfer contract. . . . In the event that the value of the investments dropped below the ability of TIGC to honor its commitment to a specific individual, the participants would not share proportionately ('pro rata') in the shortfall.

However, the definition of security does not turn on whether the investor receives a variable or fixed rate of return.

Profits can be either "capital appreciation resulting from the development of the initial investment" or earnings contingent on profits gained from the use of investors' funds. The mere fact that the expected rate of return is not speculative does not, by itself, establish that the property transfer contracts here are not "investment contracts" within the meaning of federal securities laws.

The aim is to prevent further exploitation of the public by the sale of unsound, fraudulent, and worthless securities through misrepresentation; to place adequate and true information before the investor; to protect honest enterprise, seeking capital by honest presentation, against the competition afforded by dishonest securities offered to the public through crooked promotion. . . .

The investors provide the capital and share in the earnings and profits; the promoters manage, control and operate the enterprise. It follows that the arrangements whereby the investors' interests are made manifest involve investment contracts, regardless of the legal terminology in which such contracts are clothed.

Here, the investors' beads were strung upon the gossamer guarantee of seemingly impossibly high returns at no risk. The fact that TIGC promised a "fixed rate of return" based upon the amount invested is irrelevant. We will not embroider a loophole into the fabric of the securities laws by limiting the definition of "securities" in a manner that unduly circumscribes the protection Congress intended to extend to investors. Rather, we must scrutinize these "property transfer contracts" in a manner that "permits the fulfillment of the statutory purpose of compelling full and fair disclosure relative to the issuance of the many types of instruments that in our commercial world fall within the ordinary concept of a security."

We must consider that Congress "enacted a definition of 'security' sufficiently broad to encompass virtually any instrument that might be sold as an investment," The securities laws were intended to provide investors with accurate information and to protect the investing public from the sale of worthless securities through misrepresentations. As noted above, TIGC accepted nearly $26.6 million from approximately 10,000 investors. TIGC persuaded those investors to part with their cash by guaranteeing the proverbial "blue sky;" fantastic profit at no risk. Of the $26.6 million raised, more than half of the money was used to satisfy the material "needs" of the individual defendants. The balance was poured down empty wells that could hardly be confused with prudent investments. TIGC realized no return whatsoever on those "investments." Given the totality of the circumstances here, the property transfer contracts clearly constitute securities.

SANDRA JARRETT, V. ERC PROPERTIES, INC.

211 F.3d 1078 (2000)

UNITED STATES COURT OF APPEALS FOR THE EIGHTH CIRCUIT

LOKEN, CIRCUIT JUDGE.

ERC owns and manages federally subsidized housing projects in various Arkansas communities. ERC hired Jarrett in May 1995 as resident site manager of the Yorkville apartment complex; she also conducted ERC's "Lend-A-Hand" educational program at another complex. In November 1995, Jarrett was promoted to site manager of four complexes in three different municipalities. She moved to the Booneville complex, where she lived next door to her new regional supervisor, Patsy Wilson. Jarrett's first supervisor, Tammy Hester, and later Patsy Wilson told Jarrett that ERC did not pay its site managers overtime. Jarrett was instructed to include only her "office time" --forty hours per week -- on her time sheets. On average, Jarrett worked considerably more than forty hours per week.

In March 1996, Jarrett complained to Robert Fikes, ERC's Vice-President of Asset Management, that Patsy Wilson's daughter had submitted a falsely back-dated application to rent an apartment at the Booneville complex, and that a properly dated application had disappeared from ERC's private office, to which Wilson and her husband had access. At the time, the federally subsidized Booneville complex had a waiting list, and falsifying a tenant's application date violated federal regulations. Fikes told Jarrett she would have to prove her allegations "beyond a shadow of a doubt" and fired her when she was unable to do so.

Jarrett filed this action in February 1998, asserting claims for willful violation of the FLSA's overtime requirements and wrongful discharge. The jury awarded her $11,970.08 on the FLSA claim and $33,715.04 on the wrongful discharge claim. The district court denied Jarrett liquidated damages under the FLSA and reduced her request for attorneys' fees from $36,360 to $21,816. Both sides appeal.

Was Jarrett an Exempt Employee under the FLSA? The FLSA requires covered employers to compensate non-exempt employees at overtime rates for time worked in excess of statutorily-defined maximum hours. The statute exempts certain employees from its overtime protections, including "any employee employed in a bona fide executive, administrative, or professional capacity." The Secretary of Labor has promulgated

extensive regulations defining the types of employees who fall within these exemption categories. For employees who earn more than $250 per week, the "administrative employee" exemption applies if the employee's primary duty consists of the performance of [office or non-manual work directly related to management policies or general business operations of her employer or her employer's customers], which includes work requiring the exercise of discretion and independent judgment.

ERC argues that Jarrett was an exempt administrative employee as a matter of law. We disagree.

This "short test" applies only to more highly compensated employees. While employed at the Yorkville complex, Jarrett earned less than $250 per week. Because the evidence supports the jury's finding that Jarrett was a non-exempt employee under the short test, we need not consider the more rigorous "long test".

Disputes regarding the nature of an employee's duties are questions of fact, but the ultimate question whether an employee is exempt under the FLSA is an issue of law. In this case, the district court submitted the entire issue to the jury with instructions that correctly summarized the definition of an exempt administrative employee set forth in the regulations.

Jarrett testified at trial that her duties at ERC included collecting applications from prospective tenants; verifying references and other application information; contacting potential applicants regarding apartment availability; preparing "reports," which she described as filling in blanks on printed forms; writing receipts and verifying rent payments; performing minor repairs and getting help for repairs she could not do; picking up trash; maintaining the grounds; cleaning the laundry room, bathrooms, and community room; locking and unlocking common rooms according to a schedule determined by her supervisor; and forwarding invoices to ERC for payment. These tasks resemble the work of non-exempt "bookkeepers, secretaries, and clerks of various kinds [who] hold the run-of-the-mine positions in any ordinary business. Most involved "routine clerical duties," and the rest were manual labor. Jarrett also testified that her work did not "require the exercise of discretion and independent judgment," and ERC introduced little or no evidence to the contrary. Though ERC argues its site managers primarily perform administrative duties, the jury's finding that Jarrett was a non-exempt employee is well-supported by this record.

ERC further argues that Jarrett as resident site manager was required to live at the complex, and therefore her time outside of normal office hours was "waiting time" that counts as administrative time in determining whether her "primary duty" was administrative. Only time spent working is considered in determining an employee's primary duty for FLSA exemption purposes Whether waiting time is work time under the FLSA is a fact-intensive question thoroughly addressed in the regulations. Those regulations create a presumption that "an employee who resides on his employer's premises on a permanent basis . . . is not considered as working all the time he is on the premises." Here, ERC did not present evidence overcoming that presumption and did not object when the jury instructions failed to include the issue of waiting time in the primary duty instruction. In these circumstances, ERC's belated suggestion that some or all of Jarrett's unpaid, non-office hours were FLSA waiting time that the jury should have classified as exempt time does not undermine the jury's verdict that Jarrett was a non-exempt employee.

Did ERC Commit a "Willful" FLSA Violation? In 1966, Congress modified the two-year statute of limitations for FLSA enforcement actions by adding: "except that a cause of action arising out of a willful violation may be commenced within three years after the cause of action accrued." Resolving a conflict among the circuits, the Supreme Court defined a "willful" violation as one where "the employer either knew or showed reckless disregard for the matter of whether its conduct was prohibited by the statute." Here, the jury found ERC's violation to be "willful." On appeal, ERC argues it is entitled to judgment as a matter of law on this issue.

At trial, Jarrett presented evidence pointing toward a willful violation. She introduced portions of ERC's Policy Manual stating that employees "are classified as non-exempt employees or exempt employees," that salaried non-exempt employees "will be paid ...overtime in accordance with the law," and that "the exempt or non-exempt status of each employee will be determined by the Vice President of Finance Administration." Jarrett testified that two immediate supervisors said she would not be paid overtime and instructed her to record only forty hours per week on her time sheets. Another former site manager, Nelda Beasley, testified that she also was told ERC would not pay overtime despite the fact that she was listed as a non-exempt employee "on my hiring paperwork."

ERC's response to Jarrett's evidence that it recklessly disregarded its FLSA obligations was to ignore the issue. No defense witness testified as to how individual site managers were classified as exempt or non-exempt employees, or how Sandra Jarrett was classified at either of her site manager positions. No defense witness contradicted, or attempted to explain, the testimony of two former site managers that they were told, categorically, by two regional supervisors, that ERC would not pay overtime --a generalization in clear conflict with the Policy Manual's recognition that this is a fact-intensive determination. On this record, there is ample basis for a reasonable jury to find that ERC willfully violated the FLSA's overtime requirements.

Jarrett was an "at-will" employee who could be fired at any time, with or without cause. However, Arkansas law recognizes a cause of action for wrongful discharge if an at-will employee "is fired in violation of a well-established public policy of the state." A claim that public policy has been violated will lie "if an employer discharges an employee for reporting a violation of state or federal law."

ERC concedes that Jarrett was fired because she reported but could not conclusively prove that her supervisor had manipulated the waiting list for federally subsidized apartments, which is a violation of federal regulations. But ERC argues that Jarrett cannot base a wrongful discharge claim on this public policy violation because she was a participant in the wrongdoing. ERC admits it has no Arkansas authority supporting this contention. We conclude the Supreme Court of Arkansas would not hold as a matter of law that an employee's participation in a public policy violation, under duress, precludes a claim for wrongful discharge. Thus, Jarrett's claim was properly submitted to the jury, and there is sufficient evidence to support its finding of wrongful discharge.

The judgment of the district court is reversed and the case is remanded with instructions to award Jarrett liquidated damages under the FLSA in the amount of $11,970.08. In all other respects, the judgment is affirmed.

TAMMY S. BLAKEY v. CONTINENTAL AIRLINES, INC., et al

164 N.J. 38; 751 A.2d 538 (2000)

SUPREME COURT OF NEW JERSEY

O'HERN, JUSTICE

Tammy S. Blakey, a pilot for Continental Airlines since 1984, appears from the record to be a highly qualified commercial airline pilot. In December 1989, Blakey became that airline's first female captain to fly an Airbus or A300 aircraft (A300). The A300 is a widebody twin-engine jet aircraft seating 250 passengers. Plaintiff was one of five qualified A300 pilots in the service of Continental Airlines. Shortly after qualifying to be a captain on the A300, Blakey complained of sexual harassment and a hostile working environment based on conduct and comments directed at her by male co-employees. From 1990 to 1993, Blakey was based in Newark, New Jersey, but lived in Arlington, Washington. According to Blakey, in February 1991, she began to file systematic complaints with various representatives of Continental about the conduct of her male co-employees. Specifically, Blakey complained to Continental's management concerning pornographic photographs and vulgar gender-based comments directed at her that appeared in the workplace, specifically in her plane's cockpit and other work areas.

In February 1993, Blakey filed a charge of sexual discrimination and retaliation in violation of Title VII of the Civil Rights Act of 1964 and the Civil Rights Act of 1991 against Continental with the Equal Employment Opportunity Commission in Seattle, Washington, her home state. She simultaneously filed a complaint in the United States District Court in Seattle, Washington, against Continental for its failure to remedy the hostile work environment. Because Blakey's major flight activities had been out of Newark International Airport, the United States District Court granted Continental's motion to transfer the action to the United States District Court for the District of New Jersey. Continental requested the transfer to New Jersey because Blakey was based in Newark, her allegations were predicated on unlawful employment practices that took place in New Jersey and the Continental personnel responsible for investigating Blakey's complaints also were based in Newark. Continental's motion to transfer was granted on May 13, 1993. At her own request, Blakey transferred to Houston in May 1993. To be relieved of the continuing stress that she had experienced in Newark, Blakey assumed a voluntary unpaid leave of absence beginning in August 1993.

In the midst of that federal litigation, her fellow pilots continued to publish a series of what plaintiff views as harassing gender-based messages, some of which she alleges are false and defamatory. From February to July 1995, a number of Continental's male pilots posted derogatory and insulting remarks about Blakey on the pilots on-line computer bulletin board called the Crew Members Forum ("Forum"). The Forum is accessible to all Continental pilots and crew member personnel through the Internet provider, CompuServe. When Continental employees access CompuServe, one of the menu selections listed in the "Continental Airlines Home Access" program includes an option called "Continental Forum." Like many other large corporations today, Continental's computer technology operations are "outsourced" or contracted-out, in this case to a company called Electronic Data Systems ("EDS"). EDS manages Continental's information systems including the CMS, which contains information on flights, crew member schedules, pay and pilot pairings. Continental requires that pilots and crew "access" the CMS in order to learn their flight schedules and assignments. To access such a system is, in essence, to call in through a computer or telephone.

CompuServe charges pilots and crew members a monthly fee for Internet access. Perhaps to enhance the appeal of its product, CompuServe provides the Crew Members Forum for pilots and crew members to exchange messages. In the parlance of the Internet, this is described as a virtual community. Community is about communication and interaction among people of shared interests, objectives or purposes. When community members such as employees communicate with each other, they build relationships. The Crew Members Forum essentially serves as an Intranet system.

Access to the Crew Members Forum is available only through CompuServe. The Forum is not accessible through the dumb terminals. The Forum is like a bulletin board where employees can post messages or "threads" for each other. Although it was said that Continental management was not permitted to post messages or reply to any messages on the Forum, its chief pilots and assistant chief pilots had access to the Forum if they signed up with CompuServe to utilize the CMS. Relying on deposition testimony of the Director of Crew Systems and Planning, plaintiff asserts that chief pilots are considered management within Continental. Although Continental may have no duty to monitor the Forum, it is possible that a jury could find that Continental had knowledge, either direct or vicarious through managerial employees, of the content of certain messages posted on the Forum.

In August 1995, Blakey sought to amend her federal complaint against Continental to add these allegedly defamatory remarks as the basis for an additional cause of action and as further support for her claim of a hostile environment. The federal court denied leave to amend because "plaintiff [had] other judicial recourse available to pursue her claims." In December 1995, Blakey filed this complaint in Superior Court seeking "other judicial recourse" against Continental and the pilots alleging defamation, sexual harassment/hostile work environment, business libel, and intentional infliction of emotional distress. In August 1996, Continental moved for partial summary judgment on the claims of defamation, business libel, and intentional infliction of emotional distress. Individual defendants Riggs, Vacca, Abdu, Farrow, Orozco, and Stivala also filed a motion to dismiss for lack of personal jurisdiction n8 . In April 1997, the Law Division granted the pilots' motion n9 as well as Continental's motion.

In December 1997, Continental filed a motion for summary judgment on the remaining hostile environment workplace claim, which was subsequently granted in April 1998.

Meanwhile, the federal litigation proceeded to conclusion.

In October 1997, a jury in the United States District Court for the District of New Jersey found in favor of Blakey on the claim of sexual harassment, awarding her $480,000 in back pay, $15,000 in front pay, and $500,000 for emotional distress, pain and suffering, but did not award any punitive damages. The jury also found that Blakey had failed to mitigate damages, and subtracted $120,000 from her back pay award of $480,000. The $500,000 award for emotional distress, pain and suffering was subsequently halved.

Concerning Continental's liability, the Appellate Division reasoned that while Continental provided pilots with the means to access the CMS, utilized that system to convey important information necessary for the pilots' performance of their jobs, and relied on its pilots to use the CMS for a variety of purposes, no such evidence was presented with regard to the Forum. Indeed, the record demonstrates that Continental did not require employees to utilize the Forum. Stated differently, the decision to use the Forum rests solely with the employee, and the employee, not Continental, bears the cost of use. Regardless of whether the threads were defamatory,

plaintiff has established no basis for Continental's liability under the doctrine of respondeat superior.

To put the issue in perspective, we need to shrink the context a bit. There was a television series a few years ago called "Wings." Wings (NBC television broadcast, April 1990 through May 1997). The program concerned a small, regional airline, its pilots, ground crew and maintenance people. If there were at that small airport a lounge used exclusively by the pilots and crew of that airline and a bulletin board in that lounge contained the same or similar comments and asides by the pilots and crew, there would be little doubt that if management had notice of messages that met the required substantive criteria of being "sufficiently severe or pervasive to alter the conditions of employment and to create an intimidating, hostile, or offensive working environment," a cause of action for hostile work environment sexual harassment could be asserted. And if there had been a nearby place frequented by senior management, pilots and crew where one of the crew was regularly subjected to sexually offensive insults and if that harassing conduct was a continuation of a pattern of harassment in the workplace, an employer that had notice of the pattern of severe and pervasive harassment in and out of the workplace, would not be entirely free to disregard the conduct.

The question in this more complex case is whether the Crew Members Forum is the equivalent of a bulletin board in the pilots' lounge or a work-related place in which pilots and crew members continue a pattern of harassment. The trial court correctly perceived the role of the Forum when it asked:

So what's the difference? What's the critical difference now we've taken it off this wood and whatever it is, cork material, that a bulletin board is made out of, and now we've electronically put it on the Internet. Now, what are the critical differences that now take it out of something that Continental could be responsible for as a workplace, or work-related item.

This Court has recognized that harassment by a supervisor that takes place outside of the workplace can be actionable.

Thus, standing alone, the fact that the electronic bulletin board may be located outside of the workplace (although not as closely affiliated with the workplace as was the cockpit in which similar harassing conduct occurred), does not mean that an employer may have no duty to correct off-site harassment by co-employees. Conduct that takes place outside of the workplace has a tendency to permeate the workplace. A worker need not actually hear the harassing words outside the workplace so long as the harassment contributes to the hostile work environment.

Although an employer's liability for sexual harassment of which the employer knew or should have known can be seen to flow from agency law, it also can be understood as direct liability. When an employer knows or should know of the harassment and fails to take effective measures to stop it, the employer has joined with the harasser in making the working environment hostile. The employer, by failing to take action, sends the harassed employee the message that the harassment is acceptable and that the management supports the harasser. Effective" remedial measures are those reasonably calculated to end the harassment. The "reasonableness of an employer's remedy will depend on its ability to stop harassment by the person who engaged in harassment.

Plaintiff alleges that she gave notice to Continental as early as March 1995 by forwarding copies of the offending "threads" to Continental's counsel as notice of the continuing harassment. If such notice was given, Continental's liability will depend on whether the Crew Members Forum was such an integral part of the workplace that harassment on the Crew Members Forum should be regarded as a continuation or extension of the pattern of harassment that existed in the Continental workplace.

Our common experience tells us how important are the extensions of the workplace where the relations among employees are cemented or sometimes sundered. If an "old boys' network" continued, in an after-hours setting, the belittling conduct that edges over into harassment, what exactly is the outsider (whether black, Latino, or woman) to do? Keep swallowing the abuse or give up the chance to make the team? We believe that severe or pervasive harassment in a work-related setting that continues a pattern of harassment on the job is sufficiently related to the workplace that an informed employer who takes no effective measures to stop it, "sends the harassed employee the message that the harassment is acceptable and that the management supports the harasser."

On remand, the trial court should first determine whether Continental derived a substantial workplace benefit from the overall relationship among CompuServe, the Forum and Continental.

The record does not disclose that Continental sought the Forum's inclusion on CompuServe's menu. Still, it appears to us that a business enterprise would derive the same benefits from having its employees connected as would a law firm, or the judiciary itself. We have become familiar with the process through which the judiciary's employees and its several jurisdictions may be connected by the Internet. That process is well known by now. The problems that developed in our fathers' offices are likely to develop in the offices of the future. Business counselors caution employers that they should have policies that deal with sexual harassment on the message centers of this changing world. That does not mean that employers have a duty to monitor employees' mail. Grave privacy concerns are implicated. It may mean that employers may not disregard the posting of offensive messages on company or state agency e-mail systems when the employer is made aware of those messages.

CompuServe's role may thus be analogized to that of a company that builds an old-fashioned bulletin board. If the maker of an old-fashioned bulletin board provided a better bulletin board by setting aside space on it for employees to post messages, we would have little doubt that messages on the company bulletin board would be part of the workplace setting. Here, the Crew Members Forum is an added feature to the company bulletin board.

To repeat, employers do not have a duty to monitor private communications of their employees; employers do have a duty to take effective measures to stop co-employee harassment when the employer knows or has reason to know that such harassment is part of a pattern of harassment that is taking place in the workplace and in settings that are related to the workplace. Besides, it may well be in an employer's economic best interests to adopt a proactive stance when it comes to dealing with co-employee harassment. The best defense may be a good offense against sexual harassment. Effective remedial steps reflecting a lack of tolerance for harassment will be relevant to an employer's affirmative defense that its actions absolve it from all liability. Surely an anti-harassment policy directed at any form of co-employee harassment would bolster that defense.

Finally, we would hope that an employer who cherishes its reputation for caring for its customers would use its good offices to resolve this long simmering disagreement among its key employees, whose harmony would appear crucial not only to efficient flight operations but to general public safety as well. The judgment of the Appellate Division is reversed. The matter is remanded to the Law Division for further proceedings in accordance with this opinion..

ANNICE CONE, et al v. NEVADA SERVICE EMPLOYEES UNION/SEIU LOCAL 1107, et al

998 P.2d 1178 (2000)

SUPREME COURT OF NEVADA

OPINION: PER CURIAM:

SUMMARY

The relevant facts in this case are not in dispute, as the parties have stipulated to them. Appellants, Annice Cone, Sharon Mallory, and Karl Schlepp (collectively hereinafter "appellants"), are nonunion employees of the University Medical Center of Southern Nevada ("UMC"), a local government employer pursuant to NRS 288.060. Appellants, as employees of UMC, are governed by a collective bargaining agreement (the "CBA") and are members of a bargaining unit that is represented by Nevada Service Employees Union/SEIU Local 1107 (the "union").

In October 1994, approximately 100 union members, including the appellants in this case, exercised their rights under article 8, section 4 of the CBA to revoke their union dues authorization forms, thereby becoming nonunion members of the bargaining unit. During this same time period, in October 1994, the union disseminated a new Executive Board Policy (the "policy"), which is at issue in this case. The policy served two purposes: (1) to establish a fee schedule for all nonmembers of the union for representation in grievance matters; and (2) to notify nonunion members that they could select outside counsel to represent them in bargaining unit matters. The policy's fee schedule provided that grievance consultation would cost a minimum of sixty dollars an hour, that the nonunion member was responsible for fifty percent of the billed fee for hearing officers and arbitrators, and one hundred percent of union attorney fees of up to two hundred dollars per hour.

The policy was authorized by article 6, section 2 of the CBA, which provides that:

The Union recognizes its responsibility as bargaining agent and agrees fairly to represent all employees in the bargaining unit. UMC recognizes the right of the Union to charge nonmembers of the Union a reasonable service fee for representation in appeals, grievances and hearings.

It is undisputed that the policy was never actually enforced against any UMC nonunion employee, including appellants. However, because appellants believed that article 6, section 2 of the CBA and the policy violated the Local Government Employee-Management Relations Act (the "act"), appellants filed a complaint with the Local Government Employee-Management Relations Board (the "board"). In their complaint, filed on March 7, 1995, appellants alleged that the policy violated the act because it "interfered with, restrained, coerced and discriminated against the [appellants] (and all other employees in the bargaining unit) in the exercise of their right, if they choose, to be nonmembers of the UNION, all in violation of NRS 288.140, 288.270(1)(a), 288.270(1)(c), 288.270(2)(a).

On January 10, 1996, the board issued a divided 2-1 decision. A majority of the board upheld the policy, concluding that it was not contrary to the provisions of NRS 288 or Nevada's Right to Work Law (NRS 613.230-300) and that, in the alternative, appellants had waived by inaction their right to object to such provisions. Further, the board concluded that the policy was neither coercive nor discriminatory in nature and did not derogate the union's statutory duty as an exclusive bargaining agent to represent all UMC employees fairly and impartially.

The board, and later the district court, concluded that NRS 288.027 did not prohibit the union from charging a nonmember costs for the union's grievance representation services. Appellants first contend that this conclusion is erroneous because the union, as the "bargaining agent" of UMC employees, is obligated by the plain language of NRS 288.027 to "exclusively" represent all UMC employees, including nonunion members, in all grievance matters without charging a fee.

NRS 288.027 defines a bargaining agent as an "exclusive" representative:

an employee organization recognized by the local government employer as the exclusive representative of all local government employees in the bargaining unit for purposes of collective bargaining.

Because of the inclusion of the word "exclusive," appellants conclude that the union is not allowed to "pick and choose" which of the representational activities that it will provide free of charge because its statutory designation as the "exclusive representative" requires it to provide all services for free. We do not agree that the mere inclusion of the word "exclusive" in and of itself prohibits a union from charging nonunion members service fees for individual grievance representation.

Further, with regard to statutory language, there is another Nevada statute, NRS 288.140(2), that explicitly authorizes a nonunion member to act on his own behalf "with respect to any condition of his employment." This statute provides an individual with a right to forego union representation. Implicit in the plain language of this provision is the requisite that a nonunion member pay for pursuing his or her own grievance, even if such payment is made to the union.

Accordingly, we conclude that there is nothing in the plain language of NRS 288.027 that would prohibit the union from charging nonmembers fees for individual representation.

Appellants next contend that the policy violates Nevada's right to work laws. Nevada's right to work laws, particularly NRS 613.250, were enacted for the express purpose of guaranteeing every individual the right to work for a given employer regardless of whether the worker belongs to a union. See Independent Guard Ass'n v. Wackenhut Servs., 90 Nev. 198, 202-03, 522 P.2d 1010, 1013 (1974). In Wackenhut, this court invalidated an agency shop agreement, an agreement to pay fees to a labor organization in lieu of membership dues, because it violated NRS 613.250 since it was equivalent to conditioning employment on union membership.

The instant policy is unlike the agency shop agreement in Wackenhut, because paying a service fee for grievance representation is not a condition of employment. Indeed, an individual may opt to hire his or her own counsel, and thereby forego giving the union any money at all without fear of losing his or her job.

Accordingly, we conclude that the policy does not violate Nevada's right to work laws.

Appellants' final argument is that the union discriminated against its nonunion members, and thereby breached its duty of fair representation set forth in NRS 288.140(1) and NRS 288.270(2) by charging nonunion members a service fee for individual grievance representation.

NRS 288.140(1) n5 sets forth the union's duty of fair representation and explicitly states that a local government employer shall not discriminate based on membership or nonmembership in an employee organization. Further, NRS 288.270(2) describes the prohibited practices of an employee organization, including that it may not:

> It is the right of every local government employee, subject to the limitation provided in subsection 3, to join any employee organization of his choice or to refrain from joining any employee organization. A local government employer shall not discriminate in any way among its employees on account of membership or nonmembership in an employee organization.

> (a) Interfere with, restrain or coerce any employee in the exercise of any right guaranteed under this chapter.

> (c) Discriminate because of . . . political or personal reasons or affiliations.

We see no discrimination or coercion, however, in requiring nonunion members to pay reasonable costs associated with individual grievance representation, and therefore conclude that the union did not violate the aforementioned statutes.

There is persuasive authority and a compelling rationale in support of our conclusion. First, several other jurisdictions have held that requiring nonunion members to pay costs for union representation was not discriminatory, coercive or restraining.

Second, we are convinced that the exclusive bargaining relationship establishes a "mutuality of obligation": a union has the obligation to represent all employees in the bargaining unit without regard to union membership, and the employee has a corresponding obligation, if permissible under the CBA and required by the union policy, to share in defraying the costs of collective bargaining services from which he or she directly benefits.

Accordingly, we conclude that the union did not discriminate against nonmembers in enacting the policy, and that the policy merely recognized the mutuality of obligation that may arise under an exclusive bargaining arrangement.

Accordingly, we hold that the policy is not violative of NRS 288.027, Nevada's right to work laws, NRS 288.140(1), or NRS 288.270(2). We therefore affirm the order of the district court.

CHAPTER 44
TO ACCOMPANY
LIABILITY OF ACCOUNTANTS 878

HAROLD TOD PARROTT V. COOPERS & LYBRAND, L.L.P

263 A.D.2d 316; 702 N.Y.S.2d 40 (2000)

SUPREME COURT OF NEW YORK, APPELLATE DIVISION, FIRST DEPARTMENT

TOM, JUSTICE

Plaintiff Harold Tod Parrott was employed as Vice President of Sales by non-party Pasadena Capital Corp, a privately held investment advisor firm located in California. A majority of the company's shares were held by its CEO, with employees, including plaintiff, holding various minority interests. Under a January 1, 1992 stock purchase agreement, plaintiff purchased 40,500 shares at $28.22 per share. The purchase agreement provided that, upon termination of plaintiff's employment, the company would purchase back these shares at fair market value to be determined on a minority basis by an independent third-party analysis conducted in accordance with the company's employee stock ownership plan.

Defendant accounting firm had provided accounting reports to the company twice annually, on December 31 and June 30, for several years. The accountants were retained by the company and reported only to the company. As per the December 20, 1993 letter of continuing engagement, the accountants valued the company on a minority interest basis, exclusive of added value or premiums in connection with the sale or proposed sale of the company. Each biannual report was based on two methodologies: a discounted cash flow method, and a market comparable method relying on the stock values of similar companies publicly traded. Under the terms of engagement, the company's management was required to keep the accountants informed of any material changes in operation, management or financing, and the company was required to review draft reports prior to issuance to verify accuracy of the analysis and conclusions.

Plaintiff was terminated on May 31, 1996. When it appeared that the repurchase provision of the stock purchase agreement would be invoked after his termination, plaintiff initially resisted the repurchase. His initial recourse, understandably, was against his former employer. Plaintiff commenced a Federal action in the Southern District of New York in August 1996 to enjoin Pasadena from exercising its right to buy back plaintiff's stock under the stock purchase agreement. He challenged the legality of his termination as well as

what he expected to be defendant's valuation, and contended that the repurchase could not be triggered by a wrongful termination. In that action, in which he also sought an independent valuation, he estimated the value at $120 per share, arising in part from an anticipated sale of the company. However, plaintiff did not allege that an identified purchaser or a pending offer for the company existed.

By letter dated September 26, 1996, the company gave notice that it was exercising its right to repurchase the stock, and explained that the value it relied on was established by defendant accountant firm in the most recent biannual report. The accountants set a value of $78.21 per share as of June 30, 1996. This represented a total company value of $117,000,000, divided by the number of shares. The result was that plaintiff was offered $3,069,208.50 payable over five years, plus interest, for stock that he had purchased for $1,143,035 in 1992.

Plaintiff next sought recourse against the accountants, and commenced the present action in 1997. The complaint sounded in professional negligence, negligent misrepresentation and aiding and abetting the employer's breach of fiduciary duty. Under the negligence and misrepresentation claims, plaintiff argued that he had reasonably relied on the accountants' misrepresentations and omissions when he stipulated to the sale of the shares. Under the breach of fiduciary duty claim, he argued that the accountants had changed the valuation methodology, at the employer's insistence, in order to reduce the price of plaintiff's shares, and that plaintiff was thereby induced to accept a lesser value for his stock.

The analysis of the malpractice claim starts from the general proposition that under New York common-law, accountants do not have a duty to the public at large (Westpac Banking Corp. v Deschamps, 66 N.Y.2d 16, 494 N.Y.S.2d 848, 484 N.E.2d 1351). Rather, traditionally, as noted by Justice Cardozo in Ultramares Corp. v Touche (255 N.Y. 170, 174 N.E. 441) in dismissing a cause of action against an accounting firm for inaccurately prepared financial statements relied on by a plaintiff having no contractual privity with the accountants, privity was the necessary predicate for accounting liability. The duty of care arose from the relationship. Among Cardozo's concerns, still applicable decades later, was that any mistake by an accountant otherwise might expose that accountant, or any accountant, to liability by a limitless class of aggrieved parties. In Ultramares, Justice Cardozo addressed and distinguished his prior ruling in Glanzer v Shepard (233 N.Y. 236, 135 N.E. 275), upon which the dissent presently relies for the proposition that liability may arise when the third party must rely on a bean counter's report. The distinction was that in Glanzer, a bean counter had affirmatively assumed a duty of care to the specified third party for a specific purpose, to wit, give accurate weight of a quantity of beans, which was not specifically a contractual obligation, and, hence, privity did not strictly apply. Those factors are not present in the case before us. These different traditional approaches to third-party liability were joined and analyzed in the Court of Appeals' landmark Credit Alliance ruling. Credit Alliance Corp. v Andersen & Co., (65 N.Y.2d 536, 493 N.Y.S.2d 435, 483 N.E.2d 110), did not overturn the common-law rule, but only expanded it modestly, reflecting the modern ubiquity of financial statements, to allow for the liability of an accountant who provides advice to a third party with whom the accountant is not in privity, but with whom a close relationship nevertheless exists. At most, Credit Alliance resolved the tension, if any, between these two lines of Cardozo jurisprudence.

Credit Alliance sets forth three criteria for establishing the liability of accountants on the basis of advice or services to clients when non-contracting third parties claim injury as a consequence of that advice: the accountants must have been aware that the financial reports were to be used for a particular purpose or purposes, upon which a known party or parties were intended to rely, and there must have been some conduct on the part of the accountants linking them to that party's or parties' reliance. These "indicia, while distinct, are interrelated and collectively require a third party claiming harm to demonstrate a relationship or bond with the once-removed accountants" Hence, although there is some conceptual overlap among the showings necessary to establish these requirements, the Court of Appeals has nevertheless set forth three discrete criteria. Evidentiary proof, in admissible form, must be offered in support of all three criteria in order to warrant trial. As with a three-legged table, remove one prop, and the entire structure must fall. So, too,

here, where I conclude that the inadequacy of the linkage between the accountants and plaintiff is fatal to plaintiff's theory of liability.

The Court of Appeals' policy-based expansion of an accountant's common-law liability to a third party, with whom the accountant has no contractual or direct relationship, turns in part on whether that plaintiff can establish the correlates of a contractual or direct relationship. This expansion, though it "permits some flexibility in the application of the doctrine of privity to accountants' liability," as noted above, does not represent a departure from traditional modes of analyzing such privity-based liability Rather, the analytical model is whether there is a "relationship sufficiently approaching privity" between plaintiff and the accountants

In the case before us, there is no indication that plaintiff ever met or even communicated with the accountants, or that the accountants were even aware that plaintiff owned company stock, or that the stock would be re-purchased by the employer-client at a value fixed by the accountants. There were no written or verbal communications between plaintiff and the accountants on the subject matter of the stock values prior to the report being issued. At best, the accountants acted pursuant to an ongoing engagement with their client - the employer - to simply appraise the stock twice yearly for employee stock ownership plan purposes generally, and this is an insufficient basis upon which to ground a relationship approaching privity with this plaintiff.

Plaintiff concededly never read nor even received the accountants' report, and none had been provided to him. The accountants did not prepare the June 1996 report with any regard to plaintiff's termination. Nor did the accountants have a copy, or even knowledge of, any stock purchase agreement between plaintiff and the company. In sum, the accountants' discharge of their routine responsibilities was completely unrelated to Pasadena's purchase of plaintiff's stock under the stock purchase agreement.

Accordingly, the order of Supreme Court, New York County entered January 13, 1999, denying defendant's motion for summary judgment dismissing the complaint, and for costs and attorneys fees, should be modified, on the law, to the extent of granting the motion to dismiss the complaint and otherwise affirmed, without costs.

JUATASSA SIMS v. KENNETH S. APFEL, COMMISSIONER OF SOCIAL
SECURITY

120 S. Ct. 2080; 147 L. Ed. 2d 80 (2000)

SUPREME COURT OF THE UNITED STATES

THOMAS , JUSTICE

In 1994, petitioner Juatassa Sims filed applications for disability benefits under Title II of the Social Security Act, and for supplemental security income benefits under Title XVI of that Act. She alleged disability from a variety of ailments, including degenerative joint diseases and carpal tunnel syndrome. After a state agency denied her claims, she obtained a hearing before a Social Security ALJ. The ALJ, in 1996, also denied her claims, concluding that, although she did have some medical impairments, she had not been and was not under a "disability," as defined in the Act.

Petitioner then requested that the Social Security Appeals Council review her claims. A claimant may request such review by completing a one-page form provided by the Social Security Administration (SSA) -- Form HA-520 -- or "by any other writing specifically requesting review." Petitioner, through counsel, chose the latter option, submitting to the Council a letter arguing that the ALJ had erred in several ways in analyzing the evidence. The Council denied review.

Next, petitioner filed suit in the District Court for the Northern District of Mississippi. She contended that (1) the ALJ had made selective use of the record; (2) the questions the ALJ had posed to a vocational expert to determine petitioner's ability to work were defective because they omitted several of petitioner's ailments; and (3) in light of certain peculiarities in the medical evidence, the ALJ should have ordered a consultative examination. The District Court rejected all of these contentions.

The Social Security Act provides that "any individual, after any final decision of the Commissioner of Social Security made after a hearing to which he was a party, . . . may obtain a review of such decision by a civil action" in federal district court. But the Act does not define "final decision," instead leaving it to the SSA to give meaning to that term through regulations. SSA regulations provide that, if the Appeals Council grants review of a claim, then the decision that the Council issues is the Commissioner's final decision. But if, as here, the Council denies the request for review, the ALJ's

opinion becomes the final decision. If a claimant fails to request review from the Council, there is no final decision and, as a result, no judicial review in most cases. In administrative-law parlance, such a claimant may not obtain judicial review because he has failed to exhaust administrative remedies.

The Commissioner rightly concedes that petitioner exhausted administrative remedies by requesting review by the Council. Petitioner thus obtained a final decision, and nothing in § 405(g) or the regulations implementing it bars judicial review of her claims.

Nevertheless, the Commissioner contends that we should require issue exhaustion in addition to exhaustion of remedies. That is, he contends that a Social Security claimant, to obtain judicial review of an issue, not only must obtain a final decision on his claim for benefits, but also must specify that issue in his request for review by the Council. The Commissioner argues, in particular, that an issue-exhaustion requirement is "an important corollary" of any requirement of exhaustion of remedies. We think that this is not necessarily so and that the corollary is particularly unwarranted in this case.

Initially, we note that requirements of administrative issue exhaustion are largely creatures of statute. Here, the Commissioner does not contend that any statute requires issue exhaustion in the request for review.

Similarly, it is common for an agency's regulations to require issue exhaustion Yet, SSA regulations do not require issue exhaustion. (Although the question is not before us, we think it likely that the Commissioner could adopt a regulation that did require issue exhaustion.)

It is true that we have imposed an issue-exhaustion requirement even in the absence of a statute or regulation. But the reason we have done so does not apply here. The basis for a judicially imposed issue-exhaustion requirement is an analogy to the rule that appellate courts will not consider arguments not raised before trial courts.

[C]ourts require administrative issue exhaustion "as a general rule" because it is usually "appropriate under [an agency's] practice" for "contestants in an adversary proceeding" before it to develop fully all issues there. Where, by contrast, an administrative proceeding is not adversarial, we think the reasons for a court to require issue exhaustion are much weaker. More generally, we have observed that it is well settled that there are wide differences between administrative agencies and courts.

The differences between courts and agencies are nowhere more pronounced than in Social Security proceedings. Although many agency systems of adjudication are based to a significant extent on the judicial model of decisionmaking, Social Security proceedings are inquisitorial rather than adversarial. It is the ALJ's duty to investigate the facts and develop the arguments both for and against granting benefits, and the Council's review is similarly broad. The Commissioner has no representative before the ALJ to oppose the claim for benefits, and we have found no indication that he opposes claimants before the Council.

Accordingly, we hold that a judicially created issue-exhaustion requirement is inappropriate. Claimants who exhaust administrative remedies need not also exhaust issues in a request for review by the Appeals Council in order to preserve judicial review of those issues. The judgment of the Fifth Circuit is reversed, and the case is remanded for further proceedings consistent with this opinion.

TIME WARNER ENTERTAINMENT CO., L.P. v. UNITED
STATES OF AMERICA

211 F.3d 1313 (2000)

UNITED STATES COURT OF APPEALS FOR THE DISTRICT OF COLUMBIA
CIRCUIT

GINSBURG, CIRCUIT JUDGE:

The Time Warner Entertainment Company and the United States appeal from portions of the judgment in Daniels Cablevision, Inc. v. United States, 835 F. Supp. 1 (D.D.C. 1993). At issue is the facial constitutionality of two provisions of the Cable Television Consumer Protection and Competition Act of 1992 (1992 Cable Act). The "subscriber limits provision" directs the Federal Communications Commission to limit the number of subscribers a cable operator may reach. The "channel occupancy provision" directs the Commission to limit the number of channels on a cable system that may be devoted to video programming in which the operator has a financial interest.

Time Warner argues that the subscriber limits provision is a content-based restriction of its ability to communicate with its audience, and as such is subject to strict scrutiny. The Government denies that the subscriber limits provision is content-based, and argues for an intermediate level of scrutiny.

In order to determine the applicable standard of review, then, we must decide whether the subscriber limits provision is content-based. In general, the principal inquiry in determining content neutrality ... is whether the government has adopted a regulation of speech because of [agreement or] disagreement with the message it conveys. A law that singles out speech based upon the ideas or views expressed is content-based, whereas a law that "confers benefits or imposes burdens on speech without reference to the ideas or views expressed" is most likely content-neutral.

As a cable operator, Time Warner exercises editorial discretion in selecting the programming it will make available to its subscribers. Time Warner argues that the congress limited its ability to speak by restricting the number of subscribers--and therefore potential viewers--it may reach with the programming it has selected. That this limitation is content-based, according to Time Warner, is evident from the Senate Report that accompanied the final version of the 1992 Cable Act.

That Report indicated the Congress was concerned about increasing concentration of ownership and control in the cable industry:

... First, there are special concerns about concentration of the media in the hands of a few who may control the dissemination of information. The concern is that the media gatekeepers will (1) slant information according to their own biases, or (2) provide no outlet for unorthodox or unpopular speech because it does not sell well, or both....
.... The second concern about horizontal concentration is that it can be the basis of anticompetitive acts. For example, a market that is dominated by one buyer of a product, a monopsonist, does not give the seller any of the benefits of competition....

Time Warner contends that the Congress's concern that media gatekeepers would "slant" information or fail to provide outlets for "unorthodox" speech reflects a preference for one type of content and an intent to suppress another, namely, the speech of cable operators. The Company likens the Congress's efforts to limit its speech to the restraints the Supreme Court held unconstitutional in Buckley v. Valeo, 424 U.S. 1, 46 L. Ed. 2d 659, 96 S. Ct. 612 (1976), and First National Bank of Boston v. Bellotti, 435 U.S. 765, 55 L. Ed. 2d 707, 98 S. Ct. 1407 (1978). Buckley involved a federal campaign finance law aimed at "equalizing the relative ability of individuals and groups to influence the outcome of elections" by limiting their political expenditures. The Court rejected "the concept that government may restrict the speech of some elements of our society in order to enhance the relative voice of others [as] wholly foreign to the First Amendment." Bellotti similarly involved a state statute that prohibited certain types of businesses from making contributions or expenditures for the purpose of influencing particular ballot initiatives. The Court reiterated the point it had made in Buckley: A state's effort to control some voices in order to "enhance the relative voices" of less influential speakers "contradicts basic tenets of First Amendment jurisprudence."

The expenditure limit at issue in Buckley, like the prohibition at issue in Bellotti, was content-based because it "was concerned with the communicative impact of the regulated speech." Turner I, 512 U.S. at 658. As the Supreme Court made quite clear in Turner I, however, making way for some speakers, in the cable context where that necessarily means limiting the speech of others, is not inherently content-based. There the Court determined that the "mustcarry" provision of the 1992 Cable Act, which required cable operators to "carry the signals of a specified number of local broadcast television stations,", was not contentbased, and applied intermediate scrutiny in its review of that provision. Although the must-carry obligation restricted cable operators' speech by limiting the number of channels they could program at will, it did so in a content-neutral fashion and for a content-neutral reason, namely, to protect the interests of non-cable subscribers in maintaining the viability of the television broadcasting industry.

According to Time Warner, the subscriber limits provision expresses a hostility to the content of large cable operators' speech that did not underlie the must-carry obligation: The subscriber limits are meant to restrict large cable operators from presenting information in accord with their own "biases," in order thereby to promote a diversity of views in cable programming. Increasing the diversity of programming is not, Time Warner argues, among the ends the Supreme Court deemed content-neutral in Turner I.

Time Warner is correct that the Court's acceptance of the must-carry obligation as content-neutral rested in large part upon the Court's understanding that the purpose of the statute was to maintain the availability of broadcast television for those without cable; that does not render Turner I wholly inapplicable, however. The Court also identified the "bottleneck monopoly power" of the cable operator, arising out of the operator's "control over most (if not all) of the television programming that is channeled into the subscriber's home," as the threat to broadcast television. In enacting the subscriber limits, the Congress was concerned that cable operators might use that same bottleneck power to exclude other providers of cable programming. As with the must-carry obligation, its concern was not with what a cable operator might say, but that it might not let others say anything at all in the principal medium for reaching much of the public. ("The First Amendment's command that government not impede the freedom of speech does not disable the government from taking steps to ensure that private interests not restrict, through physical control of a critical pathway of communication, the free flow of information and ideas"). The must-carry obligation and the subscriber limits provision both preserve for consumers some competition in the provision of programming. The must-carry obligation preserves competition between broadcasters and the cable operator, while the subscriber limits preserve competition between the cable operator and its affiliated programmers on the one hand and unaffiliated providers of cable programming on the other. By placing a value upon diversity and competition in cable programming the Congress did not necessarily also value one speaker, or one type of speech, over another; it merely expressed its intention that there continue to be multiple speakers.

Finally, Time Warner argues that the subscriber limits provision improperly singles out for regulation the cable medium, as opposed to other video programmers such as Direct Broadcast Satellite (DBS) operators. Here it refers us to Turner I, where the Court observed, "Regulations that discriminate among media, or among different speakers within a single medium, often present serious First Amendment concerns." According to Time Warner, with the subscriber limits the Congress "targeted a small number of [the various] speakers" capable of purchasing and providing video programming, without providing any justification for limiting the regulation to the cable medium.

In Turner I, however, the Court rejected Turner Broadcasting's claim of discrimination, stating that "it would be error to conclude ... that the First Amendment mandates strict scrutiny for any speech regulation that applies to one medium (or a subset thereof) but not others." Indeed, the same unique characteristic of the cable medium that justified the imposition of the must-carry obligation is also invoked by the Government to justify the subscriber limits, namely, "the bottleneck monopoly power exercised by cable operators." In Turner I this bottleneck power was seen to jeopardize the viability of broadcast television; in this case, it arguably threatens diversity and competition in the provision of cable programming. As the Government notes, other video programmers such as DBS lack the bottleneck power of cable operators; nor do they reach nearly as many households as does cable.

In sum, upon examination of the statute, the Senate Report that accompanied it, and the Supreme Court's analysis of the must-carry provision at issue in Turner I, we conclude that the subscriber limits provision is not content-based. In order to determine whether it is constitutional, therefore, we apply intermediate, rather than strict scrutiny.

The channel occupancy provision requires the Commission to establish limits upon "the number of channels on a cable system that can be occupied by a video programmer in which a cable operator has an attributable interest." Time Warner likens this provision to "a law prohibiting newspapers from devoting more than a fraction of their columns to editorial content of their own." That this restriction is content-based, it argues, is evident from the Senate Report:

Vertical integration in the cable industry .... gives cable operators the incentive and ability to favor their affiliated programming services. For example, the cable operator might give its affiliated programmer a more desirable channel position than another programmer, or even refuse to carry other programmers.

[The channel occupancy provision] is designed to increase the diversity of voices available to the public. Some [MSOs] own many programming services. It would be unreasonable for them to occupy a large percentage of channels on a cable system.

The intent of this provision is to place reasonable limits on the number of channels that can be occupied by each MSO's programming services.

Time Warner argues that because the Congress expressed concern that cable operators might favor their affiliated programming services the legislature's "stated design was to suppress cable operators' speech," and to advance the speech of nonaffiliated programmers. Again analogizing itself to a newspaper publisher, Time Warner argues that a cable operator has a constitutional right to favor its own speech. By interfering with that right in order to alter the mix of programming available on cable, the Congress has impermissibly regulated the content of cable operators' speech.

A cable operator is unlike a newspaper publisher, however, in the one respect crucial to the Congress's reason for enacting the channel occupancy provision: A newspaper publisher does not have the ability to exclude competing publications from its subscribers' homes. The cable operator's bottleneck monopoly is a physical and economic barrier to such intra-medium competition. The channel occupancy provision responds in kind, without regard to the content of either the cable operator's speech or that of the unaffiliated programmer for which it secures an outlet. See TurnerI.

Nor does the Congress's wanting to ensure a multiplicity of voices on cable inherently bespeak a preference for or a bias against the content of any speech. That is why, in Time Warner, we upheld under intermediate scrutiny the "leased access provision" of the 1992 Cable Act. That provision requires cable operators to set aside a percentage of their channels for commercial use by unaffiliated programmers in order both to bring "the widest possible diversity of information sources" to cable subscribers and "to promote competition in the delivery of diverse sources of video programming."

Time Warner now argues that whereas the objective of the leased access provision was to promote speech from various sources without regard to content, the channel occupancy provision is meant to limit speech

from a particular type of source and therefore necessarily imposes a content-based restriction. Here it refers us to the statement in the Senate Report that cable operators may have "the incentive and ability to favor" their own or an affiliate's speech. In response, the Government explains, and we agree, that the legislative concern was not with the speech of a particular source but solely with promoting diversity and competition in the cable industry. Like the leased access provision, that is, the focus of the channel occupancy provision is upon the source of speech, not its content. the qualification of nonaffiliates to lease time on a cable operator's channels depends not on the content of their speech, but on their lack of affiliation with the operator, a distinguishing characteristic stemming from considerations relating to the structure of cable television.

We recognize, of course, the possibility that a seemingly neutral limitation may have been crafted in such a way as to single out for regulation the speech of some group that the legislature finds objectionable. There is not a shred of evidence, however, that such an illicit consideration underlies the channel occupancy provision, and indeed Time Warner stops well short of claiming otherwise. We are therefore confident that the channel occupancy provision is content-neutral and subject only to intermediate scrutiny.

Finally, Time Warner argues that the channel occupancy provision is unnecessary in light of the anti-discrimination provision of the 1992 Cable Act as well as the antitrust laws. As we noted earlier, however, a prophylactic, structural limitation is not rendered unnecessary merely because preexisting statutes impose behavioral norms and ex post remedies.

For the foregoing reasons, we conclude that the subscriber limits and channel occupancy provisions do not run afoul of the first amendment. The judgment of the district court is reversed insofar as it held that the subscriber limits provision is unconstitutional, and affirmed insofar as it held that the channel occupancy provision is constitutional.

FRIENDS OF THE EARTH, INCORPORATED, ET AL. v. LAIDLAW
ENVIRONMENTAL SERVICES (TOC), INC.

120 S. Ct. 693; 145 L. Ed. 2d 610 (2000)

SUPREME COURT OF THE UNITED STATES

GINSBURG, JUSTICE

In 1972, Congress enacted the Clean Water Act (Act), also known as the Federal Water Pollution Control Act. Section 402 of the Act provides for the issuance, by the Administrator of the Environmental Protection Agency (EPA) or by authorized States, of National Pollutant Discharge Elimination System (NPDES) permits. NPDES permits impose limitations on the discharge of pollutants, and establish related monitoring and reporting requirements, in order to improve the cleanliness and safety of the Nation's waters. Noncompliance with a permit constitutes a violation of the Act. § 1342(h).

Under § 505(a) of the Act, a suit to enforce any limitation in an NPDES permit may be brought by any "citizen," defined as "a person or persons having an interest which is or may be adversely affected." Sixty days before initiating a citizen suit, however, the would-be plaintiff must give notice of the alleged violation to the EPA, the State in which the alleged violation occurred, and the alleged violator. The purpose of notice to the alleged violator is to give it an opportunity to bring itself into complete compliance with the Act and thus . . . render unnecessary a citizen suit. Accordingly, we have held that citizens lack statutory standing under § 505(a) to sue for violations that have ceased by the time the complaint is filed.

In 1986, defendant-respondent Laidlaw Environmental Services (TOC), Inc., bought a hazardous waste incinerator facility in Roebuck, South Carolina, that included a wastewater treatment plant. (The company has since changed its name to Safety-Kleen (Roebuck), Inc., but for simplicity we will refer to it as "Laidlaw" throughout.) Shortly after Laidlaw acquired the facility, the South Carolina Department of Health and Environmental Control (DHEC) granted Laidlaw an NPDES permit authorizing the company to discharge treated water into the North Tyger River. The permit, which became effective on January 1, 1987, placed limits on Laidlaw's discharge of several pollutants into the river, including -- of particular relevance to this case -- mercury, an extremely toxic pollutant. The permit also regulated the flow, temperature, toxicity, and pH of the effluent from the facility, and imposed monitoring and reporting obligations.

Once it received its permit, Laidlaw began to discharge various pollutants into the waterway; repeatedly, Laidlaw's discharges exceeded the limits set by the permit. In particular, despite experimenting with several technological fixes, Laidlaw consistently failed to meet the permit's stringent 1.3 ppb (parts per billion) daily average limit on mercury discharges. The District Court later found that Laidlaw had violated the mercury limits on 489 occasions between 1987 and 1995

On April 10, 1992, plaintiff-petitioners Friends of the Earth (FOE) and Citizens Local Environmental Action Network, Inc. (CLEAN) (referred to collectively in this opinion, together with later joined plaintiff-petitioner Sierra Club, as "FOE") took the preliminary step necessary to the institution of litigation. They sent a letter to Laidlaw notifying the company of their intention to file a citizen suit against it under § 505(a) of the Act after the expiration of the requisite 60-day notice period, i.e., on or after June 10, 1992. Laidlaw's lawyer then contacted DHEC to ask whether DHEC would consider filing a lawsuit against Laidlaw. The District Court later found that Laidlaw's reason for requesting that DHEC file a lawsuit against it was to bar FOE's proposed citizen suit. DHEC agreed to file a lawsuit against Laidlaw; the company's lawyer then drafted the complaint for DHEC and paid the filing fee. On June 9, 1992, the last day before FOE's 60-day notice period expired, DHEC and Laidlaw reached a settlement requiring Laidlaw to pay $100,000 in civil penalties and to make "'every effort'" to comply with its permit obligations

On June 12, 1992, FOE filed this citizen suit against Laidlaw under § 505(a) of the Act, alleging noncompliance with the NPDES permit and seeking declaratory and injunctive relief and an award of civil penalties. Laidlaw moved for summary judgment on the ground that FOE had failed to present evidence demonstrating injury in fact, and therefore lacked Article III standing to bring the lawsuit.

Laidlaw also moved to dismiss the action on the ground that the citizen suit was barred by DHEC's prior action against the company. The United States, appearing as amicus curiae, joined FOE in opposing the motion. After an extensive analysis of the Laidlaw-DHEC settlement and the circumstances under which it was reached, the District Court held that DHEC's action against Laidlaw had not been "diligently prosecuted"; consequently, the court allowed FOE's citizen suit to proceed. The record indicates that after FOE initiated the suit, but before the District Court rendered judgment, Laidlaw violated the mercury discharge limitation in its permit 13 times. The District Court also found that Laidlaw had committed 13 monitoring and 10 reporting violations during this period. The last recorded mercury discharge violation occurred in January 1995, long after the complaint was filed but about two years before judgment was rendered.

The District Court noted that "Laidlaw drafted the state-court complaint and settlement agreement, filed the lawsuit against itself, and paid the filing fee." Further, "the settlement agreement between DHEC and Laidlaw was entered into with unusual haste, without giving the Plaintiffs the opportunity to intervene." The court found "most persuasive" the fact that "in imposing the civil penalty of $100,000 against Laidlaw, DHEC failed to recover, or even to calculate, the economic benefit that Laidlaw received by not complying with its permit.

On January 22, 1997, the District Court issued its judgment. It found that Laidlaw had gained a total economic benefit of $1,092,581 as a result of its extended period of noncompliance with the mercury discharge limit in its permit. The court concluded, however, that a civil penalty of $405,800 was adequate in light of the guiding factors listed in 33 U.S.C. § 1319(d). . In particular, the District Court stated that the lesser penalty was appropriate taking into account the judgment's "total deterrent effect." In reaching this determination, the court "considered that Laidlaw will be required to reimburse plaintiffs for a significant amount of legal fees." The court declined to grant FOE's request for injunctive relief, stating that an injunction was inappropriate because "Laidlaw has been in substantial compliance with all parameters in its NPDES permit since at least August 1992."

According to Laidlaw, after the Court of Appeals issued its decision but before this Court granted certiorari, the entire incinerator facility in Roebuck was permanently closed, dismantled, and put up for sale, and all discharges from the facility permanently ceased.

Laidlaw contends first that FOE lacked standing from the outset even to seek injunctive relief, because the plaintiff organizations failed to show that any of their members had sustained or faced the threat of any "injury in fact" from Laidlaw's activities. In support of this contention Laidlaw points to the District Court's finding, made in the course of setting the penalty amount, that there had been "no demonstrated proof of harm to the environment" from Laidlaw's mercury discharge violations.

The relevant showing for purposes of Article III standing, however, is not injury to the environment but injury to the plaintiff. To insist upon the former rather than the latter as part of the standing inquiry is to raise the standing hurdle higher than the necessary showing for success on the merits in an action alleging noncompliance with an NPDES permit. Focusing properly on injury to the plaintiff, the District Court found that FOE had demonstrated sufficient injury to establish standing. For example, FOE member Kenneth Lee Curtis averred in affidavits that he lived a half-mile from Laidlaw's facility; that he occasionally drove over the North Tyger River, and that it looked and smelled polluted; and that he would like to fish, camp, swim, and picnic in and near the river between 3 and 15 miles downstream from the facility, as he did when he was a teenager, but would not do so because he was concerned that the water was polluted by Laidlaw's discharges. Curtis reaffirmed these statements in extensive deposition testimony. For example, he testified that he would like to fish in the river at a specific spot he used as a boy, but that he would not do so now because of his concerns about

Other members presented evidence to similar effect. CLEAN member Angela Patterson attested that she lived two miles from the facility; that before Laidlaw operated the facility, she picnicked, walked, birdwatched, and waded in and along the North Tyger River because of the natural beauty of the area; that she no longer engaged in these activities in or near the river because she was concerned about harmful effects from discharged pollutants; and that she and her husband would like to purchase a home near the river but did not intend to do so, in part because of Laidlaw's discharges. CLEAN member Judy Pruitt averred that she lived one-quarter mile from Laidlaw's facility and would like to fish, hike, and picnic along the North Tyger River, but has refrained from those activities because of the discharges. FOE member Linda Moore attested that she lived 20 miles from Roebuck, and would use the North Tyger River south of Roebuck and the land surrounding it for recreational purposes were she not concerned that the water contained harmful pollutants. In her deposition, Moore testified at length that she would hike, picnic, camp, swim, boat, and drive near or in the river were it not for her concerns about illegal discharges. CLEAN member Gail Lee attested that her home, which is near Laidlaw's facility, had a lower value than similar homes located further from the facility, and that she believed the pollutant discharges accounted for some of the discrepancy. Sierra Club member Norman Sharp averred that he had canoed approximately 40 miles downstream of the Laidlaw facility and would like to canoe in the North Tyger River closer to Laidlaw's discharge point, but did not do so because he was concerned that the water contained harmful pollutants.

These sworn statements, as the District Court determined, adequately documented injury in fact. We have held that environmental plaintiffs adequately allege injury in fact when they aver that they use the affected area and are persons "for whom the aesthetic and recreational values of the area will be lessened" by the challenged activity.

In contrast, the affidavits and testimony presented by FOE in this case assert that Laidlaw's discharges, and the affiant members' reasonable concerns about the effects of those discharges, directly affected those affiants' recreational, aesthetic, and economic interests. Unlike the dissent, we see nothing "improbable" about the proposition that a company's continuous and pervasive illegal discharges of pollutants into a river would cause nearby residents to curtail their recreational use of that waterway and would subject them to other economic and aesthetic harms. The proposition is entirely reasonable, the District Court found it was true in this case, and that is enough for injury in fact.

For the reasons stated, the judgment of the United States Court of Appeals for the Fourth Circuit is reversed, and the case is remanded for further proceedings consistent with this opinion.

UNITED STATES OF AMERICA v. MICROSOFT
CORPORATION, et al

97 F. Supp. 2d 59 (2000)

UNITED STATES DISTRICT COURT FOR THE DISTRICT OF COLUMBIA

JACKSON, DISTRICT JUDGE.

These cases are before the Court for disposition of the sole matter presently remaining for decision by the trial court, namely, entry of appropriate relief for the violations of the Sherman Act, §§ 1 and 2, and various state laws committed by the defendant Microsoft Corporation as found by Court in accordance with its Findings of Fact and Conclusions of Law. Final judgment will be entered contemporaneously herewith. No further proceedings will be required.

The Court has been presented by plaintiffs with a proposed form of final judgment that would mandate both conduct modification and structural reorganization by the defendant when fully implemented. Microsoft has responded with a motion for summary rejection of structural reorganization and a request for months of additional time to oppose the relief sought in all other respects. Microsoft claims, in effect, to have been surprised by the "draconian" and "unprecedented" remedy the plaintiffs recommend. What it proposes is yet another round of discovery, to be followed by a second trial - in essence an ex post and de facto bifurcation of the case already considered and rejected by the Court.

Microsoft's profession of surprise is not credible. From the inception of this case Microsoft knew, from well-established Supreme Court precedents dating from the beginning of the last century, that a mandated divestiture was a possibility, if not a probability, in the event of an adverse result at trial. At the conclusion of the trial the Court's Findings of Fact gave clear warning to Microsoft that the result would likely be adverse, yet the Court delayed entry of its Conclusions of Law for five months, and enlisted the services of a distinguished mediator, to assist Microsoft and the plaintiffs in reaching agreement on a remedy of some description that Microsoft knew was inevitable. Even assuming that Microsoft negotiated in utmost good faith in the course of mediation, it had to have in contemplation the prospect that, were mediation to fail, the prevailing plaintiffs would propose to the Court a remedy most to their liking and least likely to be acceptable to Microsoft. Its failure to anticipate and to prepare to meet such an eventuality gives no reason to afford it an opportunity to do so now.

Despite their surprise, compounded no doubt by the Court's refusal on May 24th to allow discovery and take testimony on the issue, Microsoft's attorneys were promptly able to tender a 35-page "Offer of Proof," summarizing in detail the testimony 16 witnesses would give to explain why plaintiffs' proposed remedy, in its entirety, is a bad idea. Within a week they added seven more.

These cases have been before the Court, and have occupied much of its attention, for the past two years, not counting the antecedent proceedings. Following a full trial Microsoft has been found guilty of antitrust violations, notwithstanding its protests to this day that it has committed none. The Court is convinced for several reasons that a final - and appealable - judgment should be entered quickly. It has also reluctantly come to the conclusion, for the same reasons, that a structural remedy has become imperative: Microsoft as it is presently organized and led is unwilling to accept the notion that it broke the law or accede to an order amending its conduct.

First, despite the Court's Findings of Fact and Conclusions of Law, Microsoft does not yet concede that any of its business practices violated the Sherman Act. Microsoft officials have recently been quoted publicly to the effect that the company has "done nothing wrong" and that it will be vindicated on appeal. The Court is well aware that there is a substantial body of public opinion, some of it rational, that holds to a similar view. It is time to put that assertion to the test. If true, then an appellate tribunal should be given early opportunity to confirm it as promptly as possible, and to abort any remedial measures before they have become irreversible as a practical matter.

Second, there is credible evidence in the record to suggest that Microsoft, convinced of its innocence, continues to do business as it has in the past, and may yet do to other markets what it has already done in the PC operating system and browser markets. Microsoft has shown no disposition to voluntarily alter its business protocol in any significant respect. Indeed, it has announced its intention to appeal even the imposition of the modest conduct remedies it has itself proposed as an alternative to the non-structural remedies sought by the plaintiffs.

Third, Microsoft has proved untrustworthy in the past. In earlier proceedings in which a preliminary injunction was entered, Microsoft's purported compliance with that injunction while it was on appeal was illusory and its explanation disingenuous. If it responds in similar fashion to an injunctive remedy in this case, the earlier the need for enforcement measures becomes apparent the more effective they are likely to be.

Finally, the Court believes that extended proceedings on the form a remedy should take are unlikely to give any significantly greater assurance that it will be able to identify what might be generally regarded as an optimum remedy. As has been the case with regard to Microsoft's culpability, opinion as to an appropriate remedy is sharply divided. There is little chance that those divergent opinions will be reconciled by anything short of actual experience. The declarations (and the "offers of proof") from numerous potential witnesses now before the Court provide some insight as to how its various provisions might operate, but for the most part they are merely the predictions of purportedly knowledgeable people as to effects which may or may not ensue if the proposed final judgment is entered. In its experience the Court has found testimonial predictions of future events generally less reliable even than testimony as to historical fact, and cross-examination to be of little use in enhancing or detracting from their accuracy.

In addition to its substantive objections, the proposed final judgment is also criticized by Microsoft as being vague and ambiguous. Plaintiffs respond that, to the extent it may be lacking in detail, it is purposely so to allow Microsoft itself to propose such detail as will be least disruptive of its business, failing which plaintiffs will ask the Court to supply it as the need appears.

Plaintiffs won the case, and for that reason alone have some entitlement to a remedy of their choice. Moreover, plaintiffs' proposed final judgment is the collective work product of senior antitrust law enforcement officials of the United States Department of Justice and the Attorneys General of 19 states, in conjunction with multiple consultants. These officials are by reason of office obliged and expected to consider - and to act in - the public interest; Microsoft is not. The proposed final judgment is represented to the Court as incorporating provisions employed successfully in the past, and it appears to the Court to address all the principal objectives of relief in such cases, namely, to terminate the unlawful conduct, to prevent its repetition in the future, and to revive competition in the relevant markets. Microsoft's alternative decree is plainly inadequate in all three respects.

Two states dissented from the imposition of structural remedies but fully supported the remainder of the relief proposed. The absence of total unanimity merely confirms the collaborative character of the process by which the proposed final judgment was formulated.

The final judgment proposed by plaintiffs is perhaps more radical than might have resulted had mediation been successful and terminated in a consent decree. It is less so than that advocated by four disinterested amici curiae. It is designed, moreover, to take force in stages, so that the effects can be gauged while the appeal progresses and before it has been fully implemented. And, of course, the Court will retain jurisdiction following appeal, and can modify the judgment as necessary in accordance with instructions from an appellate court or to accommodate conditions changed with the passage of time.

It is, therefore, this 7th day of June, 2000,

ORDERED, that the motion of defendant Microsoft Corporation for summary rejection of the plaintiffs' proposed structural reorganization is denied; and it is

FURTHER ORDERED, that defendant Microsoft Corporation's "position" as to future proceedings on the issue of remedy is rejected; and it is

FURTHER ORDERED, that plaintiffs' proposed final judgment, as revised in accordance with the proceedings of May 24, 2000 and Microsoft's comments thereon, be entered as a Final Judgment herein.

EBAY, INC. vs. BIDDER'S EDGE, INC.

2000 U.S. Dist. LEXIS 7287 (2000)

UNITED STATES DISTRICT COURT FOR THE NORTHERN DISTRICT OF
CALIFORNIA

WHYTE, JUDGE

eBay is an Internet-based, person-to-person trading site. eBay offers sellers the ability to list items for sale and prospective buyers the ability to search those listings and bid on items. The seller can set the terms and conditions of the auction. The item is sold to the highest bidder.

Users of the eBay site must register and agree to the eBay User Agreement. Users agree to the seven page User Agreement by clicking on an "I Accept" button located at the end of the User Agreement. The current version of the User Agreement prohibits the use of "any robot, spider, other automatic device, or manual process to monitor or copy our web pages or the content contained herein without our prior expressed written permission." It is not clear that the version of the User Agreement in effect at the time BE began searching the eBay site prohibited such activity, or that BE ever agreed to comply with the User Agreement.

eBay currently has over 7 million registered users. Over 400,000 new items are added to the site every day. Every minute, 600 bids are placed on almost 3 million items. Users currently perform, on average, 10 million searches per day on eBay's database. Bidding for and sales of items are continuously ongoing in millions of separate auctions.

A software robot is a computer program which operates across the Internet to perform searching, copying and retrieving functions on the web sites of others. A software robot is capable of executing thousands of instructions per minute, far in excess of what a human can accomplish. Robots consume the processing and storage resources of a system, making that portion of the system's capacity unavailable to the system owner or other users. Consumption of sufficient system resources will slow the processing of the overall system and can overload the system such that it will malfunction or "crash." A severe malfunction can cause a loss of data and an interruption in services.

BE is a company with 22 employees that was founded in 1997. The BE web site debuted in November 1998. BE does not host auctions. BE is an auction aggregation site designed to offer on-line auction buyers the ability to search for items across numerous on-line auctions without having to search each host site individually. As of March 2000, the BE web site contained information on more that five million items being auctioned on more than one hundred auction sites. BE also provides its users with additional auction-related services and information. The information available on the BE site is contained in a database of information that BE compiles through access to various auction sites such as eBay. When a user enters a search for a particular item at BE, BE searches its database and generates a list of every item in the database responsive to the search, organized by auction closing date and time. Rather than going to each host auction site one at a time, a user who goes to BE may conduct a single search to obtain information about that item on every auction site tracked by BE. It is important to include information regarding eBay auctions on the BE site because eBay is by far the biggest consumer to consumer on-line auction site.

On June 16, 1997, over a year before the BE web site debuted, Peter Leeds wrote an email in response to an email from Kimbo Mundy, co-founder of BE. Mundy's email said, "I think the magazines may be overrating sites' ability to block. The early agent experiments, like Arthur Anderson's BargainFinder were careful to check the robots.txt file on every site and desist if asked." (underline in original). Mundy wrote back: "I believe well-behaved robots are still expected to check the robots.txt file.... Our other concern was also legal. It is one thing for customers to use a tool to check a site and quite another for a single commercial enterprise to do so on a repeated basis and then to distribute that information for profit."

It is unclear who Peter Leeds is, except that his email address at the time was <peter£biddersedge.com>.>ENDFN>

In early 1998, eBay gave BE permission to include information regarding eBay-hosted auctions for Beanie Babies and Furbies in the BE database. In early 1999, BE added to the number of person-to-person auction sites it covered and started covering a broader range of items hosted by those sites, including eBay. On April 24, 1999, eBay verbally approved BE crawling the eBay web site for a period of 90 days. The parties contemplated that during this period they would reach a formal licensing agreement. They were unable to do so.

In late August or early September 1999, eBay requested by telephone that BE cease posting eBay auction listings on its site. BE agreed to do so. In October 1999, BE learned that other auction aggregations sites were including information regarding eBay auctions. On November 2, 1999, BE issued a press release indicating that it had resumed including eBay auction listings on its site. On November 9, 1999, eBay sent BE a letter reasserting that BE's activities were unauthorized, insisting that BE cease accessing the eBay site, alleging that BE's activities constituted a civil trespass and offering to license BE's activities. eBay and BE were again unable to agree on licensing terms. As a result, eBay attempted to block BE from accessing the eBay site; by the end of November, 1999, eBay had blocked a total of 169 IP addresses it believed BE was using to query eBay's system. BE elected to continue crawling eBay's site by using proxy servers to evade eBay's IP blocks. ("We eventually adopted the rotating proxy servers.")

The parties agree that BE accessed the eBay site approximate 100,000 times a day. eBay alleges that BE activity constituted up to 1.53% of the number of requests received by eBay, and up to 1.10% of the total data transferred by eBay during certain periods in October and November of 1999. BE alleges that BE activity constituted no more than 1.11% of the requests received by eBay, and no more than 0.70% of the data transferred by eBay. eBay alleges that BE activity had fallen 27%, to 0.74% of requests and 0.61% of data, by February 20, 2000. eBay alleges damages due to BE's activity totaling between $45,323 and $61,804 for a ten month period including seven months in 1999 and the first three months in 2000. However, these calculations appear flawed in that they assume the maximal BE usage of eBay resources continued over all ten months. Moreover, the calculations attribute a pro rata share of eBay expenditures to BE activity, rather than attempting to calculate the incremental cost to eBay due to BE activity. eBay has not alleged any specific incremental damages due to BE activity

eBay now moves for preliminary injunctive relief preventing BE from accessing the eBay computer system based on nine causes of action: trespass, false advertising, federal and state trademark dilution, computer fraud and abuse, unfair competition, misappropriation, interference with prospective economic advantage and unjust enrichment. However, eBay does not move, either independently or alternatively, for injunctive relief that is limited to restricting how BE can use data taken from the eBay site.

eBay asserts that it will suffer four types of irreparable harm if preliminary injunctive relief is not granted: (1) lost capacity of its computer systems resulting from to BE's use of automated agents; (2) damage to eBay's reputation and goodwill caused by BE's misleading postings; (3) dilution of the eBay mark; and (4) BE's unjust enrichment. The harm eBay alleges it will suffer can be divided into two categories. The first type of harm is harm that eBay alleges it will suffer as a result of BE's automated query programs burdening eBay's computer system ("system harm"). The second type of harm is harm that eBay alleges it will suffer as a result of BE's misrepresentations regarding the information that BE obtains through the use of these automated query programs ("reputational harm").

As noted above, eBay does not seek an injunction that is tailored to independently address the manner in which BE uses the information it obtains from eBay. Even without accessing eBay's computer systems by robot, BE could inflict reputational harm by misrepresenting the contents of eBay's auction database or by misusing eBay's trademark. Moreover, allowing frequent and complete recursive searching of eBay's database (which would presumably exacerbate the system harm), requiring appropriate disclaimers regarding the accuracy of BE's listings, or limiting BE's use of the eBay mark would all reduce or eliminate the possibility of reputational harm, without requiring the drastic remedy of enjoining BE from accessing eBay's database. n9 Since eBay does not move independently or alternatively for injunctive relief tailored toward the alleged reputational harm, the court does not include the alleged reputational harm in the balance of harm analysis, nor does the court address the merits of the causes of action based on the alleged reputational harm in the likelihood of success analysis.

According to eBay, the load on its servers resulting from BE's web crawlers represents between 1.11% and 1.53% of the total load on eBay's listing servers. eBay alleges both economic loss from BE's current activities and potential harm resulting from the total crawling of BE and others. In alleging economic harm, eBay's argument is that eBay has expended considerable time, effort and money to create its computer system, and that BE should have to pay for the portion of eBay's system BE uses. eBay attributes a pro rata portion of the costs of maintaining its entire system to the BE activity. However, eBay does not indicate that these expenses are incrementally incurred because of BE's activities, nor that any particular service disruption can be attributed to BE's activities. eBay provides no support for the proposition that the pro rata costs of obtaining an item represent the appropriate measure of damages for unauthorized use. In contrast, California law appears settled that the appropriate measure of damages is the actual harm inflicted by the conduct:

Where the conduct complained of does not amount to a substantial interference with possession or the right thereto, but consists of intermeddling with or use of or damages to the personal property, the owner has a cause of action for trespass or case, and may recover only the actual damages suffered by reason of the impairment of the property or the loss of its use.

Moreover, even if BE is inflicting incremental maintenance costs on eBay, potentially calculable monetary damages are not generally a proper foundation for a preliminary injunction. Nor does eBay appear to have made the required showing that this is the type of extraordinary case in which monetary damages may support equitable relief.

eBay's allegations of harm are based, in part, on the argument that BE's activities should be thought of as equivalent to sending in an army of 100,000 robots a day to check the prices in a competitor's store. This analogy, while graphic, appears inappropriate. Although an admittedly formalistic distinction, unauthorized robot intruders into a "brick and mortar" store would be committing a trespass to real property. There does not appear to be any doubt that the appropriate remedy for an ongoing trespass to business premises would be a preliminary injunction. More importantly, for the analogy to be accurate, the robots would have to make up less than two out of every one-hundred customers in the store, the robots would not interfere with the customers' shopping experience, nor would the robots even be seen by the customers. Under such circumstances, there is a legitimate claim that the robots would not pose any threat of irreparable harm. However, eBay's right to injunctive relief is also based upon a much stronger argument.

If BE's activity is allowed to continue unchecked, it would encourage other auction aggregators to engage in similar recursive searching of the eBay system such that eBay would suffer irreparable harm from reduced system performance, system unavailability, or data losses. BE does not appear to seriously contest that reduced system performance, system unavailability or data loss would inflict irreparable harm on eBay consisting of lost profits and lost customer goodwill. Harm resulting from lost profits and lost customer goodwill is irreparable because it is neither easily calculable, nor easily compensable and is therefore an appropriate basis for injunctive relief. Where, as here, the denial of preliminary injunctive relief would encourage an increase in the complained of activity, and such an increase would present a strong likelihood of irreparable harm, the plaintiff has at least established a possibility of irreparable harm.

"If 30 or 40 companies spring into existence using similar business models, what will be the total load and impact on eBay's servers?"

"One crawler may currently use 1% of eBay's resources. What if hundred of users used similar crawlers?"

"Given that Bidder's Edge can be seen to have imposed a load of 1.53 % on eBay's listing servers, simple arithmetic and economies reveal how only a few more such companies deploying rude robots [that do not respect the Robot Exclusion Standard] would

be required before eBay would be brought to its knees by what would be then a debilitating load."

As discussed below, eBay has a established a strong likelihood of success on the merits of the trespass claim, and is therefore entitled to preliminary injunctive relief because it has established the possibility of irreparable harm. Accordingly, the court does not reach the issue of whether the threat of increased activity would be sufficient to support preliminary injunctive relief where the plaintiff has not made as strong of a showing of likelihood of success on the merits.

BE correctly observes that there is a dearth of authority supporting a preliminary injunction based on an ongoing to trespass to chattels. In contrast, it is black letter law in California that an injunction is an appropriate remedy for a continuing trespass to real property. If eBay were a brick and mortar auction house with limited seating capacity, eBay would appear to be entitled to reserve those seats for potential bidders, to refuse entrance to individuals (or robots) with no intention of bidding on any of the items, and to seek preliminary injunctive relief against non-customer trespassers eBay was physically unable to exclude. The analytic difficulty is that a wrongdoer can commit an ongoing trespass of a computer system that is more akin to the traditional notion of a trespass to real property, than the traditional notion of a trespass to chattels, because even though it is ongoing, it will probably never amount to a conversion. The court concludes that under the circumstances present here, BE's ongoing violation of eBay's fundamental property right to exclude others from its computer system potentially causes sufficient irreparable harm to support a preliminary injunction.

Accordingly, the court concludes that eBay has demonstrated at least a possibility of suffering irreparable system harm and that BE has not established a balance of hardships weighing in its favor.

As noted above, eBay moves for a preliminary injunction on all nine of its causes of action. These nine causes of action correspond to eight legal theories: (1) trespass to chattels, (2) false advertising under the Lanham Act, (3) federal and state trademark dilution, (4) violation of the Computer Fraud and Abuse Act, (5) unfair competition, (6) misappropriation, (7) interference with prospective economic advantage and (8) unjust enrichment. The court finds that eBay has established a sufficient likelihood of prevailing on the trespass claim to support the requested injunctive relief. Since the court finds eBay is entitled to the relief requested based on its trespass claim, the court does not address the merits of the remaining claims or BE's arguments that many of these other state law causes of action are preempted by federal copyright law. The court first addresses the merits of the trespass claim, then BE's arguments regarding copyright preemption of the trespass claim, and finally the public interest.

I. Trespass

Trespass to chattels "lies where an intentional interference with the possession of personal property has proximately cause injury." Trespass to chattels "although seldom employed as a tort theory in California" was recently applied to cover the unauthorized use of long distance telephone lines. Specifically, the court noted "the electronic signals generated by the [defendants'] activities were sufficiently tangible to support a trespass cause of action." Thus, it appears likely that the electronic signals sent by BE to retrieve information from eBay's computer system are also sufficiently tangible to support a trespass cause of action.

In order to prevail on a claim for trespass based on accessing a computer system, the plaintiff must establish: (1) defendant intentionally and without authorization interfered with plaintiff's possessory interest in the computer system; and (2) defendant's unauthorized use proximately resulted in damage to plaintiff. Here, eBay has presented evidence sufficient to establish a strong likelihood of proving both prongs and ultimately prevailing on the merits of its trespass claim.

a. BE's Unauthorized Interference

eBay argues that BE's use was unauthorized and intentional. eBay is correct. BE does not dispute that it employed an automated computer program to connect with and search eBay's electronic database. BE admits that, because other auction aggregators were including eBay's auctions in their listing, it continued to "crawl" eBay's web site even after eBay demanded BE terminate such activity.

BE argues that it cannot trespass eBay's web site because the site is publicly accessible. BE's argument is unconvincing. eBay's servers are private property, conditional access to which eBay grants the public. eBay does not generally permit the type of automated access made by BE. In fact, eBay explicitly notifies automated visitors that their access is not permitted.

Even if BE's web crawlers were authorized to make individual queries of eBay's system, BE's web crawlers exceeded the scope of any such consent when they began acting like robots by making repeated queries

Although the court admits some uncertainty as to the precise level of possessory interference required to constitute an intermeddling, there does not appear to be any dispute that eBay can show that BE's conduct amounts to use of eBay's computer systems. Accordingly, eBay has made a strong showing that it is likely to prevail on the merits of its assertion that BE's use of eBay's computer system was an unauthorized and intentional interference with eBay's possessory interest.

b. Damage to eBay's Computer System

A trespasser is liable when the trespass diminishes the condition, quality or value of personal property. The quality or value of personal property may be diminished even though it is not physically damaged by defendant's conduct.

eBay is likely to be able to demonstrate that BE's activities have diminished the quality or value of eBay's computer systems. BE's activities consume at least a portion of plaintiff's bandwidth and server capacity. Although there is some dispute as to the percentage of queries on eBay's site for which BE is responsible, BE admits that it sends some 80,000 to 100,000 requests to plaintiff's computer systems per day. Although eBay does not claim that this consumption has led to any physical damage to eBay's computer system, nor does eBay provide any evidence to support the claim that it may have lost revenues or customers based on this use, eBay's claim is that BE's use is appropriating eBay's personal property by using valuable bandwidth and capacity, and necessarily compromising eBay's ability to use that capacity for its own purposes.

BE argues that its searches represent a negligible load on plaintiff's computer systems, and do not rise to the level of impairment to the condition or value of eBay's computer system required to constitute a trespass. However, it is undisputed that eBay's server and its capacity are personal property, and that BE's searches use a portion of this property. Even if, as BE argues, its searches use only a small amount of eBay's computer system capacity, BE has nonetheless deprived eBay of the ability to use that portion of its personal property for its own purposes. The law recognizes no such right to use another's personal property. Accordingly, BE's actions appear to have caused injury to eBay and appear likely to continue to cause injury to eBay.

Bidder's Edge, its officers, agents, servants, employees, attorneys and those in active concert or participation with them who receive actual notice of this order by personal service or otherwise, are hereby enjoined pending the trial of this matter, from using any automated query program, robot, web crawler or other similar device, without written authorization, to access eBay's computer systems or networks, for the purpose of copying any part of eBay's auction database. As a condition of the preliminary injunction, eBay is ordered to post a bond in the amount of $2,000,000 to secure payment of any damages sustained by defendant if it is later found to have been wrongfully enjoined. This order shall take effect 10 days from the date on which it is filed.

Nothing in this order precludes BE from utilizing information obtained from eBay's site other than by automated query program, robot, web crawler or similar device.

VILLAGE OF WILLOWBROOK, ET AL v. GRACE OLECH

120 S. Ct. 1073; 145 L. Ed. 2d 1060 (2000)

SUPREME COURT OF THE UNITED STATES

OPINION: PER CURIAM.

Respondent Grace Olech and her late husband Thaddeus asked petitioner Village of Willowbrook to connect their property to the municipal water supply. The Village at first conditioned the connection on the Olechs granting the Village a 33-foot easement. The Olechs objected, claiming that the Village only required a 15-foot easement from other property owners seeking access to the water supply. After a 3-month delay, the Village relented and agreed to provide water service with only a 15-foot easement.

Olech sued the Village claiming that the Village's demand of an additional 18-foot easement violated the Equal Protection Clause of the Fourteenth Amendment. Olech asserted that the 33-foot easement demand was "irrational and wholly arbitrary"; that the Village's demand was actually motivated by ill will resulting from the Olechs' previous filing of an unrelated, successful lawsuit against the Village; and that the Village acted either with the intent to deprive Olech of her rights or in reckless disregard of her rights.

The District Court dismissed the lawsuit pursuant to Federal Rule of Civil Procedure 12(b)(6) for failure to state a cognizable claim under the Equal Protection Clause. Relying on Circuit precedent, the Court of Appeals for the Seventh Circuit reversed, holding that a plaintiff can allege an equal protection violation by asserting that state action was motivated solely by a 'spiteful effort to "get" him for reasons wholly unrelated to any legitimate state objective. It determined that Olech's complaint sufficiently alleged such a claim. We granted certiorari to determine whether the Equal Protection Clause gives rise to a cause of action on behalf of a "class of one" where the plaintiff did not allege membership in a class or group. *

We note that the complaint in this case could be read to allege a class of five. In addition to Grace and Thaddeus Olech, their neighbors Rodney and Phyllis Zimmer and Howard Brinkman requested to be connected to the municipal water supply, and the Village initially demanded the 33-foot easement from all of them. The Zimmers and Mr. Brinkman were also involved in the previous, successful lawsuit against the Village, which allegedly created the ill will motivating the excessive easement demand. Whether the complaint alleges a class of one or of five is of no consequence because we conclude that the number of individuals in a class is immaterial for equal protection analysis.

Our cases have recognized successful equal protection claims brought by a "class of one," where the plaintiff alleges that she has been intentionally treated differently from others similarly situated and that there is no rational basis for the difference in treatment. In so doing, we have explained that "'the purpose of the equal protection clause of the Fourteenth Amendment is to secure every person within the State's jurisdiction against intentional and arbitrary discrimination, whether occasioned by express terms of a statute or by its improper execution through duly constituted agents.'"

That reasoning is applicable to this case. Olech's complaint can fairly be construed as alleging that the Village intentionally demanded a 33-foot easement as a condition of connecting her property to the municipal water supply where the Village required only a 15-foot easement from other similarly situated property owners. The complaint also alleged that the Village's demand was "irrational and wholly arbitrary" and that the Village ultimately connected her property after receiving a clearly adequate 15-foot easement. These allegations, quite apart from the Village's subjective motivation, are sufficient to state a claim for relief under traditional equal protection analysis. We therefore affirm the judgment of the Court of Appeals, but do not reach the alternative theory of "subjective ill will" relied on by that court.

JOSEPH BENIK, ET. AL. V. BRANDON HATCHER, A MINOR, ET AL.

358 Md. 507; 750 A.2d 10 (2000)

COURT OF APPEALS OF MARYLAND

BELL, CHIEF JUSTICE

The genesis of this case was a complaint that alleged that five year-old Brandon Hatcher, the respondent, suffered lead poisoning while living in apartment # 310 in an apartment building located at 1411 Division Street, owned by Joseph Benik, the petitioner. Brandon and his family moved into the apartment in January 1990 and in December 1990, an inspection of the apartment revealed that lead paint was present in several areas throughout the apartment. After the discovery of the lead paint, the family moved to another apartment in the same building.

Brandon's mother received Section 8 assistance to subsidize her rental payments while she and her family lived at 1411 Division Street. Thus, consistent with Section 8 procedures, on January 2, 1990, prior to the family moving into the apartment, an inspection of the unit was conducted by a Section 8 housing inspector. That inspector testified at trial that the apartment passed the Section 8 inspection, which included inspecting each room in the unit for the presence of chipping or flaking paint. Confirming the inspector's testimony the petitioner testified that he had painted the apartment several weeks before the inspection. He also testified that Mrs. Hatcher was in the apartment and inspected it herself before entering into the lease. Further, the petitioner stated that, several months earlier, when she rented another apartment in the same building, Mrs. Hatcher signed a statement that she had received a booklet regarding the hazards of lead-based paint.

> Section 8 is a federal program whereby the United States Department of Housing and Urban Development subsidizes a tenant's rental of housing by paying the landlord the difference between what the tenant has been determined to be able to pay and the fair rental value of the premises.

The testimony of both the Section 8 inspector and the petitioner was contradicted by the testimony of Chakeda Hatcher, Brandon's sister. Twelve years old when the Hatcher's moved into the unit, Chakeda stated that the apartment was not freshly painted when the family moved in. She described chipping paint on the wall, ceiling, around the door frame, and the windowsills. She also stated that she saw chipping paint in the bathroom and in two bedrooms. Chakeda further testified that she witnessed Brandon with a chalky substance around his hands and mouth after he had been playing near holes located at the baseboard of the apartment. She specifically stated that the holes were present when they moved into the apartment. Finally, Chakeda testified that the petitioner was in the apartment before the lease began, talking to her mother.

Chakeda's testimony was corroborated by Brandon's aunt, Eileen Hatcher, who testified that she resided in apartment # 214 the entire time her sister and nephew lived in apartment # 310. Ms. Eileen Hatcher testified that she visited her sister within the first month of her moving into apartment # 310 and observed, at that time, that the unit was not freshly painted. She further stated that, on different occasions, when she visited the apartment, the paint on the windowsill of the middle room and kitchen was peeling and flaking.

On October 17, 1990, Brandon was diagnosed with lead poisoning, having been found to have an elevated blood lead level. At that point, the family moved out of their apartment and into another unit. Brandon's blood lead level began to decline once the family moved out of apartment # 310.

Suit was filed in the Circuit Court for Baltimore City against the petitioner. At the end of the case, the trial court gave the following instruction as to the Consumer Protection Act:

"Plaintiff has made a claim under the Maryland Consumer Protection Act. In order to recover damages under this act, the Plaintiff must prove more likely than not the following: One, that at the beginning of the lease of Apartment 310, there was chipping and flaking lead-based paint; and two that Mr. Benik was aware of the chipping and flaking lead-based paint, and also aware that its condition may constitute an unreasonable risk of harm to the tenants. And three, that despite the above, the Defendant, Mr. Benik failed to disclose the hazardous condition to Linda Hatcher at the beginning of the lease. And Four, that Brandon Hatcher was injured as a direct, proximate result of the alleged hazardous condition that existed at the time of the lease; that is chipping or flaking lead based paint. If any of the above elements are missing, the claim hereunder should be decided in favor of the defendant."

The respondent excepted to this instruction, asking the court to give his proposed instruction instead. The respondent's proposed instruction did not require the jury to find scienter on the part of the petitioner, that the petitioner be aware that the chipping and flaking paint was lead-based paint or that the condition was an unreasonable risk to the respondent.

The petitioner's primary argument is that, where the landlord does not have actual knowledge or reason to know of the condition, the CPA does not impose strict liability on a landlord in lead-based paint cases for failing to inform tenants at the inception of the lease that the premises contain chipping or flaking lead-based paint. [H]e contends that "a required element of any claim for personal injury under the CPA based on an alleged omission is scienter, or that the landlord know, or have reason to know, of the alleged hazard or condition." That is consistent, he maintains, with the common law requirement that a landlord have notice of a defect and the opportunity to correct it before being held liable.

The petitioner argues, alternatively, that any error that the trial court may have committed in instructing the jury with respect to scienter was harmless. Pointing out that the jury found for the petitioner on the negligence count, he submits that, necessarily having weighed the evidence in deciding that count, "the jury could not have found for defendant on the negligence claim without deciding that the paint was in good condition at the inception of the lease."

The instruction in this case required that, in order for the landlord to be liable for breach of warranty under the CPA for the tenant's injuries, there must have existed in the apartment at the inception of the lease, chipping and flaking lead-based paint, of which the landlord was aware and did not inform the tenant, even though he was aware that the condition may constitute an unreasonable risk of harm to the tenant, and that the chipping and flaking lead-based paint was the proximate cause of the tenant's injuries. The correctness of that instruction - the determination whether it sets forth the applicable law - requires analysis of sections of the Baltimore City Code, the CPA and our cases elucidating those enactments.

The purpose of the Baltimore City Housing Code is to:

"establish and maintain basic requirements, standards and conditions essential for the protection of the health, safety, morals and general welfare of the public ... in the City of Baltimore; to establish minimum standards governing the condition, use, operation, occupancy and maintenance of dwellings...in order to make the dwelling safe, sanitary and fit for human habitation"

After examining the foregoing provisions of the Baltimore City Code this Court concluded:

"It is clear that it is unlawful to lease a dwelling with flaking, loose or peeling paint and that no premises are to be leased for human habitation, except those that are fit for human habitation, i.e., those that are kept in good repair and safe condition as defined in the Baltimore City Code. To be sure, § 706 prohibits the use of lead-based paint for interior painting in a dwelling unit; however, neither it nor §§ 702 or 703 limits the prohibition of flaking, loose or peeling paint to lead-based paint. To be a violation, all that must be shown is that there was flaking, loose or peeling paint, without any further showing as to the content of the paint. Moreover, none of the provisions of the Housing Code premises violation on the landlord's knowledge of the hazards of lead-based paint."

It is the correctness of the jury instruction given in connection with this aspect of the case and the proper application of the CPA that are at issue.

As we have seen, a landlord leasing or agreeing to rent a dwelling intended for human habitation is deemed to covenant and warrant that it is fit for human habitation. Thus, the provisions of the City Code, i.e., §§ 702, 703, and 706, setting minimum standards and thereby giving meaning to the implied warranty, rather than §§ 301 and 303, the notice provisions, are the ones that are relevant. To prove a violation of the CPA premised on the breach of the implied warranty of habitability, it must be shown that, at the inception of the lease, the landlord made material misstatements or omissions, which either had the tendency to or, in fact, did, mislead the tenant. Thus, the landlord must have knowledge, constructive or actual, of the condition of the premises at the time of the lease.

The implied warranty provisions establish a threshold for the lease of premises and that threshold is based on the purpose of the Baltimore City Housing Code, to "make dwellings safe, sanitary and fit for human habitation," for the benefit of "the health and safety of the people." These provisions, like the Code of which it is a part, are applications of the police power of the City of Baltimore. They are examples of public health and safety regulations. The City has a vital interest and public purpose in ensuring the habitability of its housing stock and in the health and safety of its people.

Ordinarily in the case of police regulations, violation gives rise to penalty, irrespective of the motive or knowledge of the violating party, "for the law, in those cases, seems to bind the party to know the facts, and to obey the law at his peril." That is not the case here, however. The City Code provides, as we have seen, for notice and prescribes a time in which any violation may be corrected. Nevertheless, ignorance of the law is no defense. It will not relieve one who commits a wrongful act from the legal consequences of that act. Indeed, everyone is "presumed to know the law regardless of conscious knowledge or lack thereof, and are presumed to intend the necessary and legitimate consequences of their actions in its light."

Here, sections 702, 703 and 706 of the City Code prescribe the standard for the lease of premises for human habitability and § 9-14.1 deems every lease of premises for that purpose to contain a warrant of their fitness for that purpose. In his pre-lease communications with the respondent's mother, the petitioner did not disclose that there was chipping and flaking paint, as the respondent's evidence showed, and may have, impliedly or expressly, represented the opposite. He argues, however, that he neither had actual knowledge of the chipping or flaking paint or reason to know of the condition.

As the owner of the premises and the landlord, on whom the law imposes specific duties and obligations in connection with the lease of the premises, including implying a representation as to the premises' condition at the time of the lease, the law imputes the requisite knowledge to the petitioner.

It is not disputed that the petitioner never informed the respondent of the presence of chipping and flaking paint on the premises at the time the premises were let, maintaining to the contrary, that no such condition existed at that time. Nevertheless, although disputed - there being testimony that the apartment was freshly painted, passed a Section 8 inspection and the respondent inspected the premises before renting it - there was evidence from which the jury could have found that there was chipping and flaking paint in the apartment at the inception of the lease. Which of the various factual scenarios to accept was for the jury to determine.

The rental of the apartment without disclosing the flaking, loose or peeling paint would violate § 13-301 (1) in that it would be a "misleading ... statement ... or other representation," having the capacity, tendency, or effect of deceiving or misleading the respondent. The implicit representation that the apartment "... [has] a sponsorship, approval ... [or] characteristic ... which [it does] not have," namely, it was in good repair and safe condition and, thus fit for human habitation, would violate § 13-301(2), because whether an apartment is in good repair and safe condition, which, as the Housing Code defines the terms, include being free of flaking, loose and peeling paint, is, to one looking for an apartment, a material fact. Moreover, the failure to disclose it could be found by a jury to deceive or to have the tendency to deceive. Accordingly, the jury could have found that the petitioner's failure to inform the respondent of the condition of the premises violated § 13-301 (3).

We have determined that the landlord who leases premises for human habitation is presumed to have knowledge of any defective condition that a reasonable inspection would have disclosed and, as previously indicated, the factual dispute that the former situation presents is a matter for the jury to determine after proper instructions.

Finally, the petitioner maintains that the jury necessarily found, by its verdict, that the apartment did not have flaking, loose and peeling paint at the inception of the lease, any error that the trial court may have committed instructing the jury was harmless. He reasons:

"the jury decided the negligence count in favor of Benik by weighing the evidence and finding that, at the beginning of the lease there was no flaking paint. There was substantial evidence, as shown by the testimony of housing inspector William Lohr, that there was no flaking paint. ... Mr. Benik and his assistant also testified that the paint was fresh and intact, when they were in the unit prior to commencement of the lease. ... moreover, Ms. Hatcher did not note any flaking paint on her pre-lease inspection. ... the Hatchers relied entirely on the testimony of twelve year old Chekeda Hatcher, sister of Brandon Hatcher, that she recalled flaking paint throughout the apartment at the beginning of the lease. ... In order to decide the negligence issue, the jury had to weigh this evidence, and must have decided that there was no flaking paint at the inception of the lease. Otherwise, the jury would have found for the plaintiff."

It is well settled that a civil judgment will not be reversed unless the complaining party shows both error and prejudice

We agree with the respondent. The jury was instructed that, to find a violation of the CPA, there must have been, at the beginning of the lease, "chipping and flaking lead-based paint" and that the petitioner "was aware of the chipping and flaking lead-based paint." As we have seen, what the Housing Code proscribes is "flaking, loose and peeling paint," not flaking, loose and peeling lead-based paint. Moreover, the jury was not asked specifically whether there was flaking, loose or peeling paint, lead-based or otherwise, and the special verdict sheet does not reflect any such finding. It is thus quite conceivable that the jury determined that there was flaking and chipped paint in the apartment at the inception of the lease, but that the petitioner was not aware that it was lead-based. As the respondent notes, the petitioner testified that he believed that if there was lead-based paint in the premises, it was covered up, encapsulated by new walls and sheet rock installed during renovation. From this, we can plausibly surmise, as the respondent contends, that "the jury simply found that the Defendant was not negligent (under the 'reason to know' standard of Richwind) and did not violate [*538] the CPA (under the flawed instructions given by the court below)."

JUDGMENT OF THE COURT OF SPECIAL
APPEALS AFFIRMED

IN THE MATTER OF THE RULES OF PROFESSIONAL CONDUCT AND
INSURER IMPOSED BILLING RULES AND PROCEDURES UGRIN,
ALEXANDER, ZADICK & HIGGINS, P.C., and JAMES, GRAY, BRONSON
& SWANBERG, P.C.

2000 MT 110; 57 Mont. St. Rep. 433 (2000)

SUPREME COURT OF MONTANA

LEAPHART, JUSTICE

In the present case, the parties do not dispute that insurers' billing and practice rules typically "impose conditions [upon an attorney appointed by an insurer to represent an insured] limiting or directing the scope and extent of the representation of his or her client." The Petitioners have focussed on the requirement of prior approval in insurers' billing and practice rules. We therefore address that condition of representation while recognizing that other conditions limiting or directing the scope and extent of representation of a client may also implicate the Rules of Professional Conduct.

As a representative set of litigation guidelines, we briefly consider the guidelines submitted by the St. Paul Companies (hereafter, St. Paul). The declared policy of St. Paul's Litigation Management Plan (hereafter, the Plan) is to "provide a systematic and appropriate defense for St. Paul and its insureds, and to vigorously defend nonmeritorious claims and claims where the demands are excessive."

St. Paul promotes a "team" approach to litigation in which each member has distinct responsibilities. The claim professional is "responsible for disposition of claims, whether in suit or not. We expect the St. Paul claim professional to take the lead in initiating settlement negotiations . . . . We also expect the claim professional to have significant input into development of the litigation strategy (i.e., settle or try)." The Plan also "recognizes that defense counsel's primary responsibility and obligation are to protect and further the interests of the insured in the conduct of the litigation. Our goal is to cooperate with the insured and defense counsel to achieve the best result possible."

However, the Plan states that "motion practice, discovery and research are items that have historically caused us some concern and which we plan to monitor closely. While we foresee very few differences of opinion, we require that defense counsel secure the consent of the claim professional prior to scheduling depositions, undertaking research, employing experts or preparing motions" (emphasis added).

Thus, the Plan expressly requires prior approval before a defense attorney may undertake to schedule depositions, conduct research, employ experts, or prepare motions. The Plan concludes that "we understand that any conflicts between the St. Paul Litigation Management Plan and the exercise of your independent judgment to protect the interests of the insured must be resolved in favor of the insured. We expect, however, to be given an opportunity to resolve any such conflicts with you before you take any action that is in substantial contravention of the Plan."

A. Whether Montana has recognized the dual representation doctrine under the Montana Rules of Professional Conduct.

Petitioners assert that the insured is the sole client of a defense attorney appointed by an insurer to represent an insured pursuant to an insurance policy (hereafter, defense counsel) and that a requirement of prior approval in insurance billing and practice rules impermissibly interferes with a defense counsel's exercise of his independent judgment and his duty of undivided loyalty to his client. Petitioners argue that because the relationship of insurer and insured is permeated with potential conflicts, they cannot be co-clients of defense counsel.

Respondents argue that under Montana law, the rule is that in the absence of a real conflict, the insurer and insured are dual clients of defense counsel. From this fundamental premise, Respondents argue that as a co-client of defense counsel, the insurer may require pre-approval of attorney activities to assure adequate consultation. Respondents argue further that defense counsel must abide by a client's decisions about the objectives of representation and that defense counsel are obliged to consult with a client about the means for the objectives of representation. Respondents also argue that under Montana law, an insurer is vicariously liable for the conduct of defense counsel and that an insurer's control of litigation justifies holding an insurer vicariously liable for the conduct of defense counsel.

We conclude that Respondents have misconstrued our past decisions. This Court has not held that under the Rules of Professional Conduct, an insurer and an insured are co-clients of defense counsel. The Montana decisions chiefly relied upon by Respondents are inapposite because each one concerns situations where the insurer had "absolute" control of the litigation. None of the Montana decisions cited by Respondents addresses whether an insurer is a co-client under the Rules of Professional Conduct.

The precise relationship is unimportant. The authorities agree that these provisions of the contract have the effect of placing absolute and exclusive control over the litigation in the insurance carrier, with "the correlative duty to exercise diligence, intelligence, good faith, honest and conscientious fidelity to the common interests of the parties."

We note that Respondents argue that insurance contracts effectively place absolute control of litigation with insurers. However, Respondents' claim of absolute control of litigation cannot be reconciled with their insistence that whenever a conflict may arise between their litigation guidelines and an attorney's ethical obligations, the attorney is to follow the ethical course of action. Respondents' assertion that defense counsel are not only free to but must follow their independent judgment is inconsistent with their claim that insurers have absolute control of litigation.

B. Whether insurers and insureds are co-clients under Montana's Rules of Professional Conduct.

We turn to the question whether an insurer is a client of defense counsel under the Rules of Professional Conduct. We note that some other courts have concluded that the insurer is not a client of defense counsel. Recognizing the general rule that an attorney will only be held liable for negligence to his client, the court determined that "the relationship between the insurer and the retained defense counsel [is] less than a client-attorney relationship." Bell, 475 N.W.2d The court further determined, however, that although the insurer is not a client of defense counsel, the defense counsel nevertheless "occupies a fiduciary relationship to the insured, as well as to the insurance company." Recognizing further that "the tripartite relationship between insured, insurer, and defense counsel contains rife possibility [sic] of conflict,", the court reasoned that "to hold that an attorney-client relationship exists between insurer and defense counsel could indeed work mischief, yet to hold that a mere commercial relationship exists would work obfuscation and injustice."

Respondents argue vigorously that the interests of an insurer and an insured usually coincide and that most litigation is settled within an insured's coverage limits.

These arguments gloss over the stark reality that the relationship between an insurer and insured is permeated with potential conflicts. Such occasions for conflict may exist at the outset of the representation or may be created by events that occur thereafter"). In cases where an insured's exposure exceeds his insurance coverage, where the insurer provides a defense subject to a reservation of rights, and where an insurer's obligation to indemnify its insured may be excused because of a policy defense, there are potential conflicts of interest.

We reject Respondents' implicit premise that the Rules of Professional Conduct need not apply when the interests of insurers and insureds coincide. The Rules of Professional Conduct have application in all cases involving attorneys and clients. Moreover, whether the interests of insurers and insureds coincide can best be determined with the perfect clarity of hindsight. Before the final resolution of any claim against an insured, there clearly exists the potential for conflicts of interest to arise. Further, we reject the suggestion that the contractual relationship between insurer and insured supersedes or waives defense counsels' obligations under the Rules of Professional Conduct. We decline to recognize a vast exception to the Rules of Professional Conduct that would sanction relationships colored with the appearance of impropriety in order to accommodate the asserted economic exigencies of the insurance market

We caution, however, that this holding should not be construed to mean that defense counsel have a "blank check" to escalate litigation costs nor that defense counsel need not ever consult with insurers. Nor, finally, should our holding be taken to signal that defense counsel cannot be held accountable for their work.

Respondents argue further, however, that even if an insurer is not a co-client of defense counsel, an insurer's control of litigation is necessary and appropriate. Respondents argue that the insurer must control the litigation in order to meet its duties to the insured to indemnify and to provide a defense. Further, Respondents argue that the insured has a good faith duty to cooperate with the insurer in defense of a claim that warrants an insurer's control of litigation, and that in any event insureds agree to insurers' control of litigation. Respondents also argue that insureds typically contract for a limited defense that does not protect their reputational interests and that they are not entitled to unlimited expenditures on their behalf. Further, Respondents assert that insurers and insureds have "aligned" interests in minimizing litigation costs and settlements.

None of these arguments is persuasive. Animating them is the deeply flawed premise that by contract insurers and insureds may dispense with the Rules of Professional Conduct.

Finally, Respondents argue that their billing and practice rules do not interfere with defense counsels' freedom of action. As previously discussed, they suggest that when an insurer denies approval for particular actions that defense counsel propose, nothing prevents defense counsel from exercising their independent judgment and doing the very thing for which the insurer has denied approval. We reject Respondents' underlying dubious premise that the threat of withholding payment does not interfere with the independent judgment of defense counsel. The very action taken by Petitioners in seeking declaratory relief in the present case is a blunt repudiation of that speculative premise. Further, if the threat of withholding payment were quite as toothless as Respondents suggest, we doubt that they would make such a threat, let alone that they would expressly incorporate it in their billing and practice rules.

C. Whether the requirement of prior approval violates the Rules of Professional Conduct.

Having concluded that the insured is the sole client of defense counsel, we turn to the fundamental issue whether the requirement of prior approval in billing and practice rules conflicts with defense counsels' duties under the Rules of Professional Conduct. The parties appear to agree that defense counsel may not abide by agreements limiting the scope of representation that interfere with their duties under the Rules of Professional Conduct.

We conclude that the requirement of prior approval fundamentally interferes with defense counsels' exercise of their independent judgment. Further, prior approval creates a substantial appearance of impropriety in its suggestion that it is insurers rather than defense counsel who control the day to day details of a defense.

Some of the usual characteristics incident to [the employer-employee] relationship cannot exist between the insurer and the attorney representing an insured. The employer cannot control the details of the attorney's performance, dictate the strategy or tactics employed, or limit the attorney's professional discretion with regard to the representation. Any policy, arrangement or device which effectively limits, by design or operation, the attorney's professional judgment on behalf of or loyalty to the client is prohibited by the Code, and, undoubtedly, would not be consistent with public policy.

A defense attorney, as an independent contractor, has discretion regarding the day-to-day details of conducting the defense, and is not subject to the client's control regarding those details. While the attorney may not act contrary to the client's wishes, the attorney "is in complete charge of the minutiae of court proceedings and can properly withdraw from the case, subject to the control of the court, if he is not permitted to act as he thinks best." Moreover, because the lawyer owes unqualified loyalty to the insured, the lawyer must at all times protect the interests of the insured if those interests would be compromised by the insurer's instructions.

We hold that defense counsel in Montana who submit to the requirement of prior approval violate their duties under the Rules of Professional Conduct to exercise their independent judgment and to give their undivided loyalty to insureds.

We emphasize that by its plain language, Rule 1.6, M.R.Prof.Conduct, extends to all communications between insureds and defense counsel and that this rule is therefore broader in both scope and protection than the attorney-client privilege and the work product doctrine.

We hold that disclosure by defense counsel of detailed descriptions of professional services to third-party auditors without first obtaining the contemporaneous fully informed consent of insureds violates client confidentiality under the Rules of Professional Conduct.

CHAPTER 53
TO ACCOMPANY
WILLS, TRUSTS, AND ESTATES

BIELAT, EXR v. BIELAT

87 Ohio St. 3d 350; 721 N.E.2d 28 (2000)

SUPREME COURT OF OHIO

COOK, JUDGE

In the "Adoption Agreement" that he signed to open this account, Chester named his sister, Stella, as the beneficiary of the account's balance upon his death. Shortly thereafter, Chester made a will containing a clause giving all of his property to his wife, Dorothy, upon his death.

In 1993, three years before Chester's death, the General Assembly codified Ohio's version of the Uniform Transfer-on-Death Security Registration Act ("Act"), R.C. 1709.01 et seq.,. The Act provides, inter alia, that "any transfer-on-death resulting from a registration in beneficiary form * * * is not testamentary." (Emphasis added.) Accordingly, the Act removes such transfers on death from the decedent's testamentary estate, and also from the purview of Ohio's Statute of Wills, which outlines the formalities that apply to testamentary dispositions. R.C. 1709.11(D) makes the entire Act applicable to registrations in beneficiary form made "prior to, on, or after the effective date of this section, by decedents dying prior to, on, or after that date."

Soon after Chester's death in 1996, Dorothy discovered that Chester had named Stella the beneficiary of his IRA. Dorothy filed a complaint in the Summit County Probate Court, seeking a declaratory judgment that she, not Stella, was entitled to the IRA proceeds. Dorothy's argument to the probate court consisted of four steps. First, Dorothy argued that Chester's IRA beneficiary clause constituted testamentary language when it designated Stella as the pay-on-death beneficiary of the account. Second, Dorothy argued that the beneficiary clause was, therefore, null and void, since the Adoption Agreement in which the clause appeared did not comply with the signature and attestation requirements of our Statute of Wills. Third, even though R.C. 1709.09(A), supra, defines beneficiary registrations such as this one as "not testamentary," Dorothy argued that the Act could not constitutionally apply retroactively to Chester's IRA beneficiary clause, which was signed a decade prior to the effective date of the Act. Finally, Dorothy averred that without the Act to validate the beneficiary clause in the IRA, the IRA account balance would be transferred not to Stella, but rather to Chester's probate estate, where it would pass to Dorothy under the terms of Chester's will.

After considering Dorothy's declaratory judgment action and Stella's motion to dismiss, the probate court concluded that the Act validated the non-testamentary transfer-on-death clause in Chester's IRA even though the beneficiary designation in the IRA was created before the effective date of the Act. Therefore, the probate court ordered the balance of the IRA to pass to Stella under the terms of the beneficiary clause that Mr. Bielat had signed in 1983.

Dorothy appealed this judgment to the Ninth District Court of Appeals. She argued that the application of the Act to the pay-on-death beneficiary registration that Chester executed prior to the Act's effective date constituted a retroactive application of the law in violation of the Ohio Constitution. The court of appeals affirmed the probate court's decision in favor of Stella. The court held that although the Act was being applied in this case to a transfer-on-death beneficiary clause executed before the Act's effective date, the Act did not impair a vested right belonging to Dorothy, and thus did not violate the Ohio Constitution's prohibition against retroactive laws.

Section 28, Article II of the Ohio Constitution prohibits the General Assembly from passing retroactive laws and protects vested rights from new legislative encroachments. The retroactivity clause nullifies those new laws that "reach back and create new burdens, new duties, new obligations, or new liabilities not existing at the time the statute becomes effective]."

This court has articulated the procedure that a court should follow to determine when a law is unconstitutionally retroactive. We emphasize the phrase "unconstitutionally retroactive" to confirm that retroactivity itself is not always forbidden by Ohio law. Though the language of Section 28, Article II of the Ohio Constitution provides that the General Assembly "shall have no power to pass retroactive laws," Ohio courts have long recognized that there is a crucial distinction between statutes that merely apply retroactively (or "retrospectively") and those that do so in a manner that offends our Constitution. We also note that the words "retroactive" and "retrospective" have been used interchangeably in the constitutional analysis for more than a century. Both terms describe a law that is "made to affect acts or facts occurring, or rights accruing, before it came into

The test for unconstitutional retroactivity requires the court first to determine whether the General Assembly expressly intended the statute to apply retroactively. If so, the court moves on to the question of whether the statute is substantive, rendering it unconstitutionally retroactive, as opposed to merely remedial.

Because R.C. 1.48 establishes a presumption that statutes are prospective in operation, our inquiry into whether a statute may constitutionally be applied retrospectively continues only after a threshold finding that the General Assembly expressly intended the statute to apply retrospectively. In this case, by its own terms, R.C. Chapter 1709 applies to registrations of securities made "prior to, on, or after" the effective date of the Act. R.C. 1709.11(D). When R.C. 1709.09(A) and 1709.11(D) are read togethertherefore, the Act declares [***9] that transfers on death resulting from those registrations in beneficiary form described therein are always nontestamentary, even if such registrations were made before the statute's effective date. The Act became effective on October 1, 1993, and Chester designated Stella as his IRA beneficiary a decade earlier, in 1983. The General Assembly expressly intended for the Act to reach back in time and apply to Chester's 1983 designation of Stella as his IRA beneficiary.

The second critical inquiry of the constitutional analysis is to determine whether the retroactive statute is remedial or substantive. A purely remedial statute does not violate Section 28, Article II of the Ohio Constitution, even when it is applied retroactively. On the other hand, a retroactive statute is substantive--and therefore unconstitutionally retroactive--if it impairs vested rights, affects an accrued substantive right, or imposes new or additional burdens, duties, obligations, or liabilities as to a past transaction. In Part A, below, we conclude that R.C. 1709.09(A) [***10] and 1709.11(D) constitute remedial, curative statutes that merely provide a framework by which parties to certain investment accounts can more readily enforce their intent to designate a pay-on-death beneficiary. In Part B, we support our conclusion that the relevant sections of the Act are remedial by demonstrating that because the statutes do not impair vested rights, impose new duties, or create new obligations, they cannot be construed as substantive provisions for purposes of the constitutional prohibition against retroactive laws.

A

In our view, R.C. 1709.09(A) and 1709.11(D) constitute remedial provisions that merely affect "the methods and procedure by which rights are recognized, protected and enforced, not * * * the rights themselves." (Emphasis added.) Our conclusion is supported by cases that have defined remedial laws as those that "merely substitute a new or more appropriate remedy for the enforcement of an existing right." is remedial, and therefore permissibly retroactive, when the legislation seeks only to avoid "the necessity for multiplicity of suits and the accumulation of costs [or to] promote the interests of all parties."

Consistent with the tests for remedial legislation the relevant provisions of R.C. Chapter 1709 remedially recognize, protect, and enforce the contractual rights of parties to certain securities investment accounts to designate a pay-on-death beneficiary. Before the Act, Ohio courts did not consistently recognize and enforce similar rights.

R.C. 1709.09(A) and 1709.11(D) remedially changed Ohio law, therefore, by resolving a conflict between the relatively informal beneficiary designation found in an IRA and the more rigid formalities required by the Statute of Wills for testamentary dispositions. By avoiding this conflict, the Act promotes the interests of the parties to the securities accounts by validating the beneficiary designation as originally agreed. The statutes do not directly affect the rights of the parties to the securities accounts; rather, they simply protect what the parties intended to be non-probate investments. Realizing that many pay-on-death beneficiary registrations were made prior to 1993, the General Assembly made the Act retroactive to recognize, protect, and enforce even those beneficiary registrations executed before then

B

Our conclusion that R.C. 1709.09(A) and 1709.11(D) are remedial is supported by the fact that the Act patently lacks the characteristics of unconstitutionally substantive legislation.

Ohio courts have consistently held, however, that in order for a retroactive law to unconstitutionally impair a right, not just any asserted "right" will suffice.

Dorothy cannot claim a vested right to the proceeds of the IRA under the law of contracts, for she was in no way connected to the IRA Adoption Agreement that Mr. Bielat executed with Merrill Lynch. Dorothy was not a party to the 1983 IRA Agreement, nor was she a third-party beneficiary or assignee of Stella's contingent rights as a designated beneficiary of the account balance. The Adoption Agreement signed by Mr. Bielat and Merrill Lynch placed valid contractual obligations upon them, with Merrill Lynch bound to pay the IRA balance to the beneficiary that Chester designated. The IRA Adoption Agreement created no rights or obligations for Dorothy. Dorothy thus had no vested contractual right impaired by the retroactive application of the disputed statutes; she had no contractual rights to impair.

Likewise, at the time of the Act's effective date, Dorothy had no vested right to the IRA proceeds as the sole beneficiary under Chester's will. This court has held that "until a * * * will has been probated * * *, the legatee under such will has no rights whatever. A mere expectation of property in the future is not a vested right." If Dorothy had no vested rights in the contract that Mr. Bielat executed with Merrill Lynch, and no vested rights in Chester's probate estate until his death, then the Act did not impair any vested rights of hers when it applied retrospectively to validate the pay-on-death beneficiary clause in Chester's preexisting contract with Merrill Lynch.

First, we conclude that the relevant statutory provisions did not retrospectively "create a new right." Dorothy contends that by reaching back in time to change pre-1993 law regarding securities accounts, and by removing pre-1993 beneficiary registrations from the requirements of the Statute of Wills, the Act retroactively conferred a power or "right" on Chester that he could not have exercised in its absence. Though we agree that the Act retroactively removed a potential legal obstacle to the enforcement of Mr. Bielat's contract with Merrill Lynch, and promoted the interests of the parties to that contract, we do not agree that this constitutes the "creation of a right" for purposes of the retroactivity analysis.

As we stated previously, the constitutional test for substantive legislation focuses on new laws that reach back in time and create new burdens, deprivations, or impairments of vested rights.

The test for retroactive substantive laws should focus, then, as it has historically, on the impairment or deprivation of rights, the creation of new obligations, or the attachment of new disabilities

The United States Constitution's prohibition of retroactive laws is contained exclusively in the Ex Post Facto Clause, Clause 3, Section 9, Article I, which pertains only to penal statutes. The Constitution grants Congress the authority to make and change the laws, which extends to the enactment of retroactive legislation. Therefore, in the civil context, a claim of unconstitutional retroactivity under the United States Constitution implicates the Due Process Clause of the Fifth Amendment, which prohibits state action depriving someone of a life, liberty, or property interest without a rational basis for doing so.

For the foregoing reasons, we hold that R.C. 1709.09(A) and 1709.11(D) of Ohio's Transfer-on-Death Security Registration Act, as applied to the pay-on-death beneficiary designation in an Individual Retirement Account created prior to the Act's effective date, do not violate the prohibition [**40] against retroactive laws in Section 28, Article II of the Ohio Constitution. Judgment affirmed.

144